Praise for *Vampires in Their Own Words*

"Positively brilliant! Michelle Belanger's collection of balanced and intimate views on life in the vampire underground is a landmark contribution to vampire history, literature, and lore. This is a fresh and exciting look into the world of vampires, how they live, what they think——and why. A superb resource for both fans and scholars."
— Rosemary Ellen Guiley, author of
The Encyclopedia of Vampires, Werewolves and Other Monsters

"Michelle Belanger brings together some of the most active and respected voices of the vampire community to present not only their ideas, but their very personal stories and experiences. Through this brave and thought-provoking work, she is building bridges and helping dispel the misunderstandings between vampires and other spiritual communities. Her work has certainly opened my eyes and changed my view of vampires for the better."
— Christopher Penczak, author of
The Inner Temple of Witchcraft and *The Mystic Foundation*

"There's no book available on the vampire culture today with the range, depth, and diversity of Belanger's *Vampires in Their Own Words*. This collection confirms that there are more ways to be a vampire than Bram Stoker ever imagined, and many of them are more satisfying than Dracula ever dreamed. That so many real-life vampires have been willing to share their stories affirms Belanger's integrity and vision. There's a vampire for everyone within these pages."
— Katherine Ramsland, author of
Piercing the Darkness and *The Science of Vampires*

"For all that has been written about vampires, the world of real vampires remains virtually unknown. In *Vampires in Their Own Words*, adding a wide spectrum of informants to her own voice, Michelle Belanger gives empathetic access to an emergen͏t cal-religious community and invites our understa͏ al, and organizational struggles to define themsel͏ nt. An important sourcebook for both the scholar ͏
— J. Gordon Melton, Director, Institute f͏ and author of *The Vampire Book: The ͏ ͏ opedia of the Undead*

About the Author

Michelle Belanger is a highly visible figure in the modern vampire community. Author of the best-selling *Psychic Vampire Codex*, Michelle is also the founder and head of House Kheperu, one of the most widely respected vampire households. She became involved in the worldwide vampire community in the early 1990s through the publication of her magazine, *Shadowdance*, and later through the International Society of Vampires. She was also involved with the Sanguinarium, contributing heavily to its publications and revising its code of ethics, the Black Veil. Belanger's 2002 version of the Black Veil remains the most widely accepted version of a vampire "Wiccan Rede."

Over the years, Michelle has worked as a bridge between the vampire community and the rest of the modern magickal subculture. Her books on magick and energy work have helped many modern practitioners gain a better understanding of the vampire as a magickal identity. She has expanded her outreach to a variety of media, including books, magazines, radio, and television documentaries.

To Write to the Author

If you wish to contact the author or would like more information about this book, please write to the author in care of Llewellyn Worldwide and we will forward your request. Both the author and publisher appreciate hearing from you and learning of your enjoyment of this book and how it has helped you. Llewellyn Worldwide cannot guarantee that every letter written to the author can be answered, but all will be forwarded. Please write to:

Michelle Belanger
⁕ Llewellyn Worldwide
2143 Wooddale Drive, Dept. 978-0-7387-1220-8
Woodbury, MN 55125-2989, U.S.A.

Please enclose a self-addressed stamped envelope for reply, or $1.00 to cover costs.
If outside the U.S.A., enclose an international postal reply coupon.

Many of Llewellyn's authors have websites with additional information and resources.
For more information, please visit our website at http://www.llewellyn.com.

Edited by Michelle Belanger

VAMPIRES
— IN THEIR OWN WORDS —

*An Anthology
of Vampire Voices*

Llewellyn Publications
Woodbury, Minnesota

First Edition
First Printing, 2007

Book design by Steffani Sawyer
Cover art © 2007 by Mike Watson Images Ltd.
Cover design by Lisa Novak
Editing by Brett Fechheimer
Llewellyn is a registered trademark of Llewellyn Worldwide, Ltd.

Library of Congress Cataloging-in-Publication Data for *Vampires In Their Own Words: An Anthology of Vampire Voices* is on file at the Library of Congress.
 ISBN: 978-0-7387-1220-8

Llewellyn Publications
A Division of Llewellyn Worldwide, Ltd.
2143 Wooddale Drive, Dept. 978-0-7387-1220-8
Woodbury, Minnesota 55125-2989, U.S.A.
www.llewellyn.com

Printed in the United States of America

Other Works by Michelle Belanger

The Black Veil

Sacred Hunger

Psychic Dreamwalking

The Psychic Energy Codex

The Psychic Vampire Codex

This book is dedicated to the memory of D'Drennan.
You gave so much and received so little.
Too many of us—myself included—
appreciated you only after you were gone.

Contents

Introduction: The World of Vampires   xi

SECTION ONE
What Is a Vampire!

SECTION TWO
Vampire Awakenings

SECTION THREE
Vampires and Feeding

SECTION FOUR
The Vampire Community

SECTION FIVE
Codes of Behavior

SECTION SIX
Vampire Traditions

SECTION SEVEN
Other Views

– INTRODUCTION –

The World of Vampires

*I*n traditional European folklore, a vampire is an undead being that nightly rises from the grave to suck the blood of the living. Hungry ghosts of the most ghoulish variety, folkloric vampires are trapped between life and death, and they seek to drag others into this shadowy existence along with them. Typically, the vampire of European folklore targets friends and family members for his or her nightly predations, leading scholars to suggest that vampirism was merely a convenient myth that grew up to explain instances of contagion, when a wasting sickness made its way through an entire extended family or village.

The vampires of modern fiction and film are far removed from their hideous cousins in folklore. Creatures of great power and beauty, the vampires of modern myth seem to represent our culture's quest for eternal youth. Seductive and forbidding, these night-dwelling creatures of fantasy also embody many of our darkest desires: forbidden sexuality, the power over life and death, the ability to surpass human limitations—freedom on every level, even from natural laws.

Through *Buffy* and *Blade,* Dracula and Lestat, most modern readers are familiar with the vampire as a fictional archetype. But the archetype of the vampire extends well beyond fiction. For individuals involved in the magickal subculture, there is another vampiric identity: the psychic vampire. Not quite as deadly as their folkloric counterparts, psychic vampires are individuals driven to feed upon the energy of others. Often unaware of their condition, psychic vampires are nevertheless potent, and occultists from Dion Fortune to the members of the Hermetic Order of the Golden Dawn offer proscriptions against them. The time-honored tradition of psychic self-defense texts continues in the works of Konstantinos, Joe Slate, and Judith Orloff, modern writers who address the reality of psychic vampirism, offering methods of protecting one's energy from individuals perceived as psychic predators.

Beyond the canon of self-defense texts, in which vampires are typically depicted as needy and clingy emotional parasites, there is another type of vampire yet. Some call themselves psychic vampires, despite the stigma that this term may possess in metaphysical circles. Others call themselves "real vampires." Still others prefer the term "vampyre," using the variant spelling to differentiate between themselves and the creatures of fiction and myth. Others use the term "sanguinarian," or blood-drinker. Some feed upon vital energy. Some drink human blood. Others simply adopt the archetype of the vampire as a potent magickal identity. All are connected by their shared identification with this compelling and ancient figure, the vampire.

The Reluctant Vampire

My own exploration of vampirism started nearly twenty years ago. It was around that time that I began to suspect that there was something unusual about the way I interacted with other peoples' energy. I would give massages to my school friends in band and choir and theater, always knowing just where to put my hands to relieve their tension and stress. It was not uncommon for people to fall asleep during one of my back massages, and everyone I massaged would comment on how I seemed to just pull the tension out of them with my fingers.

I had an instinctive understanding of where and how to use my hands, and I was always drawn right to the problem areas as if I could sense the knots and sore spots through the skin. The moment I put my hands on another person, I would often get images in my mind, as if I could somehow "see" inside them, perceiving muscle groups, damage, and swirls of light and dark energy. Instinctively, I also knew how to manipulate this energy, and the way I relaxed my subjects so completely was to take some of their energy into myself. Knots and other problem areas manifested to me as dark or clogged-looking patches in the flow of energy. I would fix these also by pulling the energy into myself, clearing out the gunk and leaving behind an unencumbered flow. I always felt revitalized after giving someone a massage like this and, at first, I believed the rising, expansive sensation I felt was simply a part of the sense of satisfaction I experienced at having helped a friend. But I was sickly all through my youth and it began to be obvious that I felt physically better for a little while after I worked on someone else's energy. Born with a life-threatening heart defect, I endured several major surgeries before the age of five; although the worst of the problem was repaired, my health was expected to be precarious. Yet somehow I improved my own vitality by touching the energy of another person and taking some of that energy in.

It took a little while for me to fully comprehend what this meant. The ability to connect with and draw upon vital energy came so easily, I never questioned it at first. As long as I had willing partners for backrubs, there was no need to consider what those partners were providing for me. But circumstances occurred the summer of my freshman year that conspired to leave me very socially isolated for most of the rest of high school. My grandmother did not approve of my circle of friends, and she did everything in her power to alienate them from me. The end result meant, among other things, that I had far fewer opportunities to give backrubs. This should not have been a problem, but in time I began to experience some unsettling issues. My health grew even worse than before, and I was sick almost all the time. My heart would skip and hammer in my chest, but I was so terrified of having to endure more surgery that I told no one about what was happening. My hands trembled sometimes and I experienced blinding headaches, especially when I was exposed to very bright lights. If I stood up too suddenly, my vision diminished to a pinprick, and I had to fight to stay standing until the wave of dizziness passed. On top of all this, I was constantly tired. If a cold was going around, I inevitably caught it and it would linger for weeks and weeks. I saw a doctor about a number of these ailments—especially the migraines, because my light sensitivity was seriously beginning to interfere with activities like driving. The doctor, however, was never able to nail down the precise nature of the problem, nor did he ever prescribe medication that solved any of the issues.

I could have attributed all of this to the depression I felt due to the isolation imposed upon me by my overprotective guardian, but there seemed to be more at work than just missing the chance to hang out with my friends. In addition to my physical problems, I started feeling restless all the time, and I craved something that I simply could not identify. It was almost as if I were thirsty, but nothing I drank could make the sensation go away. It felt a little like being hungry, but nothing I ate seemed to help the issue either. Most food just made me feel sick, as if it were the last thing my body needed.

Shifts in mood and even physiological changes are hardly unusual for a teenager. But all this seemed very distinct from the pangs of adolescence I had already experienced. I found myself, spontaneously and uncontrollably, becoming aware of the energy of those around me. It was much like the images I would "see" when giving people backrubs—I was aware that I was looking at a person, and seeing them in a physical, "real" way. But on some other level, there was this other perception of light and flows of energy. If it had stopped just at the perception of vital energy, I might never have made the connection to vampirism. But I *wanted* this energy. I felt a compelling need to take it into me.

There is no way I can describe this craving in words that would not sound ridiculous and melodramatic. I will say that it was this growing, enervating need that made me first associate my condition clearly and irrevocably with that of the vampire. So many of the books and movies I had been exposed to went on and on about the vampire's terrible hunger, the unquenchable thirst that could only be sated with the life of another being. Almost all of the fictional portrayals of the vampire at that time were also very negative about this hunger. The hunger is what made the vampire a predator. It was portrayed as a "curse" the vampire must endure for some unspeakable evil committed in the past. On the rare occasion that a vampire was portrayed in a sympathetic light, the vampire was only a good guy because he was struggling against this need.

It's no surprise that my first identification with the vampire was hardly a positive one. I was afraid of what I felt welling up within me. I did not know where it was leading, and I did not trust it to be something I could control. I was a National Merit Scholar, a star student involved in the Honor Society who actively participated in a great deal of community and volunteer work. The dark image of the vampire portrayed in popular culture stood in stark contrast with all of this. I couldn't be a vampire. I was one of the good guys!

My initial response was to deny and repress this unsettling urge, but doing so immediately led to problems. On more than one occasion, I caught myself feeding unconsciously, daydreaming in class and focusing on the person in front of or across from me. One girl I did this to fell asleep at her desk, her head dropping down with an audible thump. Another student complained suddenly of feeling nauseated and dizzy, asking to be excused so she could go to the infirmary. These were hardly isolated instances. I tried to actively resist the urge to connect with other peoples' energy, but I noticed immediately that resisting the urges made me feel even worse.

Since I had obviously failed to quash the urge to take energy from others, I tried instead to deny its fundamental reality. I wasn't a vampire, I reasoned with myself. This was all in my head, some belief I had cooked up to express other internal issues I wasn't willing to confront in another form. My great-aunt was a social worker, so I had more than a passing familiarity with psychology. I was especially aware of how psychosomatic illness worked—how one's beliefs, fervently held, can manifest in apparently real, physical symptoms. At this point, I decided that my vampirism was nothing more than some psychosomatic effect.

I had a million excuses for why the vampirism was all in my head: Holly, who passed out at her desk, was going to fall asleep anyway. I simply hadn't noticed how tired she looked and, in my need to assert my delusion, I erroneously connected her sudden bout of sleepiness to my own actions. I decided I was committing the typical error of someone desperate to believe in something—taking random coincidences and attributing my own meaning to them. I considered that perhaps I was telegraphing my intention through facial expression or body language, and others were responding unconsciously. I even considered the possibility that I was telepathically manipulating those around me to behave a certain way—anything to avoid the possibility that vampirism was real and I was truly taking other peoples' vital energy.

This desperate skepticism led me into dangerous moral territory. To prove to myself that the vampirism was all in my head, I started to willfully experiment on the people around me. I did so covertly, because I wanted there to be no opportunity for setting up expectations in my subjects, no chance that I was simply manipulating them into sharing my own deluded belief. This meant taking energy from randomly selected people with neither their knowledge nor their consent. Eventually, it meant taking a significant amount of energy as forcefully as possible, since this was the only way I could guarantee a visible response that I could judge from a distance. If I hit someone fast and hard on this ephemeral level of energy and they did not respond, clearly there was nothing to these strange beliefs beyond my own little delusion, and I would be able to rest happy in the belief that I was just insane. And yet, time after time, people responded, often in very extreme ways. It was so much easier for me to accept that I was delusional that I still found ways to deny what I saw, to deny that it had anything to do with me.

The ethical implications of these experiments will horrify some readers—and rightly so. The only excuse I can offer is the fact that it is easy to overlook the impact one has upon others when one refuses to believe in the very reality of one's actions. I really had trouble accepting that what I was doing was real, and therefore it was equally hard to accept the reality of what this was doing to the people around me. Eventually, I came to accept that this act of taking energy from others was not just a delusion—at which point I had to wrestle with a lot of guilt concerning the impact of my actions.

These early years of self-acceptance and discovery have made me sympathetic to all the unconscious psychic vampires out there who simply cannot accept that they are the ones taking energy from others. I understand how, in this culture, one can remain ignorant of the existence of energy, even when one is drawn to it like a moth to a flame. I especially comprehend the unique thought processes that go with being simultaneously aware of this energy and yet also completely in denial of it. I rode that fence for years myself, much to the detriment of those around me. In many ways, I was a textbook case of a "bad" psychic vampire, someone who attacks others and takes against their will, repeatedly and remorselessly. If things had gone differently, I might still be that type of psychic vampire, hiding what I am even to myself and thoughtlessly preying upon those around me. What turned me around and gave me the strength to fully believe in this strange, disturbing capacity—and therefore, to control it—was discovering that there were others like me.

Vampire History

It may seem like a tale out of *Underworld* or *Blade*, but beneath the surface of our materialistic and mundane world, there exists a secret underground culture. It is a culture of vampires. No one in the modern vampire community can say with certainty when this culture truly got its start. There are tales of groups that existed in the 1970s. Certain rumors that are even harder to pin down assert that clandestine groups of vampires were gathering as far back as the early part of the twentieth century, among the flappers and rum-runners of the twenties and thirties. Some whisper that the origins are even earlier still, possibly tying back to the Romantic poet Lord Byron. A letter written by Byron's ex-lover, Lady Caroline Lamb, suggests that the eccentric poet indulged in blood-drinking at least occasionally. Although Byron himself wrote about vampires and was clearly fascinated by them, the purpose of this sanguinary indulgence remains unclear, its connection to real vampirism an issue of conjecture.

In the late nineteenth century, members of the Hermetic Order of the Golden Dawn were taught about psychic vampires in their so-called "Flying Rolls," instructional texts that detailed the theories and methods of the magickal order. Aleister Crowley, a former member of this organization, taught a method of sexual vampirism to higher-ranking members of his own organization, the Ordo Templis Orientis. Although both Crowley and the Golden Dawn may have laid the groundwork for some of the theories and practices of the modern vampire community, neither of these traditions offers evidence to suggest that organized groups of self-proclaimed vampires existed at that time.

✘   ✘

History is defined by the written record. If we apply this definition to vampire history, then the first recorded references to living individuals who identified themselves as real vampires began to appear in the late 1970s and early 1980s. In his 1984 book *Vampires Are*, Dr. Stephen Kaplan provides a fascinating if overly credulous view of self-identified blood-drinkers as well as supposed immortals. Following Kaplan, folklorist Norine Dresser references at least one organized group of self-identified vampires in her 1989 book *American Vampires: Fans, Victims, and Practitioners*. According to Dresser, her contacts, based out of New York, had been actively pursuing their brand of vampirism for a number of years.

On the magickal front, the Temple of Set, founded by Michael Aquino in 1975, contains within it the Order of the Vampyre. This group embraces the persona of the vampire as a means to personal power, adding that it contains a potential route to personal immortality. The brainchild of Aquino's wife, Lady Lilith Aquino, the Order dates back to 1979. In recent years, the Order's website has taken pains to draw very clear lines between the Order's version of vampirism and the vampirism that exists in the modern vampire community. There are some veiled implications that those uninitiated into the Order's mysteries who claim to be vampires are deluded or mistaken.

This puts some common ground between the Order of the Vampyre and another left-hand path magickal organization, the Temple of the Vampire. Founded a decade after the Order of the Vampyre, the TOV has distinct ties to the Church of Satan, sharing many high-ranking members in common. This vampire temple claims to be the only means by which an individual can become a true vampire and achieve actual physical immortality. For a healthy sum, one can order their Vampire Bible and related texts to learn their secrets. The monetary price is not the highest cost the TOV exacts from its members. Members are expected to give total obedience to the Temple's shadowy elders, maintaining absolute secrecy. If a member communicates with other vampires who are not a part of the Temple, they are threatened with excommunication.

Both of these groups were some of the first organizations to openly work the vampire archetype into their magickal practices, but they have had little to do with the modern vampire subculture. As strict members-only organizations, they have kept their distance from the growing vampire community, alienating many members of that community by asserting that their particular brand of vampirism is the only one that is right. Interestingly, as the vampire community has gained more exposure and acceptance in recent years, these two magickal orders have grown even more insular. If there is more history concerning the roots of the vampire movement, neither of these organizations seems willing to share it outside of their own membership.

Stranger than Fiction

When considering the start of the real vampire movement, one cannot divorce it entirely either from folklore or fiction. Both mythic and fictional portrayals of vampires have had a significant impact on the real vampire community, helping to shape the aesthetics, practices, and philosophies of its various members. This aspect of the community has direct ties to Lord Byron, who decisively imported the concept of the vampire to English literature. The supernatural 1960s soap opera *Dark Shadows* played a significant role as well; through the sympathetic character of Barnabas Collins, the program allowed vampires to be seen as more than just charnel-house monsters. Barnabas, the first "reluctant vampire," undoubtedly influenced the imagination of writer Anne Rice, who then furthered the appeal of the vampire archetype through the characters in her *Vampire Chronicles*—starting with the publication of *Interview with the Vampire* in 1976. The vampire Lestat, depicted as a modern rock star, drew the vampire archetype out of moldering graveyards and into popular consciousness, transforming this complex archetype from a fearsome monster to a sex symbol and, for some, even a role model.

For those just beginning to hesitantly—and somewhat guiltily—identify themselves as vampires in the late eighties and early nineties, the long tradition of fiction and folklore was at once confusing and compelling. Many people drawn to the image of the vampire wrestled with all of the trappings that had come to be associated with the archetype over the years. Some adopted the image eagerly, dressing up as vampires complete with fangs and capes, while others rebelled against this stereotype, instead combing through the folklore for the grain of truth that made them feel a connection to this powerful word "vampire," despite their own ambivalence toward the traditional representations.

The vast majority of the nascent vampire community had nothing to go on save their own experiences, underscored in some by a strange, instinctual knowledge that even they could not explain. The only way these isolated individuals even came to develop into a community was due to their need for answers—answers that could only be gleaned from others who experienced similar things. It started in fanzines and newsletters like *The Midnight Sun* and *The DarkRose Journal*. These publications were devoted, at first, to the *idea* of vampires and later to addressing vampirism more openly as a reality. The community began in organizations such as Eric S. Held's Vampire Information Exchange, groups and networks that sought to connect people of like minds and interests as pen pals or for dating. It started in private letters and impromptu meetings—often held in the unlikeliest of places.

In keeping with the real vampire's complicated identity straddling truth and fiction, early members of the vampire community often started out meeting one another at horror conventions or at role-playing games. These were the places where vampirism could be spoken about openly at a time when even the vampires themselves wrestled with belief. When people had finished discussing the vampire in fiction and folklore, then they might just be able to raise the question of the vampire as a reality. If the individuals involved in the discussion exhibited the same hesitant curiosity about what vampirism might really be, then the conversation might take off in an entirely new direction. Reluctantly, fearfully, real vampires would admit their suspicions to one another. Through these hesitant, guarded communications, vampires began to build the foundations of a real community, bound together through common experiences and beliefs.

In the years before the Internet, this process was slow. People were limited by geography, and not everyone was comfortable meeting to discuss vampirism face to face. Secrecy was safety for many of the early members of the community, especially considering what a belief in vampirism might mean if outed at a workplace or even to one's family. Once vampires found their way onto the World Wide Web, however, things changed suddenly and radically.

One of the most influential—and controversial—vampire groups in the mid-nineties, the Sanguinarium, was very openly patterned on the network of vampires featured in the novels of Anne Rice. The Sanguinarium was one of many vampire networks to come out of the shadows and onto the Internet in the mid-nineties. The Sanguinarium's influence was not due to any widespread belief that it had all the answers on vampires or vampirism. Rather, its influence stemmed from sheer visibility and the persistence of its founder. A highly controversial figure, the founder of the Sanguinarium is a man of changeable passions. Known variously to the world as Sabretooth, Father Sebastian, Father Todd, and most recently, Sebastiaan Van Houten, the mention of his name inspires strong—and not always positive—reactions from members of the community. Nevertheless, he remains one of the main reasons the community is as visible as it is today.

Father Sebastian was a New York City–based club promoter and fangmaker who had both the desire and the resources to publish material about real vampires. Although the accuracy of some of this material can be debated, Sebastian compiled a lexicon of vampire terms that is still largely in use today.

He dreamt up a complicated court system of vampire groups and houses that, in its very romanticism, appealed to many who were seeking a more formal sense of community than they were getting through pen pals and impromptu meetings at coffeehouses. Ultimately, he published his views in the *Vampyre Almanac*, first released in 1998. This digest-sized book was part vampire encyclopedia and part club resource, but it remains one of the earliest and most widespread publications by a vampire for the growing community of vampires.

The years 1996 and 1997 saw such a profusion of real vampire webpages that many researchers have been tempted to link the start of the vampire community with these early appearances on the Internet. In addition to the Sanguinarium, there was the Coven Organization, founded by an individual who went by the name Osiris and who had ambivalent connections with Father Sebastian. Damien DeVille's Vampire Church followed soon after. Sanguinarius set up her website offering support and advice for "real vampires," as did Sphynxcat, Vyrdolak, Hirudo, as well as others whose names have since faded into anonymity. There was a lot of confusion in those early days between vampire role-playing sites and those pages devoted to vampirism as a serious and personal reality. This led to something of a rift between the two communities, with role-players speaking out loudly against people who, in the opinion of the role-players, had simply taken the game a little too far. The vampires, in turn, began to make it abundantly and somewhat bitterly clear in the first few paragraphs of their webpages that they were not role-players, nor would vampire role-playing be tolerated on their sites.

The intensity of emotion led many individuals on both sides to willfully forget or obscure how intertwined both communities once were. As an example, the Black Veil, a vampire code of conduct first devised by Father Sebastian, was originally patterned on the Traditions of the Masquerade, a code of conduct used within the vampire role-playing game *Vampire: The Masquerade*. That role-playing game, published in 1991 by White Wolf Publishing, was, for its part, partly inspired by its creator's observations of the social games playing out in a Gothic club in Atlanta. The club, known as the Masquerade, was one of the many places where real vampires met and interacted during the early days of the modern community. At least one writer from White Wolf, Sam Chupp, has come forward and openly admitted that he drew upon his

Pagan and magickal beliefs to inspire certain aspects of his work. Art imitates life, which imitates art in a never-ending cycle.

The *Codex* and the ISV

My magickal—and wholly unethical—experiments in vampirism occurred throughout the late eighties. It was not until the fall of 1991 that I encountered a few others who identified as I did. Once I met others who shared my experiences, I had to face the ethical reality of what I was doing. Vampirism was not all in my head, and my actions had a palpable impact on the people around me—an impact for which I realized I needed to take responsibility. The early nineties saw the start of my involvement in developing an ethical way of meeting my needs. I did not want to be the kind of psychic vampire one reads about in books like Dion Fortune's *Psychic Self-Defense*. Knowledge is power, and so I sought as much knowledge and understanding about my condition as possible, with the hope that I could ultimately harness my innate interaction with energy toward something positive for both myself and those around me.

There were several Pagans, Wiccans, occultists, and even a few vampires in the new social circle I discovered once I was in college. Although I was thrilled to finally have others to discuss my theories and experiences with, it quickly became apparent that most of these people knew as little as I myself did, or even less. One older man claimed to be able to cure my vampirism through sex magick. He generously offered to give me a personal injection of potent life energy—I declined. Another woman, only a few years older than me, became convinced that I had "embraced" her after she allowed me to feed upon her. I thought the claim was ridiculous—no one had made me a vampire, and I was almost certain that my vampirism was an inborn quality. It was not something one could "catch" like a cold, or pass on as fictional vampires did in the movies. Nevertheless, she persisted in her belief, going on to become involved in the vampire community in her own right. She founded the Vampire/Donor Alliance and later told a colorful version of her "embrace" to *FHM Magazine*.

Somewhat displeased with the quality of people in my immediate surroundings, I continued to hope that there were others out there who actually knew what this strange ability was and how best to handle it. This led me, in

December 1991, to start a magazine called *Shadowdance*. On the surface, this self-published 'zine was devoted to art, literature, and poetry with dark and vampiric themes. Underneath that surface, I hoped to find others who, like myself, described through fiction and poetry the beliefs and experiences they dared not speak aloud in any other form. I quickly learned that there were many others who found themselves in my position—isolated, confused, and searching. The small-press magazines, and the voluminous correspondence that occurred behind the scenes, were my first introduction to the vampire community.

It took many years for anything that truly resembled a community to grow out of the hesitant letters and loose networks of people that surrounded the various small-press publications. For my part, I kept searching for people who had answers about how vampirism worked, what caused it, and why we were the way we were. Mostly, I met with more questions. From the general responses I got, I started to think that I knew as much as anyone out there, and perhaps because I had taken the time to experiment with my abilities and observe the results, I knew a little bit more. Ethics, especially, had become very important to me, particularly considering the unethical practices I had engaged in while still coming to terms with what I was. I was unhappy with the negative portrayals of psychic vampires in the self-defense texts and among Pagans in general, and I became determined to elaborate on methods that made it possible not only to feed ethically but to take the energy exchange and turn it into something positive and transformational for all parties. All of this led me to my major contribution to the vampire community as it exists today: a book called *The Psychic Vampire Codex*.

By 1994, the network of vampires writing to one another behind the scenes of my literary magazine *Shadowdance* had grown to the point where this exchange of information needed a publication all its own. Late in that year, I started formalizing this network of pen pals into a loose organization, which became the International Society of Vampires, or ISV. The ISV was a membership-based organization with a monthly newsletter, *The Midnight Sun*. The newsletter started publication in 1995. In addition to the newsletter, members were to have access to a work I had been preparing for publication since 1994. I had referred to it by several names, including *The Codex Sanguin-*

icus and *The Codex Vampiricus*. Mostly, it just got abbreviated to the *Codex*. This was a collection of my theories and observations on vampirism, derived from both experiments and personal intuitions. One of the main points addressed by the *Codex* was the fact that vampirism was something that could be harnessed in a positive fashion. One did not have to be an energy predator but, with awareness and discipline, could come to harness the ability to connect to other peoples' energy in a way that was helpful and even healing to both the vampire and the donor. The work was circulated at first in small sections to save on printing costs. The cost of printing was always an issue, both with *Shadowdance* and with the *Midnight Sun*. This cost, together with rising postage rates and growing issues with the postal system itself, led me to stop publication of both the magazine and the newsletter in 1996.

There were also larger issues involved in my decision to bring nearly five years' worth of work to an end. Nineteen ninety-six was the year of the vampire in the media, and this was not a good thing. In Florida, a troubled young man named Rodney Farrell drove to a friend's house and bludgeoned her parents to death. He claimed to be a vampire. Susan Walsh, a woman who did freelance work for the *Village Voice* in New York, disappeared while doing an exposé on New York City's growing vampire culture. Rodney Farrell's actions led him to become the youngest person on Florida's death row. Susan Walsh has never been heard from again.

This might have been the end of the story for me, but the vampire community wouldn't let me fade away so easily. While I was publishing newsletters for people in Britain, Germany, and as far away as Turkey, many other individuals had begun forming their own groups and organizations as well. New York City was a hotbed of such activity, as were several other large cities in the United States, including Los Angeles and New Orleans. The community in each city had its own distinct development, flavored by the attitudes of the city itself as well as the main movers in that city's scene. Many of the vampires in New York had a romanticized ideal of courtly culture, which led the community there to become very formal and elegant, with a focus on fashion, high society, and etiquette. Father Vincent, Father Sebastian, and the metalsmith D'Drennan were all main forces behind the early New York scene, each adding his flair for the dramatic to the overall aesthetics of what became known as the Court of Gotham.

The vampires in New Orleans fought a battle of love and hate with the image of that city as portrayed in the novels of writers such as Anne Rice and Poppy Z. Brite. Thanks to these writers, New Orleans was seen by many as a city of vampires; the undead, in addition to spirits and voodoo, became a part of the French Quarter tourist scene. Some vampires, like Lord Chaz, decided to capitalize on this, running genuine vampire tours of the city. Others resented such ventures, feeling that they trivialized the reality of their vampirism.

Los Angeles developed in almost direct contrast to New York, with the vampires in Los Angeles resisting any formalization of their community. They rejected the haute couture of the New York scene, seeing it as trite and frivolous. Daemonox, a main inspiration in the community on the West Coast, remains someone who eschews all the popular imagery of the vampire, especially the hierarchical court structure so typical of New York City vampires.

✖   ✖

All of this was happening well away from my small hometown in Ohio. However, by 1998 events conspired to bring me into contact with Father Sebastian of the Gotham scene. Much to my surprise, he had heard of me and the ISV. He and others urged me to move my work onto the Internet. This was also when I was introduced to Sebastian's version of the Black Veil. He had been using it as a code of conduct mainly at the New York nightclub where members of the Sanguinarium met. With the tragedies of Rodney Farrell and Susan Walsh still fresh in my mind, I felt that this ethical code could have much wider applications. I asked permission to rewrite it completely, moving it away from its primary code of secrecy and excising any remaining traces of the influence of *Vampire: The Masquerade*. Hoping that this could eventually become the vampire version of the Wiccan Rede, I wrote thirteen tenets that focused on mutual respect, ethical behavior, and a positive sense of community. We launched the new version of the Black Veil in 2000, and it instantly gained widespread popularity.

Also in that year, Father Sebastian published a version of the *Codex* as a companion piece to that year's installment of *The Vampyre Almanac*. The book became so popular among members of the growing community that I then donated a version to the Internet Sacred Text Archive, an online resource. With its information on feeding techniques, it encouraged vampires to be aware of their needs and to make educated decisions about how, when, and where to feed. Although an expanded edition of the *Codex* was picked up by Weiser Books in 2004, the online version can still be found for free on countless vampire websites.

I am not entirely comfortable singing the praises of my own book, but at this point it is almost impossible to have a discussion of the modern vampire subculture without mentioning the *Codex*. What the book did for the vampire community was to put in plain and accessible terms that which most vampires were already doing. It explained the process of feeding, approaching this as something that could be done positively, with willing and informed donors. It did not have to be the equivalent of psychic rape and it could, in fact, be an intimate and beautiful sharing. The Order of the Vampyre and the TOV may have been teaching metaphysical techniques for taking energy for many years, but they tended to approach the vampire as a predator, encouraging members to learn vampirism as a way of gaining power over others. In addition to this negative practice, what information they had was reserved for paying members exclusively. I felt the information should be out there and free so vampires could decide for themselves to practice ethically.

In the earliest stages of the community, many vampiric individuals felt a need for life without ever understanding or even questioning why. I stopped to question—I needed to understand that the need was more than just a delusion in order to accept it. And in my search for answers, I found many underlying metaphysical principles in the energetic and mystical traditions of other cultures, from the yoga of the Hindus to the Taoism of the Chinese. Vampirism, as I discovered, was hardly new, unusual, or strange. In most Asian traditions, it is accepted as fact that people interact with energy all the time. The confusion, for vampires born here in the West, comes more from a complete lack of context for this need. I wrote the *Codex* because I wanted vampires like myself to know they were not alone, and I wrote it because I hoped to save some of them from the bitter mistakes I made while learning to control my own needs.

Vampires and Energy

For the most part, the individuals involved in the modern vampire community identify with the figure of the vampire because that word "vampire" is one of the few words we have in the English language to indicate someone who feeds upon life. Western culture doesn't have much context for the idea of life energy. Almost all of the words and terms that we use currently are borrowed from other cultures. *Prana* is a Hindu word that means "breath and spirit," and it is connected with certain energy-raising techniques in the discipline of yoga, such as the potent breathing technique *pranayama. Chi,* another word that will often appear in discussion of life energy, is a Chinese term. *Chi* is a fundamental concept in many aspects of Taoism, and it plays a role in everything from martial arts to traditional Chinese medicine. *Ki,* the Japanese version of *chi,* is connected to the practice of Reiki, a kind of laying-on-of-hands method of healing that was imported to the West from Japan via Hawaii. A part of the very word "Reiki," *ki* refers to the energy being harnessed by the healer using the technique.

Only in the past few decades have techniques like Reiki and yoga gained popular acceptance here in the West. Many people remain skeptical about them, but major hospitals and clinics have nevertheless been integrating these time-honored traditions into their more standard therapies. The Cleveland Clinic, a world-renowned institute of healing, has run experiments to test the impact of energy upon the healing process, and hospitals around the country have started to suggest yoga and T'ai Chi as part of a healthy exercise routine. For the most part, the underlying energetic principles of these techniques remain mysterious to most Western thinkers, but gradually the idea of vital energy is sneaking into our culture.

Vampires like myself had no choice but to develop some understanding of that vital energy early in our lives. We often had no idea what to call it, but the instinct to take it remained—and that instinct was reinforced by distinct repercussions on our health and well-being when we failed to give in to the impulse. There has been much debate—both within the vampire community and outside of it—as to what makes a person vampiric. Many non-vampires who nevertheless believe in magick and vital energy argue that there is enough energy in the Universe to go around, and the act of taking vitality from another is an affront to the generosity and intended balance of divinity. Time and again, I have encountered Pagans and Wiccans who simply cannot accept the idea of a vampire's need—when that need is exactly what has convinced most of the people in my community to adopt the term "vampire" in the first place.

While there are certainly some people in the modern vampire community who identify with the archetype, not because they themselves are vampiric but because they find the archetype of the vampire seductive and personally empowering, there remain a number of individuals for whom the term "vampire" has very real and very personal repercussions. Psychic vampires, as well as some blood-drinkers, believe that their very health depends upon the act of taking another person's energy. That belief has been formulated through repeated experiences during which, abstaining from that energy, the vampire's health has gone into decline. It is worth noting that many vampiric individuals were, like myself, born with serious health conditions and birth defects. One way I have been able to put vampirism into context is by comparing it to healing, only in reverse. In energy-healing techniques such as Reiki, the healer places his or her hands on the patient and channels energy into that person in order to help alleviate illness, disease, or pain. A vampire engages in a proactive version of this selfsame healing. Instead of waiting for a healer to come to them, vampires connect with the energy of others, drawing this energy into themselves and using it to heal their own complaints.

The next question I inevitably encounter is "Why take energy from people? Isn't there abundant energy in the earth, stars, even trees?" The answer to this question reveals why—even though I am not always comfortable with the word—the term *vampire* really fits people like me. We wouldn't be tempted to call someone a vampire if they had this overwhelming energetic need but only fed upon trees. Witches and other magickal practitioners draw energy from natural sources all the time, especially when raising energy for ritual. Ordinary people also take energy from their environment as a natural part of living. Just as we breathe oxygen and take in food for nourishment, so do our bodies need energy in order to maintain healthy functioning. But vampires are vampires because there is a significant and distinct limitation in the type of energy that fulfills our needs. Although many vampires have the ability to sense and harness energy of other types, only the energy of other human beings seems adequate for maintaining our health and well-being.

I have spent long hours trying to determine why this is true. As far as this issue goes, there are almost as many theories in the vampire community as there are vampires to voice those theories. When I was first trying to deduce the cause of vampirism, I often noticed that many vampiric people exhibited significant damage or deformity in key energy centers—particularly the second chakra, at the navel, though sometimes in other areas as well. Sometimes this damage seemed like scarring; sometimes it was the result of very severe energetic blockages. Sometimes it just seemed as if that particular person's chakra functioned differently. Whatever the root cause, the end result meant that the chakra in question processed energy in a way that was impaired or changed. Vampirism resulted when that impairment or change impacted that way the person connected to, processed, or otherwise "digested" outside energy.

Other vampires appeared to have a more or less normal energetic system, but they burned through energy so quickly that they had to take massive amounts of it in almost constantly. Think of such people as individuals with hyperactive spiritual metabolisms. If energy were food, then they needed their food in the most potent and efficient form possible in order to keep up with their heightened need. Energy that we draw upon from outside ourselves still has to go through a process much like digestion, during which it is turned from earth or tree energy to energy keyed for a human system. What is more efficient, then, but to take the energy directly from its source, thus cutting out the need to "digest" it at all?

Another theory I encountered through a Taoist friend. In Taoism, Qi Gong, and related Asian practices, energy workers are taught to draw their power from the natural world. Mountains, clear and powerful rivers, expansive forests—all of these are potent sources of energy. Now consider our Western culture. How many of these natural sources have become diminished? How many people have access to pristine, natural spaces? Even if they have access, how many people bother to take the time? But the body still needs energy, and so it adapts naturally to its environment. Of natural, living things, what is the most abundant and widely available source in a city? People. Other human beings comprise the most widespread source of vital energy in any urban environment. My Taoist friend suggested that vampires are not strictly *limited* to human vital energy. Human energy is simply the most abundant form of energy to which they have access in an increasingly metropolitan world. Given that so many vampires live in big, bustling cities, I had to admit that I saw the reasoning behind his ideas.

Having worked with a large number of vampires over many years, I think there is more than one answer, and the answers vary from person to person. This is to say nothing of the vampires who feel a need for human blood, a topic on which I cannot pretend expertise.

The psychic abilities of vampires may also be a contributing factor to heightened energetic need. Most vampires do much more than just feed. As the term should suggest, psychic vampires are highly sensitive to psychic energy, and they exhibit a wide variety of paranormal abilities, drawing upon these as if they were second nature. Telepathy, psychometry, energy healing, spirit mediumship—many psychic vampires have one if not all of these abilities. Witches know to raise energy when working magick. The energy fuels the working. If psychic abilities require a similar kind of fuel, it seems that psychic vampires have a preference for raising that energy from the people around them. The root cause for that preference can be debated, but most vampires agree that it is not a choice. Most vampires have tried and failed to get what they need from other sources, relying on the energy of others because there seems to be no other option for fulfilling their needs. The best most of us can do is to find a way to do it positively, giving back in whatever ways we can.

The Magickal Significance of the Vampire

As a Wiccan, Pagan, or light-worker, you might be wondering why you should read this book. Vampires are interesting, to be sure, but what relevance does the modern vampire community have to you? Simply put, you probably know at least one vampire. In all likelihood, this person knows what they are, but has never dared to tell the other members of their circle, coven, or study group. Not all vampires are Pagan, but there are a lot of vampires in the Pagan and magickal communities. Because there is very little understanding or acceptance of vampirism within these communities, most of those vampires operate in secrecy. If only to better understand these individuals, you should read the articles collected in this book.

But there are other reasons. The vampire community, as it has grown and evolved, has started to produce its own particular belief systems. The vampire is a potent mythic archetype, and some people have adopted it as a magickal identity in much the same way that the founders of modern witchcraft adopted the term *witch*. Not everyone in the vampire community makes vampirism a part of their religious path, just as not everyone who is vampiric adopts the archetype of the vampire as part of their fashion or self-image. But there are enough magickal orders and vampire covens operating now in the United States and abroad to warrant attention as a specific spiritual movement. Most of these have their roots in neo-Paganism, although some are connected more intimately with chaos magick or left-hand path traditions. Quite a few have simply adapted traditional Pagan practices to something more palatable to their vampiric experience of the world.

Individuals who identify with the vampire archetype are no longer isolated as they once were, and they no longer have to labor under the mistaken assumption that they are the only one of their kind. The result has been a rich and diverse growth of belief systems, philosophies, and practices that have evolved around the concept of the vampire as a magickal identity, as an energetic disorder, even as a personal aesthetic. Encompassing individuals who identify themselves as psychic vampires, blood-drinkers, lifestylers, and vampire magickal workers, the vampire community is as fascinating as it is extensive.

Navigating that community can be a daunting task, especially for those who are standing on the outside looking in. Vampires themselves are not always forthcoming to strangers, and their practices can, at least on the surface, seem bizarre and off-putting. In the interest of promoting understanding and acceptance, a variety of vampires have come together in this book to share their views, reveal their practices, and tell their personal stories. It is my hope that this book will help build bridges between the members of the various magickal communities, so that Wiccans, Pagans, light-workers, and vampires can all respect one another's differences while also learning to recognize their common ground.

A Chorus of Vampire Voices

If I made one mistake when writing the *Psychic Vampire Codex*, it was to write expressly from the perspective of my own tradition. At the time, I didn't feel as if I had the authority to write from any other perspective—after all, I could only speak with certainty about my own experiences. But I've since learned that a more general approach might have been less confusing, at least for some people. The beliefs of the vampire community extend in many directions beyond the beliefs covered in the *Codex*. For some people, vampirism isn't even about belief. They see it more as an attribute or even as a lifestyle. Every group (and often every individual) active in the vampire community has a different take on what vampirism really is and how it applies to them.

This book is my attempt to provide a wider perspective on the vampire community. Because I still believe that each person is naturally biased by his or her own experiences and thus can really only speak from the perspective of those experiences, I have not authored many of the articles that appear in this book. Instead, I have invited a chorus of vampire voices to speak up and tell their own tales. In the pages that follow, you will hear from both the founders of houses as well as from individuals who view their vampirism as a condition akin to psychic diabetes; you will also meet those who view vampirism as a sacred and glorious spiritual path. Vampires who feed on the energy of other people will share their ideas alongside those who express their vampirism by drinking human blood.

Throughout all of this, I will be your guide, introducing the various writers and offering commentary on words and concepts that might be foreign to those readers who are approaching vampirism from the outside. If there is a word or phrase in an article that baffles you, flip to the end of that essay and look for the term in the definitions. These definitions will help not only to explain unfamiliar terms but also to give them context within the history and development of the vampire community as it exists today. I have done my best to be balanced and fair in these annotations, but please be aware that I can only speak about the things I know myself. I am speaking from over fifteen years' experience now, but I acknowledge that there are details of our history and development that I did not witness and thus cannot accurately recount. Some groups are very secretive, and so any statements one can make about them are necessarily very generalized and may not encompass the nuanced complexities of their actual beliefs.

Nevertheless, these annotations remain a solid resource that will provide a starting point for your explorations into the vampire community and its myriad beliefs. I have been fortunate in the fact that many community leaders have participated in this project, trusting me enough to send me their writing for inclusion in this book. A good starting point for anyone researching the community of modern vampires would be to look these individuals up on the Internet and read more of their work. Many host websites and message boards where you can ask further questions and receive answers directly from the horse's mouth.

In section 6, I focus on several individuals as well as their groups. In this spotlight section, these community leaders share a little of their personal history: what brought them to the vampire community, how they interpret being a vampire, and why their vampirism is important to them. Each of these individuals provides a solid example for different aspects of the community. Rev. Vicutus is a left-hand-path occultist. Madame X reveres the fashion and aesthetic of the vampire as much as its spiritual dimension. Gabrielx couldn't care less about the fashion, but is very devoted to the idea of community. And Eclecta just wants to know the *why*s of vampirism.

There are many other individuals I would have liked to include in this spotlight section—but it would take a whole series of books to represent adequately every vampire who has something significant to say. As you read these sections, please understand that these people represent some but not all of the various groups within the community. As with every aspect of human belief, there are always different ways of doing things and different interpretations.

The final section of the book, section 7, contains articles that look at the community from the outside. Many of these writers are not even vampires, although several know members of the community and have interacted with vampire groups. I collected these articles to help put vampires in context for those readers who are also looking in from the outside. If you happen to be a vampire, don't think you should skip over these exceptional articles. The insight they offer into our community might surprise you. Often when someone approaches a topic from a totally different perspective, that person sees things that those who are working from a more traditional viewpoint might miss completely. This concept underscores the real heart of this work: in any human endeavor, we cannot see the whole picture when we are looking as one person alone. It takes many views and many voices to adequately capture the intricacies of ideas and beliefs. No one writer (myself included) whose work appears in this book has all the answers about who and what vampires really are. But in lifting our voices together, we come much closer to presenting an accurate view.

SECTION
– ONE –

What Is a Vampire?

Kris Steaveson has been a practitioner of magick in many forms for nearly ten years. Like many vampires who are also ethical witches, Kris "awakened" to her nature shortly after she began practicing, and struggled to reconcile her nature with her beliefs. She is currently leader-in-standing of a magickal order, an author, and an artisan. For the last six years, she has run a business from home, making ritual tools by hand. Despite being open about her beliefs and practices, she lives a private life.

My Experience of Vampirism

by Kris Steaveson

Vampirism, as I have experienced it, is a condition preventing the normal generation and circulation of energy in the body. The average person by right of birth has the ability to generate and process their own energy as well as energy from other natural sources. For some reason we, as vampires, don't. For some people, this manifests as the need (or perceived need) to feed on blood, a very powerful carrier of human energy. For others, it manifests as the need for that energy directly, in the form of *prana* or *chi*, a need that can be even more devastating.

The classical vampire has such a romantic image these days. Suave, slick, androgynous, and desirable. Anyone who sees these seductive beings comes under a glittery thrall and is penetrated, willingly, in the ultimate way. The vampire of fiction and film is the ultimate lover, as well as the simultaneous image of Angel and Devil.

And then there is the psychic vampire. The psychic vampire is a functional person most of the time, as mortal and graceless as any. Yet because of that powerful need for human energy, the psychic vampire may also seem like a junkie, shuddering in the corner, in dire need of their energetic fix.

For us there is no pill, no therapy, no treatment—except to feed and to continue to feed. There is no room for romance, no glittering Hollywood façade. We are seen as leeches, as wanton attackers, and as people doing this for the thrill. Few people understand that our need is like the need for food. While some people indulge their need for food to a fault, everyone must eat a minimum to maintain their health. Psychic vampires must feed in order to maintain themselves.

Discovering who and what I am was a long and painful process. I spent several years manic-depressive with a severe heart condition. I was wracked by a feeling of weakness, lethargy, and the desire, on bad days, to lie down and die. One night, I felt myself reach out and draw energy from something. The energy cured my ills as nothing else had done in all my life. From then on I did my best to do this in an ethical way, and I have kept my health up as a result. As it is for so many people today with their eating requirements, it has been a slow process for me, learning to keep a proper balance between health and gluttony.

I did a lot of online research, often checking it against my own feelings and other sources. I found out that I wasn't like others; my experiences were specific and my feeding even more so. Blood was appealing but not what I *needed*. I did not make strong bonds with those I fed upon. I could draw energy from the environment if I concentrated and did so consciously. I did not have to feed on other people, but in general it was better for me if I did.

Feeding has a sensation to it that is hard to describe. It is not a thrill by any measure. I liken the sensation to inhaling a very deep breath of fresh air. My body wakes up, gets back some barely perceptible feeling. The difference between "before" and "after" is marked. My attitude and vitality improves. My mind clears up, and I tend to think on my feet a bit better. Energy is my morning cup of coffee, and anyone who has had to get up at some unholy hour to do their daily grind will understand that sensation.

Initially, my beliefs were affected by this revelation. As an ethical witch, I struggled, when I first realized I was a vampire, to reconcile my needs with my faith. Feeding, to me, fell under some archetypal idea of "harm" . . . and at the time I very much bought into the mass-market "Wicca" that professed that you should never so much as think an unkind thought. As time went on, I developed a more organic view of spirituality. Animals hunt and kill to sustain themselves, but they do so without cruelty. To me, this is the essence of any living being and something people should strive for: survival without cruelty.

This has changed the way in which I practice my faith, because I can no longer pretend that all actions are without harm. Even eating a peanut butter sandwich deprives someone else (or at least deprives bacteria) of that sandwich. You're doing harm to spores when you breathe. You're performing bacterial genocide when you wash your hands. The list could go on. Similarly, anyone working a spell is taking up and expending energy, either from themselves or the area. That deprives someone, somewhere of that energy.

Vampirism puts me in an interesting position in ritual. It makes it both easier and harder to work with others. I work with energy more easily, and can network the energies of others unconsciously. However, when they feel my energy at work or when they find out what I am, they tend to want me gone. Vampirism is about as popular in Pagan circles as fundamentalist Christianity. This is slowly changing, but there are people still bound and determined to make a monster out of you when vampirism is just a part of who you are.

Vampirism, to me, is a condition of the soul that can be caused by only two things: by being spiritually inhuman or by severe and lasting damage to the spiritual bodies. In either case, I think that the vampirism itself is caused by the ill fit of the energy body to the human body. In some cases, the body is shaped to fit these changes, and the result is serious physical illness in the person. We're affected by a spiritual diabetes that has no cure and can only be managed with the equivalent of spiritual insulin.

Psychic vampirism has changed the way in which I view the world quite dramatically, because I identify the various differences (and similarities) between not only bodies and minds, but between souls as well. It makes me, by nature, more accepting of the feelings and beliefs of others—because if I dare to believe my soul is formed differently, then I had damned well better accept that someone else's can be nonhuman, or the wrong gender for their body.

It has made me more aware of the unseen side of things. Energy, spirit, and matter are all in a very delicate and awesome interplay. I am awed and humbled by this web of reality. I cannot ignore it any more than I can ignore my own limbs. I am obligated to be aware.

Definitions

Psychic vampire: An individual who regularly and actively needs to take in human vital energy in order to maintain his or her physical, mental, emotional, or spiritual well-being. Most psychic vampires believe that they need to supplement their own systems with this vital energy for one of three reasons: they themselves do not produce enough of this energy, their systems burn through this energy far too quickly, or they are unable to process other sources of energy outside of the human spectrum. A psychic vampire can take in energy over a distance or through physical touch.

Wiccan Rede: The core of ethical principles at the heart of the Wiccan faith, the Wiccan Rede states: "An it harm none in word, thought, or deed, do as thou wilt." For many Wiccans, psychic vampirism is seen as unethical because the act of taking vital energy from another human being is perceived as inescapably harmful.

Sedona is a familiar face for many in the online vampyre community. Hailing from the courtly system of vampyres in New York City, Sedona first became part of the community through House of Illusions, with which she is no longer associated, in early 2001. Inspired by the website Darkness Embraced, she founded Phantasmagoria Syndicate, an educational branch of House of Illusions. She is also part of the Aetherium, which aims to educate those who seek knowledge about vampirism. Sedona helped found House Aeterno, and she runs her own website at www.freewebs.com/madamesedona.

Vampirism Associated with Energy Signatures

BY SEDONA OF HOUSE AETERNO

In the general sense, most people who study vampirism divide it into two main categories: sanguine and pranic. Sanguine vampyres are individuals who meet their needs by drinking blood. Pranic vampyres take living energy instead.

But where does our education on such things end and our own thinking begin? In truth, who doesn't know how to pick up a book, read it, and parrot back its information? One of the great things about vampirism is its ability to provoke deep thought due to its ambiguity. Yet many people take what is read in books to heart without pausing to question or doubt the information. Too often, the words of one or two authors are looked upon as something that should never be changed. Certainly, when most of us choose to follow someone else's beliefs on a subject, we do so because that person happens to share very similar ideas to our own. But how identical are these beliefs, really? Too many people dare not to venture out and disagree with "popular" beliefs due to the fear of being ostracized, criticized, or ridiculed for their ideas.

This essay is about questioning those interpretations of vampirism that have been offered to us by a few, and learning to discover what we believe for ourselves.

Behind the Words

When we look at the word *vampyre*, we cannot help but picture a being looming behind shadows—a pallid figure with elongated fangs, dressed in a cloak of crimson and black. This is mainly the image that has been implanted into our heads from historical myths, stories, and Hollywood depictions. As we know, modern-day vampyres do not necessarily fit this image. Yet even to many modern vampyres, vampirism is little more than an aesthetic look or something for role-playing. Many accept the persona of the Hollywood or mythical vampyre rather than seriously sitting down and asking themselves what they think a vampyre is beyond the legends and stories. There is a philosophy and a spirituality hiding beneath the Hollywood façade that has much more to it than capes and fangs.

If we leave the Hollywood depictions behind, what is a vampyre? A modern vampyre is a being who has the ability to absorb the energy from living, nonliving, and elemental things. I personally believe that everyone and everything, especially living organisms, naturally exchange energies between themselves, mother nature, and their general environment. We can feel changes in our HEF (human energy field) as the weather changes, when we eat or drink, when we interact with animals and plants, and even as the earth moves through its cycle of days, months, and years. When we take energy from the environment, it can occur in the form of eating, drinking, meditating, sleeping—even listening to birds singing in the morning. All of these activities supply us with a type of sustenance that we, as humans, need to survive. Vampyres also need this sustenance. But compared to a mundane, a vampyre needs to take in extensive amounts of outside energy. The amount is so great that a vampyre becomes aware of the activity of taking energy, whereas most people simply interact with energy without ever realizing that they are doing so.

Why does a vampyre need to take in so much energy? There is a belief that the physical body acts as an earthly anchor for the soul/spirit. The physical body binds our spiritual energy to this earth. Sometimes, something traumatic or shocking occurs that can weaken and cause rifts in the physical shell. Parts of that spiritual energy might escape, get damaged by outside negative forces, or just shut down. Once the physical shell is able to repair itself, it starts to suffer from the lack of that absent energy, showing the symptoms of vampirism.

A person with this condition will discover that the routine methods for gaining energy—such as eating, drinking, or sleeping—do nothing to improve the situation. The energies provided by these actions are no longer enough to make up for the loss of the spiritual energy. In that respect, vampyres need an additional source to sustain themselves. It is the need for this outside energy—not any Hollywood trappings—that defines someone as a vampyre.

DEFINITIONS

Role-playing and vampires: Role-playing has fairly negative connotations within the vampire community. This is largely the result of the complicated relationship between the vampire subculture and a role-playing game called *Vampire: The Masquerade*. First published in 1991 by creator Mark Rein-Hagen, *Vampire: The Masquerade* allows participants to play vampires struggling to survive in the modern world. The relationship between *V:TM* and the vampire community is very similar to the relationship between the earlier role-playing game *Dungeons & Dragons* and the Pagan community. Both games appeal to certain members of these communities. Both games have a reflexive relationship with certain terminology, themes, and aesthetics that appear within their respective non-role-playing communities. And both have attracted writers either overtly or covertly involved in the non-role-playing side of each community. The integration into role-playing games of ideas, terms, and definitions drawn from the real-life vampire community further muddies the waters between what is real and what is the game. The most striking example of this is the case of the Black Veil, the most widely known set of vampire ethics. At its inception, this code was originally patterned after *Vampire: The Masquerade*'s "Traditions of the Masquerade," a set of rules that the vampires in the game world were expected to uphold.

Pranic vampirism: Alternate term for energy vampirism. *Prana* is a Sanskrit word related to breath, life, and the vital force. A pranic vampire, then, is an individual who feeds upon this vital force. In recent years, there has been some confusion between "pranic" and "Tantric" techniques, leading some vampire websites to incorrectly identify pranic vampires as individuals who feed through sex.

Vampire **vs.** *vampyre:* In the 1990s, several groups within the vampire subculture began using the more archaic word *vampyre* to distinguish a real, modern vampire from the vampires of fiction and folklore. The most notable of these groups was the Sanguinarium, which initially started out as a society of lifestylers—individuals who adopted the Romantic aesthetic of the vampyre. The Sanguinarium eventually developed into the dark spiritual society now known as the OSV—the Ordo Strigoi Vii. Groups or individuals influenced by either the old Sanguinarium or the new Strigoi Vii typically retain the "vampyre" spelling. It is also a spelling favored by the Temple of Set for their Order of the Vampyre.

Midnight Childe is a thirty-nine-year-old psychic vampire, or psi-vamp, who has been aware of her nature since her teens. Her early searches for community led her to the Sanguinarium, but she has widened her studies of vampirism to include many other groups and houses, learning more and more about herself as she goes.

Discovering and Defining Vampires

BY MIDNIGHT CHILDE

A vampire is an actual living person with a need to replenish a lost energy. This loss can occur on many levels; I personally relate it to damaged energy centers. There is something missing that does not allow us as vampires to process energy effectively—thus, we have the need to feed on alternate energy sources to maintain our own well-being. Failure to do so regularly can result in various symptoms, ranging from mere mood swings to severe sickness. The severity of this need varies from one vampire to another.

As a psi-vamp, I feed on energy, or *chi*. The technique I use primarily is touch: not just basic touching, but a more focused type of physical contact. I use my hands and mouth for this form of feeding, often choosing to feed from the chakra points of my donor. I use my hands to initiate contact, and my mouth to "breathe in" the energy. I have used other methods of feeding as well, such as ambient feeding and deep feeding. Ambient feeding serves only as a "quick fix" for my needs. Deep feeding, although far more sustaining, can create such potent psychic ties between people that it must be practiced with care. I reserve deep feeding exclusively for my husband.

When I feed, I get a hot feeling in my hands that surges throughout my entire body as the feeding progresses. I can feel the energy that I am taking from my donor flow into my body and begin to disperse. Sometimes, although

I am not sanguine, I have had the coppery taste of blood in my mouth during feeding.

My husband serves as my primary donor, and he has reported that the effects of my feeding vary from one feeding to the next, depending on how deeply I draw and how long the process lasts. He has told me that when I feed he feels his energy flowing out of him, and it is comparable to having a deep cut that bleeds profusely. He can actually feel his "life" draining out of him. He says it feels different from, for example, fighting sleep, as he can actually feel the drain actively taking place. I have noticed that my feeding is best done when my husband is sitting or lying down. I found out the hard way that initiating feeding while he was standing up landed him pretty quickly on the ground!

Since I do not practice sanguinarian ways, the safety measures I take are quite simple:

- Use common sense when feeding.
- Know your donor and their limits.
- Never take too much at one time.
- Always be aware of how your donor is reacting.
- If things are not going smoothly, stop.
- Always, first and foremost, be considerate of your donor's concerns.
- Never force feed, and always know when to say enough is enough.

Vampirism is not a choice. Being a vampire is a condition of the soul. Some people see vampires as negative, but I think that we, as vampires, were created for a specific purpose. What that is we may never really know, but I feel we are all connected for some reason. I believe that we vampires have been around for several thousand years just as humans, and perhaps even before humanity. I do not feel that our vampirism in any way makes us superior to "normal" human beings, as many may seem to think. Rather, I think it sets us apart from everyone else. I think that as vampires we have lived many, many past lives, and that we will continue to live again. In that way, vampires are immortal—not in the physical sense, but in a spiritual sense. I have always felt that past lives play a vital role in vampirism as well. Many of the non-vampires I have met can recall a few past lives, but many vampires I have met can recall a whole chain of selves leading back into the distant past.

Definitions

Chi: Chinese term for life energy. *Chi* is one of three main energies at work in the human body, according to Taoist beliefs. For Westerners, the most familiar technique for working with chi appears in T'ai Chi, a style of moving meditation that elegantly combines physical exercise with internal work to cultivate and encourage healthy chi flow. Chi is also fundamental to the principles of the Chinese healing technique known as *Qi Gong*.

Chakras: From a Sanskrit word meaning "wheel," chakras are energy centers believed to occur within the subtle body. Most modern traditions identify seven such "wheels of light" that run in a line down the center of the body parallel to the spine. First referenced in the Hindu sacred text known as the Upanishads, chakras are believed to process vital energy between the physical and subtle bodies.

Psi-vamp: Abbreviated term for *psychic vampire*. Due to the many and varied permutations of definitions that pop up on the Internet, there has been a recent though not widely accepted fad for identifying a psi-vamp as someone who vampirizes psychic energy, and a psychic vampire as a vampire who is also psychic. These terms are usually interchangeable.

Ambient energy: The human body runs on energy, from the bioelectrical charge that fuels the nervous system—measurable through galvanic skin response—to more subtle energies, like the chi harnessed in martial arts and Qi Gong. Just as all living beings naturally take in energy from the environment, they cast off energy into the environment as well. The ambient energy that ethical psychic vampires target is energy generated by people. However, like heat radiating from a candle's flame, this energy is no longer directly a part of the person from whom it originated. No longer attached to any specific person, most ethical psychic vampires feel that it is morally safe to freely draw on this energy in order to feed.

Past lives: Individuals in the vampire community do not assert that they are physically immortal. However, many who identify with the vampire archetype do espouse a belief in spiritual immortality. This is a belief that goes beyond the concept of reincarnation and treads upon ideas of rebirth. Many vampires believe that they retain a near-constant thread of personality and memory through successive lives. Individuals who espouse this view also typically believe that their vampirism manifests in each of these lives.

Spiritual immortal: A belief that an unbroken thread of personality and memory can be attained spiritually, so that the soul of a person realizes its identity and retains that identity regardless of physical incarnation. This is slightly different from the notion of standard reincarnation, for it asserts that, despite different bodies, the person remains essentially and fundamentally the same. In several Eastern traditions, most notably Taoism, spiritual immortality is seen as a state of high spiritual development, attained only by the spiritual elite. In the Hindu system, a spiritual immortal is termed a *bodhisattva,* and the role of such a person is linked to the spiritual realization of the entire human populace.

Michelle Belanger is author of the groundbreaking Psychic Vampire
Codex *and founder of House Kheperu. Author of the widely accepted version of the* Black Veil, *Michelle has been involved in the vampire community since the early nineties. Featured on numerous documentaries, including A&E's* Vampire Secrets *and the French release* Vampyres: When
Reality Surpasses Fiction, *Michelle has worked for years to dispel the
myths and misconceptions about the worldwide vampire community.*

In Defense of Psychic Vampirism

BY MICHELLE BELANGER OF HOUSE KHEPERU

It is a common belief among Pagans—and Wiccans in particular—that
psychic vampirism is an aberration or an outright crime. It is understood
to be something done willfully by the psi-vamp, and it is seen as something typically done for power, self-indulgence, or maliciousness. While there
are certainly individuals who engage in learned vampirism for pleasure or
sport, the existence of such people in no way invalidates the reality of those
who have an actual and legitimate energetic need.

Those Pagans and/or Wiccans who are willing to accept the notion that
some people may naturally require the taking of energy will typically draw the
line at human vital energy (often better known as chi) with the reasoning that
there are all kinds of energy that people can tap into, so a psi-vamp should be
able to go out and basically eat a tree.

So what is a psychic vampire if not someone who is addicted to the taking
of energy or who takes it simply because they can?

Some people do not naturally produce enough vital energy to sustain
optimal physical, spiritual, and mental well-being. Such individuals must
actively take energy from the environment around them to supplement their
personal vital energy.

If such a person is able to consistently draw upon the energy of nature, the earth, celestial energy, elemental energy, or some other outside source that *does not include* other people, then he or she is what I'd label a *partial* psi-vamp. Such a person can sustain their physical, mental, and spiritual well-being without taking the vital life force from other people, but he or she still has a distinct energetic need.

A full-blown psi-vamp is an individual who has this energetic need but is additionally *limited* almost exclusively to sustaining themself through the vital energy of other people. This energy can be taken through sexual interactions; it can be taken ambiently from crowds; it can be taken in the form of emotional energy; and some will take it through the medium of blood.

The defining factor of a full-blown psi-vamp is that the vampire cannot adequately sustain his or her basic physical, mental, and spiritual well-being by taking any outside energy *except for* human vital energy. This person will need to actively take such energy on a semi-regular basis (once a week to once a month on average, depending on activity, metabolism, severity of need, and so forth), or else suffer a loss of overall health and well-being. To be cut off from such energy will cause general lethargy, depression of the immune system, and a host of other ills.

In defense of the Pagans who have formulated such a negative opinion of vampires, it is certainly true that unconscious psychic vampires who have no idea what they are doing can be exceptionally destructive to those around them. Typically, a lot of unawakened psi-vamps will unconsciously create emotionally charged and melodramatic situations expressly to feed off of the energy that results. They are attention-getters, drama queens, and *oh-poor-mes*.

The untrained and unawakened tend to be in the vast majority, so it's from experiences with these that most metaphysicians have formulated their opinions of psychic vampires as a whole. And having had to deal with some stubbornly unawakened psi-vamps, I can understand to a point where these negative opinions come from. Such people are indeed a royal pain in the butt.

However, the fact that such poor souls exist is no good reason to reject the entire community as a whole, nor is it reason to judge all of us by someone's bad behavior. Psi-vampirism is a very real phenomenon. It is often as difficult for the awakening psi-vamp to realize that he or she has an actual and legitimate need for human energy as it is for a Pagan, Wiccan, or New Ager to accept that some people can only be sustained by a very limited spectrum of energy. It is far easier to take the utopian view of reality and believe that the Universe, in its wisdom, has provided adequately for all beings. And yet we know in reality that this is untrue, for even though there is an abundance of food that grows on our planet, many people still starve. Some starve because of the selfishness of others. Some starve because their geographic location simply does not provide the bounty required for a sustainable existence. Still others starve even with an adequate supply of food because somewhere in their own digestive systems there is a malfunction that prevents the proper assimilation of nutrients.

Too often, magickal workers who are reluctant to accept the reality of vampirism seek to discount all information about it being a real and legitimate need. Those who object to the very existence of psychic vampires should not attempt to obscure the subject or suppress what little information is available to those awakening to what they are. Instruction and awareness are the two best tools to combat those pesky psi-vamps who run around creating head-aches for everyone. A person cannot make ethical choices about applying a need they have yet even to acknowledge within themselves. Only when a person is fully educated and aware of such an ability can that person choose when and where to feed.

Taking energy from an unwilling target is indeed unethical. But learning to consciously take energy is the only thing that will enable true psi-vamps to make ethical decisions about their feeding habits. Once psi-vamps have achieved awareness and self-control, then they can harness what they are more positively, seeking out willing and able donors instead of randomly taking energy from anyone who crosses into their space.

Telling a psychic vampire that their need is not real, is all in their head, or is some manner of learned addiction (I've heard all that said far too many times, even from well-meaning friends and mentors) only prevents the psychic vampire from achieving the understanding needed to develop a healthy approach to who and what they are.

Definitions

Vital energy: The notion that there is a subtle something that galvanizes the human body lies at the heart of most metaphysical traditions. This vital energy, having many different names in many different cultures, is tied to breath, life, and spirit. At least as old as the Hindu Upanishads, this belief goes hand in hand with a belief in the soul. For many people, the soul is perceived as a kind of energy, something that can detach from the body and survive it after physical death. Although vital energy is not typically equated with the soul itself, it is seen as the key force that animates the physical body when the soul is in residence.

"Real" vampires: From the moment when someone first identified with the vampire as a magickal identity, there have been heated debates about what constitutes a "real" vampire. Left-hand path organizations, such as the Temple of Set's Order of the Vampyre, decry the members of the modern community as nothing more than poseurs, asserting that only the learned vampirism taught within their systems is legitimate. Within the modern community, individuals tend to differ significantly in their beliefs about what constitutes a "real" vampire. Most default to the definition of vampirism as a need for vital energy, but some groups do not limit this exclusively to human energy, identifying a person as a vampire if they exhibit a marked need for any kind of outside energy, including elemental energy, the energy gleaned from storms, and even energy drawn from technological devices.

Vampire ethics: This phrase might sound like a contradiction of terms, but within the modern vampire community, ethical behavior is a big deal. The social aspect of the vampire community depends on everyone working together and getting along, and this includes respecting the rights of others when it comes to their personal energy. It's considered very bad manners to take energy from someone without their consent, and most vampire organizations require that those associated with them adhere to ethical guidelines such as the Black Veil or the Donor Bill of Rights.

Jodi Lee has written articles online to help dispel the myths and misun-derstanding that surround real vampirism. She worked for six years as an editor for an online community, achieving the position of senior managing editor. For five years, she was editor-in-chief of 3Sides Electronic Publish-ing, now 3Sides Literary Agency. Active as a writer in both the vampire and Pagan communities, Jodi is currently a submissions editor with Apex Science Fiction and Horror Digest. *She lives in Canada.*

Vampires: Dispelling the Myths

BY JODI LEE

What are some of the stories you've heard about vampires? Surely, in this day and age, there isn't a person out there who hasn't heard of or read about Dracula. That undead, night-prowling Count of immense powers and unlimited appeal has caused quite a stir—and perpetuated the frightening myths that can make reality hard to live in.

Holy water, silver, sunlight, and garlic are banes to the Hollywood vam-pire. But being a real vampire does not give you an automatic allergy to silver. Holy water does not burn like acid, and garlic does not keep you at bay. The only myth that seems to hold some grain of truth to it has to do with sunlight. Sunlight will hardly reduce a real vampire to ash, but for myself, I do easily burn. I only burn once a year, though, and that turns into a deep enough tan that I don't burn again. However, I don't like being outside in the sunlight simply because it hurts my eyes, even when I wear heavy-duty sunglasses. I won't sit out in the sun for more than half an hour at a time. This is true for summer or winter. Cloudy days are often just as bad.

Real vampires are not immortal, although many of us seem to have (or claim to have) strengthened immune systems and tend to look younger than our years. Again, this is not the case for everyone, since I have had grey hair since I was in my mid-teens, and I certainly look like I'm in my thirties. The fellow who carded me at a local bar didn't seem to think so, but I believe that I look my age. In my opinion, whether you're a vampire or not, you can't battle genetics! If the family genetics indicate early aging, you're going to age early.

While vampires tend to be nocturnal, sleeping in a coffin from dawn until dusk is a myth. Although, there again, I do know someone who did sleep in a coffin for several years. He didn't absolutely *have* to, and eventually I think he grew out of it. Frankly, I couldn't stand sleeping in a coffin—there just isn't enough room to sprawl out!

Why are vampires night owls? Most of us just generally function better during the night. I know this is true for me. I write and research mainly between ten PM and three AM. So there is something to the notion that vampires are "children of the night."

Are vampires bloodthirsty predators, stalking "victims" to drain the lifeblood from them? The only time I ever stalked a "victim," it was a game of sorts that we had agreed upon ahead of time. And even when I caught him, I hardly drained him dry.

On that whole "draining dry" bit, they say that drinking more than an ounce or two of blood will make a person physically sick. To my knowledge, no vampire takes more than an ounce or two from a donor. For myself, I've never gone beyond an ounce and that was spread out over a few hours. When I drank from my first donor I was close to being completely drunk (and no—not from alcohol, but it's the only way I can describe the feeling) after only a few sips.

How different is a vampire from an ordinary person, really? You could very well know a vampire. You could work with one or even have one in your family. You won't see them manifest any of the tell-tale signs depicted in the movies. If they didn't tell you what they are, you would never know.

DEFINITIONS

Dracula: Most modern vampires are quick to point out that they have little in common with Dracula, the character that Irish writer Bram Stoker based upon the historical Wallachian warlord Vlad Tepes. Despite this, there remains an amusing and wholly unintentional connection between modern vampires and Bram Stoker's famous book. The year 1997 was the one hundredth anniversary of Bram Stoker's *Dracula*. Coincidentally, 1997 was also the year that many of the most well-respected real vampire sites went up on the Internet.

Sunlight: As depicted in both fiction and folklore, vampires are not universally sensitive to sunlight. Bram Stoker, for example, has Dracula running around London during the day. His powers are muted, but he hardly turns to ash. Cinematic portrayals of vampires solidly established the "seared by sunlight" stereotype, starting with F. W. Murnau's 1922 classic *Nosferatu*. Despite this, many modern vampires complain of a marked sensitivity to sunlight. Are they taking the stereotype a little too seriously? Many psychic vampires are highly sensitive to a variety of energies, so an argument can be made that some energetic aspect of sunlight is simply too much for them. Whether their sensitivity is real or imagined, many real vampires avoid direct sunlight.

Larae is best known as the founder and owner of Darkness Embraced (www.darknessembraced.com), an extensive website resource that is maintained for individuals interested in vampires, witchcraft, and the occult. An active webmistress and moderator for several online vampire pages, Larae is a prolific individual whose work is distinguished by her charming blend of elegance and down-to-earth sentiment.

Am I a Vampire?

BY LARAE OF DARKNESS EMBRACED

Being a vampire is not about power, beauty, or romance. There are no Frank Langellas or female equivalents in our realms. No one is going to appear outside your window in the darkest hours of the night with a billowing mist rising behind them. No one is going to embrace you in an eternal kiss and take you away from all your pain. As romantic as this may seem, this type of magic exists only on a Hollywood set. There are various downsides to our nature that creates hardship for many of us, and it leaves much to be desired.

Real vampirism is a condition that is often accompanied by chronic physical symptoms such as lethargy, insomnia, or migraines. When a medical professional is consulted, no specific physical condition can be found to explain these symptoms, and no traditional treatment suffices to make them go away. Only by feeding does a vampire alleviate these symptoms, and if a vampire does not regularly feed, the symptoms recur. This is hardly the glamorous existence of Anne Rice's Lestat.

Before deciding that you are a vampire, consider that many of the traits typically associated with vampirism may also be symptoms of potentially life-threatening illnesses. Your collection of symptoms should be addressed by a physician before you even consider vampirism to be the cause. Speak to your parents or family practitioner about your symptoms (although you should leave out the part about believing yourself to be a vampire). Get yourself a thorough examination, just to be certain that vampirism is what's really going on. In the long run, you will be glad that you did.

If you are an adolescent, please understand that your body is going through immense changes. These changes will continue all the way into your early twenties. There are so many things going on in your body that could have a tremendous impact on your physical and emotional state that it may be premature to blame vampirism. Even things that may be considered bizarre to most are nothing more then your body reacting to these chemical and hormonal changes. If you experience symptoms along with severe bouts of depression and anger, then you may require a little extra help from the medical profession to assist you in coping and getting through all these changes. It's absolutely nothing to be ashamed of, and it's more common than you may think. Don't make yourself suffer needlessly. Talk about your problems and get appropriate help.

If you are still certain that you are a vampire, educate yourself. Doing so is especially important if you are considering drinking blood. Before you even conceive of the notion of drinking blood, please educate yourself on safety, blood issues, first aid, and any other information surrounding bloodletting! Drinking someone's blood is a very serious thing. There are a variety of horrendous things that could happen both to you and to the person you engage in bloodletting with if you don't know what you are doing. Irresponsible bloodletting could have ramifications ranging from blood-borne diseases like HIV or hepatitis to acute injuries, scars, infections, and even death. Also, please understand that cutting yourself and drinking your own blood will by no means validate your vampirism. If you have an obsession with cutting yourself, please seek out help.

If you still wonder whether or not you are a vampire, take at least an hour out of your day to reflect upon your feelings and your inner self. One option that can assist you in this quest is to record, in a journal or notebook, any questions you have that have led you to make this query about yourself in the first place. Make comparisons and abstracts, jot down thoughts, experiences, or anything that you feel pertinent to discovering the answer for yourself. Over considerable time, you will become proficient in drawing your own conclusions as well as learning some new things about yourself along the way. In the mean time, seek out others and ask questions. Observe conversations taking place on various forums and e-lists online, and follow threads that seem pertinent to you. Even if you ultimately decide that you are not a vampire, you will benefit from these extensive personal inquiries, learning much about who you really are.

Validation from Others

Some websites will declare that only other vampires will be able to tell you for certain whether or not you are a vampire. This is simply not true. The only grain of remote truth in such a statement is that vampires are sometimes drawn to other vampires. Sometimes, we are pulled to others of our kind unconsciously without any logical surface explanation. We may see a person in a crowded room and feel drawn to them without being able to put a finger on the exact reason why.

It is important to realize that those we feel strongly drawn to may not always automatically be of a vampiric nature. What you are responding to is something different about that person—a difference that comes out in their energy. They could be Therian, Otherkin, an old soul, or someone who is a natural energy worker, such as a witch or shaman. We can be drawn to all such people because of our shared parallels with enlightenment and sensitivity to energy. Sometimes, narrowing someone down as being a vampire can be complex; for this reason, the latent should be left to awaken on their own.

Interference from a vampire validating who they "believe" to be another "vampire" can be destructive. Ultimately, it can interfere with the latent's growth and spirituality, especially if that person is misled down a path that is not meant for them. In my opinion, this can cause a lot of turbulence during awakening—a process that is already difficult and unsettling enough for most. Telling people what they are should be avoided as much as possible. It's perfectly fine for a vampire to offer subtle support and guidance while keeping their speculation secret, but an awakening individual's vampirism should not be validated outright by anyone save for the awakened soul themselves.

If you are truly a vampire, you will come to know this in your own time. No one will need to confirm or validate it for you.

DEFINITIONS

Donor: An individual who willingly provides sustenance to a vampire. Donors are highly respected within the vampire community, as they are not always easy to come by. Donors can provide energy, blood, or a combination of both to a vampire. Even if a donor is only providing energy, it is a widespread practice to ensure that both donor and vampire are tested for any disease. A donor does not have to be in any sort of romantic or sexual relationship with a vampire in order to provide what that vampire needs.

Latent vampire: An individual whose vampirism has not yet been fully realized. Latent vampires still feed, but all of their vampirism is unconscious and instinctual. A latent vampire must go through the process of awakening to realize what he or she is. Often, this awakening is sparked by an intense energy exchange with another vampire, an experience that has helped perpetuate the myth of "turning."

Therians and Otherkin: Therians and Otherkin are an offshoot of the modern magickal movement. These individuals feel a spiritual tie to something other than humanity. In the case of Therians, this is a strong tie to a specific animal. For Otherkin, the tie is often to a mythological creature, such as a dragon or a griffin. The level of identification goes beyond that of an animal totem. Most Therians and Otherkin feel that, underneath their human bodies, they really are this other thing. The "otherness" typically expresses itself as a magickal identity, influencing psychic abilities and other powers. The vampire community is divided in its acceptance of these beliefs.

Sylverë ap Leanan has been involved in the vampire community since the mid-1990s. She is the facilitator of one of the community's oldest Internet-based support groups, the Real-Vampires Community Alliance (http://groups.yahoo.com/group/real-vampires/). Originally involved in the Vampire/Donor Alliance, Sylverë has appeared in the British television documentary American Vampires *and on the Internet radio program* Nightwatch. *She is a mother of two and lives in Kansas City with her family.*

To Bleed or Not To Bleed

What Makes a Vampire Real?

BY SYLVERË AP LEANAN

Are you a vampire if you drink human blood? Or are you a vampire if you feed upon energy? In the years I've been involved with the vampire community, I have heard the blood drinker versus psychic feeder argument so often that it's become nearly passé. Even so, it still has the capacity to both infuriate and incite what amounts to a verbal brawl among those who are active in the community. I confess I will never understand why there is any debate at all, much less why the sanguinarians seem to feel that ingesting blood somehow elevates them to a superior status. To understand my perspective, the reader must first understand my definition of *vampire* and how I arrived at the conclusion that I am, in fact, a vampire who feeds psychically.

A vampire is a person who experiences a deficiency in energy that cannot be attributed to any known medical cause such as leukemia, lupus, hypoglycemia, porphyria, or Epstein-Barr virus; nor is it the result of engaging in magic(k)al practices to an excessive degree. It is a deficiency that cannot be alleviated by typical methods, including eating a balanced diet, resting, and routine social contact with friends. This deficiency can only be corrected by ingesting blood (typically human) or other bodily fluids, or by absorbing energy through various meditative, spiritual, or "psychic" practices.

Vampirism is the condition that causes the need for—and the act of—drawing out and ingesting human bodily fluids for the purposes of gaining the living energy (alternately called *prana*, *chi*, *ki*, or breath) contained therein, or absorbing that same energy through psychic and/or spiritual means in order to maintain one's health at optimum levels. Some people may engage in vampire-like practices, but such people are not real vampires if the consistent need to do so in order to ensure good health is absent. The difference is subtle, and is often overlooked or misunderstood by those who are not truly vampires.

All vampires require living energy above and beyond what is generally considered normal for a human. The only difference is the means by which they acquire it. While some vampires prefer or require blood as a focal point, others are more adept at or have a preference for drawing the energy from other sources. These sources may include, but are not limited to, the ambient energy of a large crowd, natural sources such as electrical storms or running water, the intense emotional states of others nearby, sexual energy, or the energy of artists in the process of performing or creating.

From my observation and experience, I propose that there is no specific set of symptoms common to all vampires beyond the inability to produce enough energy to meet the needs of the body through the usual methods of balanced diet, rest, and recreation. Many vampires exhibit traits such as extreme sensitivity to light or temperature, a persistent feeling of hunger or thirst that is not alleviated by food and water, or detrimental health effects such as migraines, nausea, or chronic fatigue, but other vampires do not experience these symptoms, or else they experience them to a much lesser degree. The defining factor in determining whether or not one is a vampire is the persistent energy deficiency that can neither be explained nor remedied by Western medicine.

There is absolutely no credible medical evidence to suggest that we as vampires harbor an unknown virus, carry a genetic mutation, suffer from an enzyme or vitamin deficiency, or are missing or have a flaw in certain mitochondria. We are not are the descendents of an ancient subspecies of proto-humans that crossbred with modern humans or an alien race that crossbred with prehistoric humans. I have seen so many spurious claims for a biological cause for vampirism, and all have left me unconvinced. Vampires are normal and generally healthy *Homo sapiens*, end of story. My personal philosophy addresses the cause of vampirism from a spiritual standpoint, but that's best left for another essay.

✠　✠

As for how I know I am a vampire, I can say that over the years I've been tested for numerous ailments—from diabetes to hypothyroidism, anemia to HIV. Other than a tendency toward low blood pressure (the low side of normal but not unhealthy) and borderline hypoglycemia, which is easily managed by monitoring my diet, I'm as healthy as the proverbial horse. I have been in counseling with a licensed mental health professional. While I do have seasonal affective disorder and trichotillomania, neither of these conditions accounts for the often debilitating physical symptoms I experience when I have not fed. Drinking blood does absolutely nothing to alleviate them. However, upon absorbing psychic energy from another person, these symptoms disappear. They recur in a cyclical manner, usually once every four to six weeks, and worsen progressively the longer the interval between feeding sessions. Since no other explanation fits, I can reasonably conclude that I am a vampire.

Now back to the argument of drawing psychic energy versus drinking blood. Not all vampires need to consume blood, and to say otherwise is foolish at best. The spiritual resonance of the energy found in blood cannot sufficiently meet the needs of all vampires. Some of us require a higher "frequency" or energy in a more pure state in order to attain any benefit from it. Others simply choose to get the energy they need from other sources due to the potentially serious health risks associated with drinking blood. This does not preclude the very real need to feed, however. We will not die if we don't feed. For that matter, neither will a vampire who chooses to drink blood die from its lack. We'll just be unhealthy, miserable, and less-than-pleasant people until we feed.

As far as I'm concerned, it's not only inaccurate to claim that psychic feeders are somehow less "real" than blood drinkers, but it is also cruel. Many vampires already feel marginalized in a world that considers us crazy if not dangerous. To those who would declare that the only real vampire is she who drinks blood, I say: who the hell are you that you feel you have the right to compound this insensitivity by dismissing us out of hand based solely on our chosen method of getting the energy we require? It could be argued that psychic feeding is the more valid method because those of us who engage in that practice have evolved beyond the need for such crass techniques as drinking blood. It is our rarefied tastes and more enlightened approach that make us the "true" vampires. However, I see no reason to stoop to that level. Wouldn't that be the pot calling the kettle black? I know who I am, and I'm secure enough that I am beyond the folly of those who want to disparage my personal reality. What I don't understand is why some feel that demeaning their peers is an acceptable means of making themselves feel special.

DEFINITIONS

Sanguinarian: Derived from the Latin word *sanguis*, meaning blood, a sanguinarian is an individual who drinks blood. A more common term is *sanguine vampire*.

Porphyria: A disease that has been linked with folktales of both vampires and werewolves as a possible explanation for the origin of these myths. A hereditary disease that afflicts the bone marrow and thus the blood, porphyria can render its sufferers highly sensitive to sunlight. There are perhaps anecdotal reports that porphyria has inspired cravings for human blood. The disease can turn the teeth a rusty color, giving the impression that the sufferer has been drinking blood. There is no evidence whatsoever that any of the members of the modern vampire community suffer from any form of this disease.

Kiera is a registered nurse and one of five founding members of the Atlanta Vampire Alliance. Her research into the vampire community as well as the esoteric field of study began in the early nineties. Until the development of the Atlanta Vampire Alliance, Kiera walked a solitary path, more intent on spiritual exploration and gathering knowledge than in joining a vampire house for social reasons.

Revelations

BY KIERA OF HOUSE AVA

I am a deeply spiritual person, although I do not align myself with a particular religion. Along the course of my quest for personal meaning, I have done research on Celtic and Siberian shamanism, Wicca, Paganism, voodoo, Taoism, Buddhism, and Native American spirituality. Although none of these paths seemed to explain everything I had encountered in my life, all of them taught me something of value.

Ever since I was a very young child, I have felt a deep spiritual connection to a Mother Earth goddess and also to the Native American path. I recently read an article written by former Harvard professor Barry Fell that links the Celts' Ogham symbols to inscribed symbols found in Native American archeological sites in New England that date to about 800 BCE. Through this archeological evidence, there is now proof of contact between Europeans and Native Americans prior to the Roman Empire, long before even the Vikings briefly settled North America.

For years I have stated that the Celtic religion and modern Wicca hold significant parallels to Native American belief systems, so in essence this article provided validation for the belief system that always felt closest to my personal vision.

Then I began reconsidering my views on modern vampirism, and this is where my revelation began:

I know some people choose to associate themselves with the term *vampire/vampyre* for many reasons, and I dare not try to touch on them all here. However, most psi-vampires state they have an energy deficit that causes them a physical hunger and a need to feed upon the life energy or emotional energy found in other people and in crowds, or the natural energy found in elemental reservoirs.

I do not necessarily doubt this particular rationale; however, I have come to believe that it is simply a manifestation of a different idea. As vampires, we delight in the decadence and pleasure of feeding, but I think often that as psi-vampires we are accused of being "leeches" who only take energy, giving nothing in return. Yet from my observations, we actually participate in a give-and-take scenario. Because of this, I feel that the more accurate term for what we now call a psi-vampire is an *energy manipulator*. We cycle energy, rather than simply consuming it.

Energy is not stagnant. It cannot be consumed without releasing energy in another form. Is our "Beacon" not a manifestation of the concentrated energy field that surrounds us? It is the flame that draws the moths to us.

Energy flows freely. Those of us who know how to channel it are at a great advantage compared with those unawakened souls who are unable or unwilling to be first swallowed up and then strengthened by the mighty currents that flow within every atom of matter on this plane of existence. Perhaps that is the truest explanation of modern vampirism, an inborn ability to harness and direct the forces of nature.

If you look throughout other cultures and time periods, there are all sorts of professions that others turn to in times of need: prophets, seers, saints, priests, faith healers, shamans, natural healers, herbalists, witches, witch doctors, even nurses. What do all of these people share in common? Through ritual or ceremony, these people raise and manipulate energy. They use this energy to heal others as well as to strengthen their own Gifts. In essence, they are energy manipulators of various degrees and archetypes.

Is that not what a psi-vampire is? A human being who is able to extract and manipulate energy for his or her own personal use? Does it matter what label we attach to it? Vampire, witch, shaman—the symptoms are all the same.

Vampires are energy manipulators in the same vein as other energy manipulators who are accepted or even embraced by societies such as shamans, healers, Reiki instructors, or various other spiritual and magickal practitioners. We *can* be beneficial, supportive, and harmonious with human communities. It is a choice each individual makes according to his or her own moral and ethical codes.

Yet vampires are still often vilified as energy suckers, energy feeders, beings who take and do not give in return. I propose that there is no difference between energy feeders and energy workers. In the end, the energy is cyclic. You cannot harbor it like a dragon guarding its treasure. Energy that seems to be destroyed is only changed.

How can it be assumed that we only reap energy from others? Do we not also give that energy back to others day after day, especially in our dayside professions? As a nurse, each patient I touch and reassure is given my energy. Often, my patients' gratitude and warmth cycles that very energy back to me. We reciprocate, healer and healed.

I know a vampire who is a massage therapist. While he may inadvertently feed on the ambient energy of a client, he is also investing a great deal of physical, spiritual, and mental energy into his daily profession. A multitude of vampires through their chosen professions have demonstrated similar investments of energy.

My argument is that this vilification is, first of all, unjust and inaccurate. Secondly, it creates a social stigma that I think many vampires wear as a mantle of guilt because of the nature of their being. Many vampires are either made to feel guilty by this stigma or find some masochistic satisfaction in symbolically flogging themselves with it. This is the classic Louis de Pointe du Lac syndrome, under which we broodingly ask, "Am I innately evil for my very nature? Is it beyond my control? Am I damned?"

The need to consume energy to alleviate a pranic deficit is not exclusive to vampirism. If you delve into shamanism, there is a concept called the Wounded Healer, wherein a healer actually suffers physical harm from the amount of energy they focus into healing another. The Practitioner expends so much of their own vital life-force energy that they become weakened, and need to gather energy in order to recharge their batteries. This is the price one pays for a Gift. Nobody rides for free.

Frankly, and this is an opinion that will probably ruffle some feathers, I don't think psi-vampires *must* have energy to survive. Due to a car accident, I spent the better part of eight months isolated from all people, alone 90 percent of the time. I did not wither up and die from lack of energy feeding. There are many elders within the vampire community who speak of times their hunger lay dormant, sometimes for lengthy periods of time. Some report they thought they had been "cured" of their vampirism—until their hunger resurfaced. It was like that for me. I had no opportunities to feed my needs, yet those needs never surfaced during that time.

In my opinion, psi-vampires enjoy feeding. They enjoy using their charisma to their benefit. They enjoy the rush. If we have an energy deficit (and this has never been proven concretely), it is a mild one. The deficit does not threaten our survival. It is something that can be lived with. Maybe we get a little distracted when we get low on energy. We get a little grumpy, but we won't die.

And when we are not able to feed off energy due to circumstances that isolate us, the symptoms we suffer are more along the lines of alcohol or drug detoxification rather than those of malnourishment. The symptoms most vampires attribute to lack of feeding are lethargy, inability to focus, and irritability. Aren't these symptoms more akin to withdrawal than starvation?

Perhaps the reason I titled this essay "Revelations" is because I think that, far too often, the vampire community as well as the individuals who comprise it forget to think outside the box. They read any number of online or published texts and accept the information within them as if they were the Holy Grail.

It has been stated that psi-vampirism results from an energy deficit, which may or may not be true and yet almost everyone takes it as the gospel truth. I believe elders and texts can be valuable assets, but that does not mean that we as vampires should simply expect to be spoon-fed our beliefs. Human beings were given a frontal lobe for a reason: to learn, to explore, and to question.

Ultimately, vampires are people too! We have professions, families, friends, responsibilities, and morals. We are all individuals and many of us subscribe to differing ethical, moral, and religious codes. There are the archetypal evil energy-sucking vampires who shamelessly prey upon people. Yet is that really any more horrific than the Jack the Rippers, John Wayne Gacys, and Jeffrey Dahmers—deviants of the "normal" dominant society? Like any other aspect of society, vampires produce their saints as well as their monsters. That's just human nature. We each make our choices, and those choices are never universally evil—or universally good.

Among vampires, there are those we would classify as good, evil, and everything in between. Most vampires are basically decent human beings who have one extra issue to struggle with, or in turn fully embrace. We just happen to be awakened to energy forces that most people either choose to ignore or are ignorant of. This gives us a greater potential for power, but also a greater responsibility to use that power wisely.

Definitions

The Beacon: Psychic vampires have distinctive energy signatures, and other psychic vampires seem to be naturally sensitive to this particular signature, even if the individual in question is unaware that he or she is, in fact, a vampire. "The Beacon" is a term used to describe this sixth sense that many psychic vampires have about one another. Coined in the earliest versions of the *Psychic Vampire Codex*, the Beacon has gained widespread use throughout the general vampire community.

Vampires and serial killers: A number of popular writers on the vampire archetype insist on identifying certain serial killers as "vampires." Some serial killers, like Jeffrey Dahmer, have been known to consume portions of their victims. The vampire subculture understandably objects to having murderers and madmen like Jack the Ripper identified as "real" vampires, but the connection persists. This is largely due to Elizabeth Báthory, the so-called Blood Countess. A Hungarian noblewoman who lived from 1560 until 1614, Báthory is often described as having slaughtered young women in order to bathe in their blood. Allegedly, she did this in order to maintain her own youth and beauty. Although the historical Blood Countess did indeed torture and kill perhaps hundreds of young women, tales of her sanguine bathing habits are related more to legend than to fact. Her ties with vampires and vampirism remain in the popular imagination, however, and these ties are made more persistent by the fact that she was distantly related to Vlad Tepes, the Wallachian hero who served as the historical inspiration for Dracula.

Louis de Pointe du Lac syndrome: In Anne Rice's *Vampire Chronicles,* Louis, the vampiric "son" of Lestat, is the quintessential "reluctant vampire" who is consumed by guilt and remorse for his very existence. In the vampire community, which cannot help but be influenced by portrayals of vampires in modern culture, someone who struggles needlessly and excessively with the supposed evils of his or her vampiric nature is sometimes compared to Anne Rice's Louis character.

Rev. Vicutus has an extensive background in magick and the occult, following a long-held tradition of Luciferianism. Founder of Ordo Sekhemu, Rev. Vicutus has dedicated his magickal organization to serious study of the more occult aspects of the vampiric condition. His writing and views are distinguished by an unfailing devotion to eloquence, aesthetic, and high magick. He runs the website www.ordo-sekhemu.org.

The Journey Is Now

BY REV. VICUTUS, DOMINUS DE ORDO SEKHEMU

Embrace thoughts. Thoughts are subtle and quick, and they depict much more than words ever will. Thoughts fade in and out of our mental abyss. They are like the patterns that are encryptions for numbers. I feel that our own individual thoughts are the origins of expression, which we inadvertently act out through kindness, compassion, anger, and other such human characteristics.

Creative and Destructive Flows

Many tend to view the opposites of Life as an absolute "goodness" and an absolute "evilness." The distance between the polarities doesn't necessarily mean that one is good and the other bad. They are simply degrees of the same state. They are outward (projective) and inward (receptive) flows of natural energies.

Should a practitioner of magick focus his Path upon the Left, and another practitioner of magick focus his Path upon the Right, that doesn't necessarily mean that one is an evildoer and the other a holy man. They are both aspired, spiritual beings living human experiences. Each individual complements the other in spirituality and fervency; therefore, they share the same state of Divine Consciousness only at a different parallel level.

Distance from the Divine Source is not negative, simply Dark. It is natural that some people (especially young students of magick) misperceive things in this manner, since their level of perception is at a different level of understanding. This is part of their spiritual growth process, and it is through these engagements that we learn and advance.

The same principle applies to all such things universally. In everything there is manifested a measured motion. The universe expands and contracts, and with it the birth and death of star systems and baby universes. This is how Nature's laws of rhythm, harmony, and symmetry affect us. Even the mental states of mankind rise and fall as one becomes like a black hole in space—absorbed. And to the mystic—absorption into Wisdom.

The outer world is simply a reflection of the inner cosmos. I have always perceived the chakras as spheres of transcendence because they represent various states of consciousness and attributes very much comparable to the cosmic planets. It is beautiful when I look at pictures of our galaxy and connect that to our innermost selves—the Inner Sanctum, our soul.

Each of us has a purpose for humanity. Earth is so beautiful and when you look upon its inhabitants, you capture a glimpse of the earth within you, surrounded by the blackness of space.

Shades

Between the polar extremes, there are gradual degrees of shades. So one asks himself, where does Light end and Darkness begin?

To Sekhrians, vampyrism is a spiritual condition. The cycling of energy is quite subtle and beautiful, especially when one hones certain abilities and uses them for the benefit of the Self and others. This exchange of goodness is the very core of Beauty. The manifestation of our healing mirrors the uniqueness of our true Selves. Through the connection with illuminated intelligences, one becomes an illuminated Power of Light—encompassing the entire polar spectrum from enlightenment to endarkment. The symbiotic connection is Divine, and this is the certainty that as vampyres we take *and* receive mental states, emotions, energy, thoughts, disease, and sensations.

Vampyres as Meta-Programmers

We are all "designed" to "re-vamp" old systems into something compatible for this new age, which is why we're called vampyres. "We are," as Sister Michelle Belanger of House Kheperu puts it, "catalysts of change in a spiritually bereft age." We are not here to destroy, cause chaos, cause ill health, or to be maleficent, but rather to spawn new ideas and new ways to improve old systems so that humanity may flow evenly.

Vampyres were once admired and respected as patrons. Today we are often frowned upon due to our uniqueness and difference. It is time to clear such misconceptions not by the publishing of material based on what one awakened individual feels true vampyrism is, but by our actions and our compassion as creatures of Beauty. Actions speak louder than words, and (unfortunately) it is by our actions that the world judges. We are judged by the Work we leave behind.

Finis Coronat! *The conclusion crowns the Work!*

I tell you all: you are all of magnetic service, unique and beautiful in your own right. We all serve individual purposes that revolve around our own baby universes, and even more than that, we all serve a "common" purpose—a purpose to assist in the growth and personal evolution of the "common man." This is truly an exciting journey!

DEFINITIONS

Left-hand path: Sometimes abbreviated to "LHP," the left-hand path of magick is often mistakenly presented as "black" or "dark" magick. Although this is the path of LaVeyan Satanists, Setians, and many dark Pagans, the left-hand path is less about the pursuit of evil and more about the pursuit of the Self. Rather than seeking out and supplicating gods and goddesses, the practitioner of the left-hand path seeks to realize his or her own godhood. A left-hand path practitioner's fundamental relationship with magick, deities, and natural forces can best be summed up as "My will be done."

Right-hand path: Sometimes abbreviated to "RHP," the right-hand path of magick seeks to work with deities and higher forces in order to empower and improve the Self. The right-hand path is often incorrectly presented as "white" magick or "good" magick. A right-hand path practitioner's fundamental relationship with magick, deities, and natural forces can best be summed up as "Thy will be done."

Endarkment: A term coined by Lady Dark Rose of House Sable Brahmin and later adopted by House Sekhemu. Endarkment is a vampiric form of enlightenment, by which an individual comes to a greater sense of understanding through a detailed exploration of his or her dark side. In a psychological sense, it can be compared to the integration of the Jungian shadow.

SECTION
- TWO -

Vampire Awakenings

Michelle Belanger is the founder of House Kheperu, a decade-old vampire organization devoted to compiling and sharing knowledge about psychic vampirism and energy work. A full-time writer and lecturer, Michelle does a great deal of community outreach, seeking to serve as a bridge between the often secretive vampire community and other magickal subcultures.

What Is Awakening?

BY MICHELLE BELANGER OF HOUSE KHEPERU

*T*here is more to the world than just ordinary, physical reality. There is not just body. There is also spirit. All of the material things around us have a vital, spiritual component that our current culture encourages us to be blind to. However, for some of us, it is impossible to remain blind. Those who we term *Awakened* have their eyes open and are able to see all of those things that make the universe a richer and more profound experience than one of just the material senses.

Awakening comes at various points in people's lives. Some of us are born Awakened, and we have known nothing else. Others come to their Awakening later in life. Most often, we are born with the capacity to Awaken, and latent talents and abilities manifest in early childhood. But as our parents, teachers, and all other authority figures in our lives repeatedly reinforce the notion that our subtle senses are just our imaginations, that spirits aren't real, and that magick doesn't exist, we start to block off this aspect of our experience.

These self-imposed mental blocks often do not start to come loose until the onset of puberty or later adolescence, when a person typically begins to develop his or her own independent identity. Sometimes, latent abilities manifest with renewed strength as puberty comes upon us, and then our sensations and perceptions become something that cannot be denied. More often, as we go through that period of individuation in adolescence when we question the rules and boundaries set by society and by our parents, we start to also question those boundaries that tell us what we can and cannot believe.

It is very common in this stage of Awakening to reevaluate the experiences and beliefs of childhood in an attempt to discern what was real and what was truly imagination. At this stage, it is also common to experiment with different belief systems in an attempt to understand what is really going on with a reality that does not seem to conform to the accepted rules. A person at this stage has a lot of unanswered questions and many experiences that seem to defy the very rules of possibility.

It is not uncommon to have spontaneous numinous experiences at this stage as well—episodes of precognition, strong moments of empathy or telepathy, visual perception of auras or spirits, and other feelings which cannot be explained.

The challenge with Awakening is breaking through those barriers built up by your parents, your society, and your birth religion so that your Higher Self begins to peek out through the façade imposed upon you. This is not an easy thing to do. It takes a strong personality and a profound belief in yourself to be able to reject the accepted paradigm and seek to define one of your own. This is one of the reasons so many Awakened people are such egoists—it takes a strong ego to survive the process of Awakening without buckling under the pressure to just disbelieve.

Belief is the crux of Awakening. There is usually a critical point at which a person who is Awakening makes a decision to believe or not to believe. If they choose to accept that there is more to reality than they have been told, then the process continues and, with work, they will eventually come to understand and even master the latent abilities that they have. If they choose not to believe, those latent abilities do not just go away. Instead, the Awakened person enters a period of deep repression that can continue their whole lives. Either way, the road before the person is not an easy one. On one hand, they must work their whole lives to believe in something most other people regard as fantasy. On the other, they must work their whole lives to forcibly keep their spiritual eyes shut, when seeing and experiencing things on that level are as natural to them as breathing.

Although many people equate Awakening with a spiritual epiphany, it's not always a matter of turning on a light in a dark room, and then you're Awakened. It's more like lighting a candle in a dark cave, only to discover that the light of this one candle reveals many more candles and a far more extensive cavern than you'd ever imagined. From that first faint light, you understand how to go about illuminating your surroundings, and the process continues for as long as you are willing to explore. Awakening was certainly like this for me. There was no single, specific incident that finally tipped the balance of belief. Rather, it was a whole lot of little things that piled up until I couldn't ignore them anymore. I could have explained one or two strange incidents away, but five, ten, or fifteen weird things all happening around me with no good explanation just couldn't be coincidence any more. Eventually, it took more mental gymnastics to deny my nature than it did to simply accept it.

I've seen this exact same process at work with others again and again. The really big, reality-popping incidents don't tip the balance of Awakening for them. The more extraordinary and extreme the event, the easier it is to convince oneself that it was nothing but wishful thinking or an overactive imagination. The day-to-day incidents, however—these are another matter entirely. In the end, it is the endless string of little intuitions, coincidences, and luck that finally make the difference for people. Crushed under the weight of a thousand everyday miracles, most people have to reassess their views on reality. They take that first step and begin to believe.

Awakening is a crucial process—not just for the individual, but for our very world. The world around us is changing, as are the people who share this changing world. There are more and more Awakened in every generation. Vampire, witch, New Ager, Indigo Child—together we are pushing the boundaries. Each time another person Awakens to the greater potential of reality, the easier it becomes for others to see past the blinders of mundane reality and make that leap toward spiritual evolution. This is the time and the place for it, and if you have the courage and the perseverance, there is something wonderful to be achieved.

Spiritual evolution: Inherent in the concept of Awakening is the idea that human beings can become more than just physical beings living in a material world. The idea of spiritual evolution suggests that there are realms and levels of experience beyond physical existence that humans can access if they cultivate the proper skills. Although the concept can be found primarily in Eastern religions as well as certain New Age circles, this model of spiritual development, geared toward becoming something better than human, flows as a distinct undercurrent within several modern magickal communities, the vampire subculture included.

Higher Self: Connected strongly to a reincarnational model of existence, the term "Higher Self" is often used to indicate that portion of an individual's personality, knowledge, and memory that transfers from life to life. Especially in New Age circles, the Higher Self is seen as a more enlightened portion of personality that remains somewhat separate from the everyday personality living from day to day in a specific life. For those who believe in reincarnation, the Higher Self is often perceived as being able to choose not only the circumstances of the next incarnation, but also the life lessons that each specific incarnation will encounter in order to further the development of the soul over time. Many vampire houses have adopted the notion of the Higher Self, viewing the Higher Self as the immortal aspect of the vampire.

Anshar Seraphim was born in Torrance, California in 1980 and currently lives in the Sierra Nevada Mountains. He has been doing energy work for over eight years and is an active member of both the Wiccan and vampire communities, writing many articles for each. In his spare time, he enjoys reading and writing poetry, painting, sculpting, crafting medieval armor, playing pool, and studying holistic medicine.

Understanding Energy: A Journey

BY ANSHAR SERAPHIM OF HOUSE LOST HAVEN

Energy. It has many forms and incarnations, some of which are known to the world at large and some of which elude us in any definitive way yet pervade our every waking moment. Energy work, as it has been called by many, is the conscious redirection and application of thought energy. It holds great meaning for many, but to some it is superstitious nonsense. In many years of energy work, I have realized that many people, including some practitioners, are only aware of it through faith and experience, akin to a religious belief. In other words, they accept what most of us cannot see. I myself am a skeptic. When I first came across energy work, I thought it was total nonsense. Only after spending a considerable amount of time in study and theory was I able to draw the conclusions that I needed in order to open my mind to its influence, and ultimately attempt to understand its origins and composition.

Being naturally empathic, I have always been accustomed to feeling the emotions of those around me. I never related any of these experiences to energy, simply because I felt that it wasn't necessary for metaphysical energy to exist for me to be able to tune into others. There is a daunting wealth of information that we do not currently know about the human brain, or even the nature of the universe, and so I simply attributed my empathy to a part of my mind that was somehow more sensitive to the thoughts of others. Later on in my life, I realized that this attitude was a necessary stepping stone to the realizations I've made in my life today.

Well, that of course brings us to the topic: What is metaphysical energy? Does it exist? If we have no way to scientifically record it with our technology—see it, smell it, taste it—what gives us pause to consider its existence? These are hard questions when they're posed at anything vaguely spiritual, since so much of what is intrinsically spiritual defies scientific logic or application. For many, this simply means it's a farce, some vagary invented by the deranged or religious to fill a gap of individuality, to provide meaning where there is none.

Being a skeptic, this was of course my initial approach. How could I believe that some measurable spectrum or quantity of energy exists around me that I cannot see, gauge, or understand? Was it necessary to have "faith" in this energy to see it, to understand it? The clear answer I've come upon is a resounding no.

I was first made aware of thought energy when a good friend of mine began to use Reiki techniques to help alleviate my headaches and muscle strain. He had offered several times before and I had refused him, telling him that I didn't buy into his "invisible healing energy." Finally, I relented, after suffering a particularly bad migraine for about three hours. My eyes had become incredibly sensitive to light, and the throbbing and nausea began to overwhelm me.

He had me lie down and began to pass his hands over me. Being the skeptic I am, I was very careful to breathe as I had been and change nothing else (other than my physical positioning, of course). If this was going to work, I wanted to know exactly why. I began to feel undulating waves of energy passing through my body, carrying my pain with it. This energy was centered around his hands, so I immediately assumed the radiant heat was having an effect on my skin, and that soft warmth was causing some kind of reaction in me. I expressed this thought to him, and with a smile he immediately began to radiate an intense cold through me, with the same effects as the first wave. This caught my attention, because it refuted my assumptions and made me examine my perception of what was happening. After about ten minutes of this, my headache was gone, and I was left with many questions about the nature of what had been done to me.

I began a process, which lasted nearly a year, to understand the nature of this energy, and to understand not only what metaphysical energy is, but how it exists and interacts with the world around us. Since, as I stated before, most information that can be found on the subject of metaphysical energy is of questionable scientific merit, I decided that there was a set of assumptions I would have to make about this energy if I intended to cogitate on a cohesive theory.

Thought energy, if it exists, may be like many other bands of energy that we cannot detect with our senses—such as radiation, radio waves, and many others. The simple fact we cannot detect it or record it may simply mean it exists in a spectrum that we currently cannot observe (much like radiation and other forms of energy must have appeared to early scientists).

Those who are adept at using thought energy and energy work have trained themselves to use and harness it. How do the energy of an untrained person and a trained person differ? Is this effect measurable? What creates this energy? Energy is a constant in our universe. Any physics student can tell you that the law of conservation of matter and energy states that energy/matter cannot be destroyed; it simply changes from one form to another. Does thought energy share this property?

As you can see, I had many tough obstacles to overcome in order to understand the nature of an invisible force, especially since that force may have spiritual ramifications. The majority of the information I knew I'd be able to gather would hardly be scientific. With this in mind, I created a logical progression to help me understand this energy and began to record my observations. What follows are conclusions I was able to reach through observation, self-study, and contemplation.

Spiritual energy/thought energy, if it exists, must adhere to the law of matter/energy conservation. It is not destroyed or created; it simply changes forms. Energy can be scattered, formed and cohesive, inactive (if thoughts and emotions aren't currently affecting it in any way), and it can be focused and directed, as it was in my experience with the headache. Spiritual energy/thought energy must adhere to the law of complexity. I can cut a glass with a diamond because the diamond's structure is far more dense and complicated, and by the same token I can overwhelm a bandwidth of radio waves with either a stronger signal or a far more complicated one on the same frequency. Thought energy gets its complexity from conscious and unconscious thought and emotion. It is assumed because of this property that people familiar with energy work can raise "shielding" around themselves. By consciously focusing on its existence, the energy becomes more complicated and dense, and prevents incoherent or coherent energy from passing through it.

That last observation was an important one. The human mind is in essence a large bio-electric computer. The brain emits waves of discernible measurable energy that can be recorded in many ways, one of which is an electroencephalogram (EEG). It is not hard to make the leap that there are bandwidths and types of energy emitted by the mind that we cannot yet detect, considering that we know so little of the human mind and have such a rudimentary understanding of the nervous system. This was the tiny leap I had to make in order to form a good thesis as to the nature of metaphysical energy and its effect on us and the world around us.

When we have an emotion, there is a physiological response and an electrochemical response. It is not hard to fathom that this phenomenon emits a type of energy, or more specifically that the mind affects the waves of energy that flow outward from us, somewhat like a large object being dropped into a lake. The ripples that channel away from us can be felt by those with increased sensitivity. Finally, I had come across a logical explanation for my empathy! I was compelled to look more into the effects of this energy and its existence. I felt as if I was finally getting somewhere.

Energy pervades us, but thought energy must gather around those with the conscious ability to think and reason. This energy would then change in intensity and composition to reflect the thoughts, emotions, and "energy history" of a being—hence the idea of an aura. One by one, the building blocks began to fall into place. The psychic phenomena that science has been at a loss to explain begin to reveal themselves on a grander scale.

Object reading would then begin to make sense. If an object is near a person or an intense experience, it would be soaked in cohesive thought energy. If people are sensitive to this energy, then they can come in contact with the object and "feel" the experiences the item has been subjected to, and they can form a picture of its use or possessor.

Finally, vampirism, as it is crudely called—and I say "crudely" simply because of the connotations the media and the world at large have placed on this term—falls into focus as well. Individuals whose thought patterns create a void within are driven to feed on the energy of others in order to stabilize their own energy. This is "psi" vampirism, or pranic vampirism as it is sometimes called, borrowing from the eastern traditions of *prana* (life energy). Being around individuals like this who are unaware of their condition can make one feel drained, sleepy, or even irritated for no reason whatsoever. They deplete the natural thought energy that a person has unconsciously accumulated. If a person with this problem doesn't "feed," there can be physical manifestations, such as the headaches with which I used to often find myself plagued.

The next question with vampires, of course, falls to the blood-drinkers or "sang" variety of vampires. These individuals literally drink the blood of those who donate to them, consuming for pleasure or need. Why the blood? Well, if I had to apply the same scientific assumptions I've made in the rest of this essay, I'd say it's because blood travels through every part of the body and is exposed to every bit of it, including the brain, and therefore has much more intense energy associated with it. It exists behind the natural wall we all erect, and therefore blood would be one of the most potent sources of this energy. Since thought energy is an expression of the will and subconscious, even the act of allowing a person to make physical contact and feed may transmit this energy. I would never presume to understand the exact nature of sanguine vampirism, as I am not one of them, but I have noticed that feeding on blood also seems to have the same effect as feeding on energy in my case. Draw your own conclusions.

Since a mind's ability to focus and direct energy is completely dependent on cohesive thought, concentration, and belief/awareness, my ability to look at metaphysical energy as a real force I can scientifically understand—instead of an invisible, unknowable force that possibly exists—has made my ability to work with energy much stronger, and has intensified my personal drive to explore. From all of these conclusions and my newfound relationship with energy, I have pursued its understanding with a renewed hunger.

Energy work has much more meaning to me than it ever did before, and every day I come to new conclusions with the understanding that thought energy is more than mumbo jumbo; it's simply another one of nature's potent forces that many do not understand. I hope this realization brings some of you into focus, and helps you all on the path of understanding that we all aspire to walk.

Definitions

Reiki: A technique of energy healing that originated in Japan. It was imported to the United States through Hawaii. In Reiki, individuals are tuned to a source of universal life energy, and they are taught to channel this energy in order to heal others. Vampires report varying results with Reiki. Many are proficient in the energy techniques that form the basis of Reiki, but when it comes to using Reiki energy to sustain themselves, most vampires quickly learn that, though they might use Reiki energy to heal others, it's another matter entirely to try to "eat" Reiki.

Empathy: By its classic definition, empathy is the ability to relate to and sympathize with another's feelings. In a magickal or psychic context, however, empathy has come to describe the extrasensory perception of others' emotions. Related in concept to telepathy, an empath is able to pick up on the energy of emotions, reading people far more accurately than even the most astute interpreter of facial expression and body language.

Electrical interference: A number of psychic vampires assert that they have an unusual impact on electrical devices in their immediate vicinity. Many uncontrollably drain watch batteries. Some regularly blow out light bulbs. Still others drain the batteries in cell phones and digital cameras. This particular side effect was demonstrated quite dramatically on the A&E Network's 2005 documentary *The Secret Life of Vampires*. While interviewing author Michelle Belanger in a Philadelphia park at dawn, the camera suddenly recorded a high-pitched whine and then went completely dead. A&E shouldn't feel bad, though. A number of film crews have experienced similar problems when trying to interview Michelle.

Born in 1985, Autumn Rain is a Canadian who has been interested in the vampire and Goth scenes since the age of sixteen. She pursued a liberal-arts degree in college and is the author of a soon-to-be published novel. She chooses not to take part in the vampire community.

Path of Discovery through Age and Energy
BY AUTUMN RAIN

When I was about fourteen years old, I realized I had a unique ability to heal. This realization came about because my mom had been recently diagnosed with fibromyalgia; she was going through a hard time and was in a lot of pain. I realized that through simple touch I could actually pull the "pain" right out of her and into me. What I was actually doing was absorbing the negative energy that was carrying or causing the pain. This led me to take an interest in reflexology.

Not long after, I was admitted into a reflexology class. In the Canadian school system, this is normally post-secondary, but I was fairly well self-taught by then. They made an exception for me, and I started to take the class when I was still just fourteen. If I had not abandoned the final exam, I would have been the youngest registered reflexologist in Canada at fifteen years old.

A significant part of this class was learning how to manipulate energy. Since I knew I already had a natural talent for this, I was fascinated and made sure to incorporate it into all the reflexology treatments I gave. I soon lost an interest in the reflexology itself, finding that it was unnecessary for me to accomplish my goal of relieving pain. By simple touch, I could relieve a chronic migraine in just one to ten minutes. There have been times when my grandmother was in tears with pain, and I was the only one who could help her. The extra-strength painkillers did nothing. She believes to this day that I have a gift from God.

I always loved the feeling I got from doing this. There was a strange rush as I felt the energy move from my patient into my hands. It's like a shiver that moves through my whole body, only it's warm and invigorating. I am usually quite lethargic, but when I heal someone it fills me with energy and makes me feel normal for a certain period of time, usually about two days. I always seem to end up the unofficial giver of massages wherever I am. People tell me they feel guilty for getting me to make them feel better. But they repay me plenty.

While always making sure to leave out the "V-word" and any implication of such, I am fairly open about what I can do. I keep no secrets about the fact that I am "sucking" the negative energy out of their bodies and taking it into myself for their and for my benefit. In this way, I can be honest and get permission for what I am doing without risking getting myself into trouble. Spiritually, I believe in the Wiccan Rede: "An ye harm none." I never use my abilities for energy manipulation to cause harm to others. The worst thing that has ever happened was that I caused someone to fall asleep.

When I was about sixteen years old, I began to discover vampire literature. I was immediately fascinated and set out to research as much as I could. It was at this time that I discovered the existence of what they call real vampires. I soon fell into a social circle that included two vampires and Otherkin. I learned quite a lot from these people, but something was missing and I began to doubt the existence of real vampires, wondering if vampirism were simply a psychosomatic response to reading too many horror novels.

Unless they're needed, I ignore my abilities for the most part. For various reasons, I'm adverse to claiming, even to myself, to be a vampire, and I choose not to take part in the community, though over the years I've learned a lot and made some valuable friends.

Definitions

The "V-word": Many individuals in the vampire community have an ambivalent relationship with the word *vampire*, occasionally referring to it simply as the *V-word* to express some of their misgivings about it. Most psychic vampires will attest that they use the word *vampire* simply because it's the best word in the English language that describes what they are and what they need to do. Every now and then, some group within the community attempts to spearhead a movement to install a new word to replace the dreaded V-word. However, these movements are typically short-lived. There is something persistent and enduring about the word *vampire*. Perhaps it's the romanticism our society has attached to the archetype, or perhaps there is a power connected with the archetype that goes beyond mere words.

Gryphon Mandrakken is a military veteran who has been studying and practicing magick for over twenty years. In the course of his magickal career, he has been a founding member of several Pagan circles, but he is most at home as a member of the Warrior caste of House Kheperu. House Kheperu encourages its members to formulate their own beliefs based upon their own experiences, sharing these views as pieces of a larger puzzle. Gryphon's particular views are an eloquent blend of his life experiences, vampirism, and magickal background.

Awakening, Immortality, and Ascension

BY GRYPHON MANDRAKKEN OF HOUSE KHEPERU

All living things (which include animals, humans, plants, and a number of other entities that often defy definition) are imbued with a soul or spirit. The energy of this soul is eternal. This eternal aspect can be compared to Isaac Newton's Law of Conservation of Energy, which states that matter and energy can be neither created nor destroyed. The form can be broken, changed, reborn, or transformed, but the basic essence is everlasting. Thus, all life, after a fashion, can be considered immortal.

However, there is a fundamental difference concerning the concept of immortality between ascended beings and non-ascended beings. Ascended beings are those who have awakened and gained a sense of self-awareness that carries over from life to life. Non-ascended beings are those who still sleep. Within the vampire community, the non-ascended are often considered "mundanes"—worldly people whose sensibilities and perceptions are tied to the physical realm. In contrast, ascended beings are individuals whose sensibilities and perceptions have moved beyond the physical, material world to focus on a worldview more refined and spiritual/energetic. Vampires, Otherkin, ritual magicians, mystics, and shamans are a few examples of potentially ascended beings.

At birth or conception (depending on your beliefs and point of view), the physical form of all living beings receives a soul. In the case of the non-ascended (the vast majority of beings), this soul is merely a random portion of the Universal Life Force. To illustrate: imagine a ladle being dipped into a great well and the liquid being poured into a vessel (the physical body).

During this being's life, all of his or her experiences, ideas, emotions, thoughts, and understandings are recorded within the soul. Upon the death of the physical body, the soul returns to the universal source and its essence is reabsorbed into the whole. To continue the previous analogy, the liquid is poured back into the well. In a manner of speaking, the soul experiences a form of death as its individuality merges with and becomes a part of the Universal Life Force once more. This is all part of a great mechanism that drives the cycle of cosmic evolution.

However, not all beings remain a part of this cycle of continuous emergence and reabsorbtion. When a being "ascends," either by design or circumstance, the soul no longer is reabsorbed into the Universal Life Force upon physical death. Instead, through force of will, an ascended soul retains the sum of its experiences and its individuality, and embarks on a spiritual and personal journey of evolution. Consider ascension the ability to achieve self-awareness in the cycle, and this realization leads to a solidification or crystallization of the individual Self. The water freezes into ice and is not easily reabsorbed.

A being that is ascended is therefore considered immortal, as its true essence or soul no longer experiences death. Depending on the soul's level of advancement along its journey, it may or may not reincarnate into another physical body. In this sort of reincarnation, the liquid is not poured back into the well, but continues, complete, to a new vessel.

This self-awareness through lifetimes, although it allows for greater powers of insight and understanding, does not set the ascended morally above the non-ascended. It must be understood that while the non-ascended are not yet continuous beings like the ascended, they are no less deserving of freedom, love, respect, understanding, and compassion. We must remember that the energy that comprises our souls was once as they are. And while not immortal, the non-ascended are no less living beings. Our immortality gives us a great responsibility, for we are the shepherds of ages to come. Ascension is responsibility, not privilege.

Ascension

Whether by the machinations of higher powers or merely the chaotic natural forces of the cosmos, evolution is not so much a slow march forward as it is a series of astounding leaps. The hallmark of these evolutionary steps is the process of "synergy," wherein the end result of an equation is greater than the sum of its parts. In these cases of synergy, logical progression does not apply. Instead of one plus one equaling two, suddenly and inexplicably it combines to three.

When we experience these leaps on the small scale of the events in our personal lives, we call it "epiphany." Even though we do not have all the information, somehow the answer comes to us. Even though we do not have all the pieces of the puzzle, we still see the big picture. These epiphanies come to all beings, ascended and non-ascended alike.

The non-ascended are separate yet united parts of a larger group mind or collective consciousness (as described by Carl Jung). They are bound rigidly to the mundane world and readily partake of ordinary reality, accepting standard social convention. Even so, there are moments in the life of non-ascended beings, when through hardship, trial, experience, and learning, they have the opportunity to step from the ordinary to the non-ordinary. Unfortunately, these moments all too often slip by virtually unnoticed.

However, upon rare occasions, these potential ascenders seize this golden moment and become something more than the sum of their parts. They become a living, breathing synergy of transformation, and ascend ordinary reality.

Tempered in the fires of knowledge, wisdom, and experience, the energy of the soul adjusts to a higher resonance of being. Since the soul is still tethered to the Universal Life Force, it still returns there upon physical death, but is no longer reabsorbed. Due to the greater strength and awareness of being, through force of will the soul remains whole and retains its individuality. In-between physical incarnations, the soul rests within the universal source and is refreshed and recharged. Eventually, the soul will reincarnate into a new physical form, retaining echoes of its past selves.

Each new physical incarnation of an ascended being carries hidden within it all the experiences, knowledge, and memories of past incarnations. Often, this wealth of information remains buried in the subconscious. However, through "awakening," much of this can be recovered. Subconscious material is brought into consciousness, and the being's journey toward ascension can continue.

The Vampiric Condition

A very small number of ascended beings in the world are vampiric. As vampires, our unique nature separates us even from other awakened, rendering it difficult for them to relate to our particular experience of the world. Our need to feed on the life force of other sentient living beings is a condition that, latent or conscious, we must eventually come to terms with and understand.

What causes the vampiric condition? Our pranic centers of energy within our bodies, typically located in the Ba or Navel (which is located in the belly, approximately two inches below the navel), are no longer connected to the Universal Life Force as are the pranic centers of other ascended beings. Whether by choice, through ritual, purposeful expansion of the soul/mind, or by circumstance—through damage to the energy body and/or spiritual evolution—our souls have become separate from the universal source of life energy. This independence comes with a price. No longer nurtured or recharged by this source, we must feed, energetically, for ourselves.

Among other things, this separation manifests as a hunger within us that is twofold. Firstly, and perhaps most immediately urgent, is the hunger to replenish the life force that sustains our being. Secondly, but no less important, is the emotional hunger to feel linked to other life forms. Our unique form of pranic feeding sates both hungers, for not only does it fill us with life energy, but the process of feeding requires that we establish a link to the donor of that energy as well.

Regardless of the cause or condition, the separation from the Universal Life Force acts as a catalyst. It requires the development, both conscious and subconscious, of the subtle skills of energy manipulation for survival. It urges us forward along our spiritual journey as we step beyond mere ascension. It places us precariously within both the material world and the spiritual world. And it inspires us to plumb the shadowy resources of our minds and cultures for answers to our inner questions.

Ascension is the first step beyond ordinary reality. It is a step shared by many mystery traditions. The vampiric condition is a step beyond even that, unique only to our kind. At some point in our many lives it is likely that we chose to ascend in this fashion. Our condition is not a curse, nor is it an affliction. We merely travel along our path, continuing toward spiritual fulfillment in a different fashion with purpose and willful intent.

Definitions

Ascension: A term with distinctly New Age overtones, *ascension* typically refers to the notion that existence is a constant process of spiritual evolution, and that our identities as physical beings are but one step along a much larger progression to spiritual perfection. Many doctrines of reincarnation are connected intricately with the idea of ascension, perceiving each successive incarnation as an opportunity to expand the soul's knowledge and experience, so that the essence of a being evolves from one form to the next.

Kheprian: Technically, a member of House Kheperu, although the term has come to refer to anyone or anything connected to the tradition established by House Kheperu within the vampire community. House Kheperu takes its name from the ancient Egyptian word for "transformation," and its members approach vampirism as a dynamic and necessary part of the energetic balance of the universe. House Kheperu addresses vampirism primarily in terms of energy, and is probably most widely known for its three-caste system of Priests, Warriors, and Counselors. The castes represent spiritual archetypes, but their application in ritual and energy work is as stages along a complete circuit.

Ba: In the religion of the ancient Egyptians, the human soul was perceived as having many parts. One of these, traditionally depicted as a bird with a human head, was the Ba. Sometimes shown as residing in the belly, the Ba was the aspect of the soul that flew forth from the corpse after death. Modern hermeticist R. A. Schwaller de Lubicz equated the Ba with the essence of a being, its life force. In the Kheprian tradition, the Ba is equated with the navel chakra and is tied to an individual's connection to universal life energy.

Khan is a former military man who now works as a private defense con-
tractor. A proud single father, he has been quietly involved in the vampire
community for many years, remaining independent of any specific vam-
pire house. Despite his independence, Khan's realistic and level-headed
wisdom is often sought out by other members of the community. He is
viewed as a trusted advisor and confidant by several well-established vam-
pire organizations.

Twenty-first Century Vampire

BY KHAN

I am a thirty-eight-year-old single father. I work as a defense contractor and part-time martial arts instructor. I am also a vampire. Using every iota of "common sense" I can muster, I ask myself, "What am I doing here?"

I was born in Chicago Heights, Illinois. From the time I was eighteen months old until I was eleven, my mother lovingly raised my younger brother and me by herself. As a child, I was always considered bright and creative. I did well in school. I bonded more with the girls I knew than with the boys. To me, they were more thought-provoking. I had nothing to prove but my intellect. My sincerity was appreciated. I had male friends, but they were few and far between. When I did bond with another boy, we were thicker than thieves.

At eleven, my mother remarried, and we moved to Virginia Beach, where I still reside at the time of this writing. We lived a "normal" life, in a "normal" town. I ran track and played baseball. My friends were a lot like me. But in my teens, I felt different in certain senses. I could, at times, finish peoples' thoughts and sentences. Sometimes, I would know what they were thinking, without a word being spoken. We all chalked this up to a sense of a close bond, and we never gave it another thought.

When I was seventeen, I enlisted in the Marine Corps. I spurned the advice of many by not going to college, but, for some strange reason, I felt compelled to join the Corps. I knew this was a path I must take. At the end of high school, I went to Parris Island, South Carolina, to start my adult life.

I had the best time of my life going through what most considered hell. I drew a sense of power, knowing that I excelled in what others would or could not. It gave me a sense of inner strength that most people never know.

After a period of studying Russian for the military, I was sent to Infantry Training School. There I met the most extraordinary individual I, to this day, have ever met. Patrick Spencer was British. He had moved to the U.S. and felt the same urge I did to be a Marine. This man was an individual who could make you laugh and smile at the worst moments of your life. His honest and upbeat attitude never seemed to wane. We became the best of friends, and spent time available with his sister and her husband in Poway, California. We were, in the greatest sense, inseparable brothers.

On September 14, 1988, my closest and dearest friend in the world died in a tragic training accident. It was graphic and painful. The moment it happened, I could feel the pain, though I was five miles away. Later that day, when I heard what happened, I stood numb. I could not understand the magnitude of what this would mean. I was never one for showing emotional weakness, and, being a Marine, I conditioned myself not to.

That night, I walked outside my barracks. I sat in the dark, away from anyone else, and looked up at the star-filled night. At that moment, I cried with a pain I had never known, much the way I am crying now, recalling this moment in my mind. For an hour, all I could do was let out this pain, as if it were my own death at hand. When I could cry no more, I closed my eyes and sat. I was not capable of doing anything else. All thought emptied from my mind, and I couldn't move. Then the most mind-boggling thing happened, something that, to this day, I can't fathom.

I had a vision in my mind, while I was awake, of an ageless Chinese man.

This man said to me, "Fear not, for there is a reason for everything. There is a path we all must take. In the end, we must all go our own Way."

I opened my eyes and looked around, wondering who was screwing with my mind. I was thinking that maybe my mind made something up to help me ease the pain. I was Jewish, and no more Chinese than the rocks around me. But at that moment, I felt a renewed strength that carries me on to this day. Not knowing how to accept all of this, I buried it in the archives of my brain.

The Holy Land

I finished infantry training as the top anti-tank gunner in my class. I was given orders to Camp Lejeune, in North Carolina, to serve with the Second Light Armored Infantry Battalion. I bonded very quickly with a good many in my Company. The company I kept was perceived as odd by the others around us. My "brothers" all looked like huge beer kegs with feet. And I was right there in the middle of them, this 160-pound twenty-year-old. But I felt invincible. I feared nothing, only because I knew my limitations. This sense about myself drew people toward me. I didn't try to figure it out. I was with people, I knew, who would take a bullet for me, just as I would for them. And I was more than adequately trained to take the lives of others for the greater good of mankind. What greater purpose could there be?

In late 1988, a detachment of us was deployed to the Mediterranean for exercises. I couldn't wait! It was a chance to see a portion of the world I had only read about and seen on TV. I hadn't done any extensive traveling. So we departed to places I'd never experienced. We saw the beaches of the French Riviera, the Coliseum in Rome, medieval castles in Italy, and places so awe-inspiring that we were grateful to take them in. Then we went to Israel.

Upon arrival, all of us wearing our civilian clothes, we boarded a charter bus with black curtains over the windows. We loaded our equipment in the storage area and took the longest bus ride of our lives. After what seemed like an eternity, we stepped out of the door into a completely barren desert. There to meet us was the local commander of the Israeli army. We discovered that we were to do some joint training with men in the Israeli army.

They learned a great deal from us, just as we did from them. We talked of different cultures, of different military mindsets, and of our homes. It was something we would all cherish for a long time. And, as most military men do, we played pranks on each other. Our commanding officer was a first lieu-tenant who was no older than we were. One night, while he went to make a head call, a few of us caught a couple of scorpions and put them in his sleeping bag. Upon his return, he opened his sleeping bag and looked around. He said, "Okay, who's the clown who did this?" We all laughed, including him, because we knew that no matter what stupid thing we did, we were all here for each other, and the pranks were merely out of kinship.

About two that morning, we awoke to tracer rounds being shot over our heads. Since none of us had seen direct combat, the adrenaline was higher than we could imagine. Coming from the hills a mile or so away, a group was shooting at us with fervor. What we didn't know was that we were right outside the Lebanese border. But during this firefight, I experienced a sensation I couldn't believe. I felt like I had been there before, doing the same thing.

After about an hour and a half, the shooting stopped. Luckily, the only casualty was some of our equipment. After a conference between the Israeli commanders and ours, it was decided that the joint exercise should come to a close. A couple of buses like the ones that brought us there arrived, and we quickly loaded them, grateful that we were lucky to escape with our lives and no major injuries. During the ride back to Haifa, I shared my odd sensation with one of my "brothers." Being on the same intellectual level as me, he said that the psychological phenomenon of *déjà vu* was common, especially during times of extreme excitement. Using that same logic, I stored the information away, not giving it another thought.

Upon our return to the coast, we debriefed and rested. We were offered the opportunity to take a tour of Jerusalem and Tel Aviv. Because of the traditions of Judaism—I didn't practice but I still believed myself to be Jewish—I jumped at the opportunity. Boy, how proud my family would be that I went to Solomon's Temple and the Wailing Wall! I took an insane number of pictures and reveled in the history that I walked upon. I went to the Wailing Wall. As is the customary tradition, I wrote my grandfather's name on a piece of paper and tucked it into a space between the bricks, asking God to keep my grandfather's spirit safe. He had passed when I was five. Though I only remembered a small bit of his time with me, I knew I owed him this service. After saying my prayer, I closed my eyes and laid my head against the wall, enjoying the emotions that passed through me. Sure enough, the image of that ageless Chinese man appeared in my head. He sat, floating in nothingness, and smiled at me. As quickly as he had appeared, the vision dissipated.

"Now this is just freakin' out of control!" I yelled at myself.

Why, in the name of something holy, would this Chinese guy appear to me at the Wailing Wall? How many floating Chinese guys go to Israel?

Again, I buried this away, vowing not to reflect on its meaning anymore. People would think I was certifiably nuts if I ever shared it.

Ancient of Ancients

After our trip to Tel Aviv, we returned to our ship in Haifa to relax in the nightlife. We got prepared to go underway again. Next stop: Alexandria, Egypt. The land of ancient Pharaohs. We hoped that Egypt would be just as exciting as Israel. We arrived in Alexandria during the spring of 1989. It smelled like dead carcasses had lined the streets for a thousand years. Garbage was piled up four feet high in the medians of the streets. Filthy kids walked around, some missing an arm or a hand. The local people looked as though there was no purpose for them other than just being there. During some maintenance of the ship, those who wanted to go got an opportunity to take a tour of the pyramids. Naturally, I knew I had to go. When would I get this chance again? Besides, it had to be a hundred times better than the armpit we were currently stuck in.

Our first stop was a carpet-making factory. In the front were beautifully crafted designs that made me stand in awe. We then went into the actual factory, and I was in utter shock. At these huge looms were little kids. They couldn't have been any older than eight or nine. And they worked like I'd never seen. Pacing the floor was their foreman, an eleven- or twelve-year-old with the most evil scowl on his face. I felt a deep sense of sorrow and despair; these kids were like slaves. I walked out quickly, with a sense of utter disgust toward mankind.

We got back on the bus and rode to Giza. The sight was something you can't understand unless you've been there in person. I just felt insignificant compared to these monstrous creations before me. There was nothing more incredible than to look upon these efforts of mankind and bask in their historic glory. We took the local tour and saw the exhibits of Nefertiti and Ramses. We then went to see the Great Sphinx.

As I stood before this huge statue, I got another funny feeling. I had been here before. But this time I had, in my mind, the perspective of looking at this statue from horseback, with a completely different feeling. Thinking that it was my mind playing another trick on me due to the heat, I discarded the thought that what I was seeing was anything different than what I had rationally explained to myself.

We boarded the bus and went back to Alexandria. Our time in Egypt was rapidly coming to an end. According to our schedule, we were off to Sardinia for some more training, and then some liberty in Toulon, France. Flowing alcohol, amorous women, and the red-light district: the anticipation couldn't be cut with a machete. En route to France, we found this was not to be.

Over the loudspeaker was the captain of the ship. He announced that we were being redirected to assist in evacuation of embassy personnel from Beirut. As much as we wanted to bask in our own debauchery, the anticipation of more trigger time was actually welcomed.

Our mission lasted about twelve hours. After much tension, that same putrid smell, and frequent gunfire, we all evacuated back to ship, unscathed. We were successful, and all lives were intact on our end. It was now off to Spain to rest up and return home. During the trip back, I spent a lot of time reflecting on all I had seen and felt—and that damned Chinese guy who kept popping up in my head at the weirdest times.

You Can Never Return

I returned to the welcome of my parents, who were ecstatic that I had come back alive. My mother was always worried I'd die in some battle. My father beamed with pride, as he saw on the surface what I had become. In my mind, though, I was becoming something different, and I didn't know what that was.

Was I becoming the stereotypical Marine, slowly losing my grip on reality due to the combat? Was I not as mentally tough as I had thought, and getting ready for a breakdown? A voice kept going in my head: "Everything has a reason. There is a path we must all take. In the end, we must all go our own Way."

In August of 1990, we were deployed to the Persian Gulf. In total, I spent a year and a half in Kuwait, Oman, the United Arab Emirates, Bahrain, and

Saudi Arabia. Though I could go on about more battles and gunfights, it was the same as before. With one exception.

As I looked down at the blood seeping from the freshly killed, it changed in color. The best way I can describe it is that it appeared to dim, as if someone had slowly turned down the dimmer switch on a light. What properties did blood have that would cause this effect? What, scientifically, did this mean? Was it light refraction? A differentiation from the heat? Was I dipping further into the uncharted depths of a warping psyche? What was I becoming?

As I stood in the desert, staring at these lost souls, all I could do was ask questions of myself. I thought about the fact that other human beings would be squeamish or nauseated by this sight, while I was standing there in complete amazement at blood seeping from a dead body in the middle of a desert, where millions of gallons have spilled over thousands of years. I had to be ill. There was no other rational explanation for it.

At the end of my enlistment in 1992, congressional budget cuts in defense spending put an end to my military career. Infantry troops were not allowed to reenlist, except in another field. After what I had been through, I couldn't become a warehouse supervisor on some remote military base. I knew it was time to move on. But what does somebody with my background do?

Treasure Hunt

A few weeks after returning to Virginia, I saw an ad in the newspaper for a security detail. Prior military experience was a must. There it was: my answer and salvation. While I waited for some kind of response, I took a security position at a local factory and met a girl who was smitten with me. We got married. Soon afterward, I got a response.

A gentleman in the Northeast wrote that he was heading to Haiti in search of treasure. He had a map and an agreement with the local government. My résumé was impressive, and he wanted me to come along for his protection. My fees would be discussed after I replied.

A treasure hunt. All of my hopes based on a treasure hunter. I had to be the biggest buffoon on the planet to put my hopes in this crap. Who did this jerk think I was? Did I sound like some idiot who would fall for this Indiana Jones garbage? I had to call this clown and give him a piece of my mind. A voice went through my head: "Everything has a reason. There is a path we all must take. In the end, we must go our own Way."

Here we go again. Why was this coming to me now? My brain must be working on its last piece of gray matter. So I called him and told him I was responding to his letter. Yet there was something about his tone that rang of passion and sincerity—not like a used car salesman, but like someone who believed that this was his purpose. He said that he liked who I was, and offered me three thousand dollars plus expenses for two weeks. For that kind of money, I didn't care if he was the incarnation of Elmer Fudd and rode on a Twinkie. I had to go. And there wasn't a soul who could convince me otherwise.

My wife called me a foolish dreamer. My parents declared that I must be dumber than a box of rocks. My Marine Corps "brothers," of course, wanted to come along for the ride. The gentleman from the Northeast said that there was an ex–Navy Seal not too far from me who would meet me at the airport, and we would all meet in New York with the rest of his team. From there we would fly to Haiti. He suggested that I pick up some things to keep myself occupied during all of the travel time. I made a trip to the local bookstore, hoping to find something that might keep my attention for longer than half an hour. Being a military man, I thought Sun Tzu's *Art of War* would be a terrific choice. As I went to pick it up, something caught my eye. A picture. A tiny picture on the binding of another book. As I neared this picture, I could not believe what I was looking at.

It was a drawing of that ageless Chinese man who had been haunting my brain for six years. The excitement and relief shed from me like a snake shedding its old skin. All because of a simple copy of the *Tao Te Ching*. As I skimmed the passages, I saw things that paralleled my life in ways I had never given much thought to. Finally, I had some guidance that I could make sense of. The ageless man I saw was none other than Lao Tzu.

✠   ✠

What was in store for me next? I was grateful that a conventional psychologist wasn't in on the treasure hunt, as I'm sure I would have been committed to some institution for my own perceived mental distortion.

Ah, to be mundane! To be a good husband with an office job that paid well. A good father to my two-point-three kids. Washing the station wagon and cutting the grass on weekends around my home surrounded by a white picket fence. Church every Sunday. Occasional fishing trips with my equally mundane neighbor. Bowling league on Tuesdays. Looking forward to meatloaf night. This Biff-and-Muffy blissful ignorance was something to aspire to. The blue pill or the red pill. I couldn't comprehend why someone wanted to be different from anybody else. Why would anyone want to live with the consequences of being eclectic and special, an eyesore to the bland fabric of "decent" society?

And yet I knew it was too late for me. I was too far down this path. All I could hope for was to be complete. The things I experienced in Haiti were almost beyond imagining, but each experience set itself up like a lesson, one more step along the path of my awakening and acceptance of the truths I had been avoiding all along. In the end, there was no denying it. I had powers others could perceive; powers they sometimes feared. I had lived before, many times, and in my travels I was often drawn to the places that had once been important to me. And there was a hunger, a restless beast inside of me. It was something I instinctively knew I should always control.

I'm not a big proponent of labels. However, I know people need them in order to identify with a group. They are especially important for the newly awakened, to help them figure out what the differences are. That being said, I can most closely be identified as an incubus, a sexual vampire with sang and psi traits. But I believe that most of our kind don't fit into only one category, and I'm no exception to that rule.

I don't proclaim to have the keys to the kingdom. I'm not all-knowing, and I have no aspirations to be the next community alpha. My story is like most, in that some of my experiences are similar to those of others while other experiences are uniquely my own.

I started writing my "vampire autobiography" so that those who had questions might have a reference and know that they're not alone. My life has been strange, and blessed, and I have no complaints. I hope others with experience will also see fit to share their tales, so that our brothers and sisters will come to know what is truly inside our beings.

Definitions

Incubus: In medieval Europe, the incubus was a spirit believed to visit men and women in their sleep and inspire sexual dreams. In some reports, the incubus was perceived as a very real entity, often a demon, who engaged in sexual acts with mortal men and women. In the modern vampire community, the term has been adopted to refer to individuals who prefer to feed on sexual energy—or, in rare cases, on sexual fluids.

THREE

Vampires and Feeding

Sphynxcat is founder of Sphynxcat's Real Vampires Support Page (http://sphynxcatvp.nocturna.org), one of the few vampire resource webpages that has existed without interruption since the mid-1990s. Sphynxcat works tirelessly to provide as much reliable information as possible on every aspect of real vampirism. A very private individual who often avoids media attention of any sort, Sphynx has graciously stepped out of the shadows to share her words here.

A Vampire's Perception of Energy

BY SPHYNXCAT

A lot of people ask me what the energy feels like when I'm working with it. I have always replied that how I feel energy won't necessarily be how anyone else feels it—and I still believe this, because there are essential differences between how I perceive things and what I see described by other sources. This doesn't mean that anyone is necessarily wrong or right—only that how we interpret things is not the same. While other people may see energy in colors or shapes or anything else, I'm aware primarily of textures and sometimes strength or temperature.

How do I perceive energy? Well, when it's flowing normally, it's very reminiscent of a light summer breeze or a light breeze from a fan indoors—very light and wispy, with little solidity to it. However, it ebbs and flows like water currents in a larger body of water—although, to me, it does not seem to be affected by phases of the moon as large bodies of water are. Sometimes, the energy even has a strong and/or variable texture (spiky/thorny, slimy, smooth, solid, spongy, squishy, and so on) when it comes from people. Part of that variance will come from others' moods, and part will come from their "inner self," what kind of person they really are. It takes time and practice to tell, but you can eventually learn which are "good people" and which are "bad people"—terms that will, by the way, always be relative to *your* frame of reference—and the "bad people" give you a bad vibe that is often described as the "creeps" or the "heebie jeebies." Most people quickly grasp gut hunches and "heebie jeebies" if you mention them, but not much beyond that point.

Natural or man-made energy may also have a texture, but it tends to be more constant—with very little variance—and is usually stronger. Lightning bolts, obviously, have a shorter "physical" duration (in this case, by "physical" I mean potentially measurable by normal physical devices) than the ambient power surrounding a generator, power plant, or high-power electrical wires.

Draining Energy

There are various ways to go about this, mainly dependent upon the visualizations that work for you. Whether you imagine a straw, a vacuum, or whatever—that part I leave entirely up to you. For me, it often feels like a breeze is blowing in my direction, or as if ghostly water is pouring over me. Sometimes there's a temperature feeling to it, and sometimes it's just like a wave of goose bumps. You may or may not experience the flow of energy in the same manner I do; you'll just have to be more aware of your feelings when draining energy to find out for yourself.

When draining from people, I prefer large groups—nightclubs, parties, roller rinks, concerts, and so forth—so I can skim off the top and pick up the cast-off excess. Large groups ensure that I'm not unintentionally having an adverse affect on any particular individual.

When I have a choice, I do prefer man-made, nonhuman, or natural sources over people—they're steadier and more constant. These sources are always the same strength, and there's more of this energy to tap into, so I worry less about the effect I will have on any particular individual.

The Energy of People

Most healthy people give off an outer layer of excess energy, sort of like a full, uncovered cup that sloshes on you while you're carrying it. There are multiple layers of this, so here's a brief rundown using my terminology (which is by no means "official"—others can and do use different terms):

Outer Level

This level rejuvenates quickly, but even normal activities such as walking will also drain it. After a night of solid rest, though, the drained person will be just fine, with no damage. My method of skimming off the top refers to energy from this level, and it is usually what is cast off (outside personal levels) by people to become part of the ambient energy in the area.

Inner Level / Life Force

This level could probably be considered the "real" life force of the person—if you're careful, neither of you will come to harm, and the primary effect will simply be tiredness. However, if you drain this level too far, the person will get tired, and you run the risk of making them sick, whether short-term or long-term, and of aggravating any existing physical illnesses they already have. During certain . . . bedroom activities. . . as well as other activities, energy from this level can be made more accessible, sort of like an adrenaline rush.

Core Level / Soul

Some say there's a third, innermost level that is closest to the person's vital essence or soul energy. Whatever it really is, I don't advise tampering with it, because it's so deep inside a person. There's a potential for harm to the person, whether immediately obvious or not, and there are plenty of other ways to get the energy you need.

DEFINITIONS

Feeding: The process by which a vampire, psychic or otherwise, acquires the vital force they need. For psychic vampires, feeding can take many forms. Although many psychic vampires enjoy the personal interactions that physical contact with a donor can provide, few psychic vampires require physical contact in order to feed. Psychic vampires, by definition, can draw energy over distances, drawing upon someone from across a room or even visiting a donor in dreams. Sanguine vampires, although they may seem limited on the surface, also feed in different ways. Some sanguine vampires acknowledge that they use blood merely as a focus, as a kind of physical vehicle for the life energy they really crave. Others assert that there is a mysterious something present in the physical blood itself that answers their needs.

Ambient energy: People are constantly interacting with their environments on an energetic level, both giving off energy and taking it in. The energy that naturally radiates from people can build up in physical areas, especially when there are a lot of people in an excited or agitated state that charges their energy with high emotion. This free-floating energy, which originated from people but is no longer directly attached to any of them, is often called ambient energy. Ambient energy is considered to be the most ethical choice for feeding, as it allows a psychic vampire to take in human vital energy without taking it directly from any single person.

Khan is an "old school" vamp who maintains amicable relations with a number of significant groups within the community, including Shadow-Lore, House Eclipse, and House Kheperu. A true independent, he has managed to steer clear of the many petty rivalries that sometimes mar the community, often remaining a voice of reason sought out by both sides.

Feeding: Facts and Myths

BY KHAN

For many who are either mundane or coming into an understanding of who they are, the term *vampire* creates a very basic image. The prevalent image on most minds is Dracula—a creature who is undead, turns into a bat, sleeps in a coffin, and bites unsuspecting people on the neck, draining their blood and turning them into vampires. Bram Stoker, Anne Rice, and others of their ilk have perpetuated these myths in their fantastic tales of fantasy.

For those of us who reluctantly claim the label of being vampiric, such myths are far from the truth. We are not undead. We don't drink people dry or have the ability to "turn" someone, or anything else along those lines. However, we do have the need to feed. The reasons for and results of this feeding, though, are quite different from what you've seen in the movies.

Why We Feed

Many of us have a deficiency in our bodies. We simply don't have the capacity to maintain the chi that allows others to live a healthy and normal life. And so we must get this life energy from another source to help us maintain a healthy existence. Would we die without it? Most likely not. However, there are adverse effects to not feeding. Lack of feeding causes chemical changes and actual physical problems. Our vampiric spirit and human bodies, though two separate entities, are in conjunction with each other. One affects the other. Our immune systems need the sustenance, just as a normal person might require the proper amount of vitamins and minerals.

Ways We Feed

The most common feeding technique is psychic. Not to be confused with palm readers and prognosticators, psychic feeding involves taking in the energy of our surroundings, whether it is the energy from a crowd at an energetic event, ambient energy from nature, or sexual energy made from desire. All of these can be taken in and used to complement the energy we already contain within. The act of psychic feeding is chronicled as far back as dakinis in the story of Buddha, and as recently as *The Vampire Psychic Codex* by Michelle Belanger. Some accounts mention the act as a natural part of the cycle of life, whereas some claim it is detrimental to existence. Most of those who feed are quite benign, although there are some who make it detrimental if they feed too much.

Then there is the more commonly known technique of blood consumption. Most important to note is that only a pint of ingested blood will make the human body vomit. There are no exceptions. For those who believe they can be drained, or that they are somehow not human, sorry to disappoint. The main reason some people feed by blood is that they are simply incapable of taking in energy through psychic means alone. Both means contain the necessary chi, but the difference between taking in chi through psychic means versus blood consumption can be explained with a simple analogy: it's like the difference between drinking coffee or sucking on a coffee bean. The means of delivery is different. The concentration is different. But the contents are the same.

Most human beings have the capability of producing extra energy, or blood, when the body gets depleted. We vampires, on the other hand, aren't afforded such luxuries. This is where reality breaks from the myth. This phenomenon is currently being researched by the American Medical Association and other medical organizations. I and many others hope that the information that results from this research becomes common knowledge, so that the fear created by eons of myth will finally be dispelled.

Definitions

Mundanes: A term often used within the vampire subculture to refer to non-vampires. The word *mundane* itself merely refers to the physical world, but in this context, it refers to individuals who are unable or unwilling to perceive more than material existence.

Dakinis: "Women who dance in the emptiness," the dakinis are fierce, sensual, and unrestrained goddesses who figure prominently in a number of visionary experiences detailed in the *Tibetan Book of the Dead*. Dakinis often appear naked, garlanded in human skulls. They have wild, flowing hair and carry a wickedly curved little blade called the *vajra*, which they use to cut through worldly attachments. They also often appear carrying a skull from which they drink human blood. This gruesome cannibalism is yet another way in which they remind us to let go of our attachment to the physical body and the ego it represents.

Processing energy: A number of occultists have argued against a vampire's intrinsic need to take energy, citing the notion that all beings are connected to an infinite energetic source. Even given the ideal that there is energy everywhere and there is always enough for everyone regardless of circumstances, there is still the problem of taking this energy in. Consider the fact that there is ample air throughout the world, and that everyone is free to breathe it. However, if there is something intrinsically wrong with a person's lungs, then that person is not going to get same benefit from this near-limitless resource of air than an individual with healthy lungs. Some theories interpret vampirism as the energetic equivalent of having bad lungs. Even if there is ample energy everywhere, a person lacking the ability to take this energy in and process it can still starve.

Raven Kaldera is a pagan priest, intersex transgender activist, parent, astrologer, musician, homesteader, and the author of books such as Pagan Polyamory: Becoming a Tribe of Hearts, Urban Primitive, *and* The Ethical Psychic Vampire. *He is the founder and leader of the Pagan Kingdom of Asphodel, the Asphodel Pagan Choir, and one of the cofounders of the Institute for Heritage Skills. Despite being open about his vampirism, Raven has maintained distance between himself and the vampire community, preferring to forge his own path.*

Ethical Vampires and Feeding

BY RAVEN KALDERA

*V*ampire is a term with very negative connotations. But, to be blunt, many of the people for whom it is an accurate term are not very nice people, and do a lot of harmful things. So I think that any attempt to whitewash the word would seem like a lie. It is an ambivalent word because this is an ambivalent condition. Even at its most ethical and healing, the danger of mis-use is always present as a possibility. We need to be honest about that.

In the process of writing my book *The Ethical Psychic Vampire*, I learned a lot more about my own vampirism. My attitude has gone from blindness about what I was doing, to bewildered denial, to acceptance, to exploration, to discipline, to usefulness. I no longer believe, as I did when I was younger, that this is some kind of curse. I see vampires as being as much a part of the psychic ecosystem as any other scavenger. It is no accident that most of the totem animals that I work with are scavengers—Raven, Skunk, Hyena. We have a purpose, one way or another.

My ideas on what causes vampirism are drawn from many interviews with people who are different sorts of vampires. Nearly all of these people did not self-identify as vampires per se; they were not part of any vampire community. Some were Pagans or magicians; some were energy workers; some were Tantrikas; some were ordinary people who grudgingly admitted that yes, this was what they did, but they didn't talk about it.

I am quite clear that there are at least two types of vampirism—basically, congenital and acquired. Congenital vampirism runs in families, including my own. My daughter is one, from before birth. I've interviewed quite a few families who have acknowledged their covert vampirism. Acquired vampirism is learned, sometimes in childhood (usually by kids in dysfunctional situations or, especially, by kids with chronic illnesses) and sometimes in adulthood—sometimes consciously and sometimes unconsciously. The two are very different in terms of what sort of energy they can use, and how they use it. Congenital (primary) vampires need it, or they become weak and logy, although they will survive if they are otherwise healthy. Acquired (secondary) vampires don't need it, although they can become dependent on it as if it were an addictive drug.

I am a primary vampire, and I can feed several ways. I can "lightfeed" by extending my auric "tentacles" and sucking up ambient energy, if there are a lot of people around getting excited. I'm careful to avoid people's auras, unless they've consented. Generally I deepfeed, though. I have done bloodletting, but I find that I don't need it much any more; if the donor allows me in past their auric boundaries, I just climb on top of them, extend all my tentacles into them, and sucker right into their spine. Sometimes it becomes deep enough that I temporarily merge with them. I breathe in and out deeply while doing this, because the breathing helps me to focus on pumping the prana into me. Then I pull out, hopefully before I've exhausted them, and roll over.

I'm a shapeshifter, meaning that I can move my astral body around in all sorts of ways—it's a shaman tool. At rest, with no attempt to shape it to match my physical form, my astral body is basically just a mass of tentacles that constantly test the air around me. People who are psychically aware have often been very disturbed by seeing these tentacles. When I change shape—heck, for that matter, when I give my astral body a human shape like my physical form—I'm basically just winding and bundling and fusing tentacles together into whatever shape I like.

I've become skilled enough at deepfeeding over the years that I can now drill into the chakras and "mainline" in a way that actually gives me more than blood. If I'm not careful, I can now suck a person straight into shock, so I depend on my donors to give me feedback so I won't harm them. I still take blood for bonding and sex, and because I love it, but it's not necessary.

I also keep my own milk goats, and milk fresh from the animal has a lot of life force, not to mention organic protein. We butcher our own animals— lamb and goat—and I make sure to get fresh meat and organic liver. We keep hens, and I eat fertile eggs. I keep my own garden, and during the summer I eat veggies straight from the stem. I have a few friends who are Reiki masters and who will give me a "shot" of Reiki, and I ground to the earth and use some of that. Those two aren't enough, though—in metaphorical terms, straight human prana is like food; Reiki is like, oh, I'd say sports water; and earth energy is like herbal tea. Useful, but not enough to sustain.

I deepfeed perhaps twice a week, with the other methods making up the difference. I have a couple of genetic illnesses that plague me, and if I am not careful about my bodily maintenance in general—eating the right foods, avoiding chemicals and allergens, getting enough sleep—I get sick. Getting enough prana is part of that maintenance. Without it, over time, I will get ill. Since one of my chronic illnesses is potentially fatal if I'm not careful, I get what I can.

DEFINITIONS

Tantrika: A practitioner of Tantra. There are two very different types of Tantric practice. Traditional Eastern Tantra, such as that practiced by Tibetan Buddhist monks, is a technique of focused visualization intended to help the practitioner integrate both male and female aspects of the personality by imagining these two aspects in sexual union. Western Tantra has developed more into a technique of sex magick, taking the symbolic union of male and female into a very physical realm. Western Tantric techniques are often used to both harness and generate energy, often with very potent results.

Sympathetic vampirism: Everyone interacts with energy, both giving it off and taking it in. In this respect, vampires are not unique. What defines a vampire is more a combination of heightened need and energetic limitation. Psychic vampires have to feed almost exclusively on human vital energy. If they could get by with energy from trees, for example, very few people would be tempted to call them vampires. However, since everyone takes in energy in one form or another, it is entirely possible for a non-vampire to learn how to vampirize the energy of other people. Certain magickal traditions, such as the Temple of the Vampire, actively teach this as a way of preying on others to increase personal power. Sometimes, individuals who have been preyed upon by a vampire over an extended period of time will unconsciously learn how to take energy in order to replenish themselves, especially if the vampire feeds faster than their system can recuperate. In some cases, even once such an individual gets away from the predatory vampire, he or she will continue to take energy from others out of habit, perpetuating the cycle of the classic needy psychic vampire.

Mairi LaPier is the founder of an international network called Shadow-
Lore, a group that connects vampires, Otherkin, and individuals of similar
interests from around the globe. Mairi is also a proud grandmother who
attends PTA meetings and ghost-hunts on the side. She has been involved
in several initiatives within the vampire community to promote communi-
cation between different houses and groups for a greater understanding of
the community as a whole.

The Blood and the Life

BY MAIRI OF SHADOWLORE

I've owned and moderated a number of vampire e-groups over the past
seven years, and of the hundreds of vampires I've spoken with who prefer to feed sanguinely, almost all were adamant that they are unable to
feed from any other type of energy other than blood.

As a vampire myself, I can and do feed from all types of energy, though
I still prefer sanguine energy. But I believe that while feeding sanguinely, I
am also feeding from my donor's psi energy. It's taken me years to figure out
what I've been doing. Only after reading the chapter on "Feeding and Energy
Exchange" in *The Psychic Vampire Codex* did it all become clear.

I believe that we have fooled ourselves into believing that the small amount of
blood we take is all we need, when in reality it is more than just the energy contained in the blood that we're feeding upon. We are unconsciously feeding from
our donor's psi energies as well as from the energy contained in the blood.

There are many vampires who can feed from sanguine means as well as
psi, but they have no idea that they are doing both at once. Or that in some
cases their need for a sanguine feeding is merely a tool they use to obtain
additional psi energies. This is not to say that there isn't a need to take the

blood of a donor; I am merely pointing out that the act creates a bridge or conduit for removing other life-force energy.

I know from my own experiences that when I remove the blood from my donor using a syringe, placing the blood in a cup and then drinking it, that I need much, much more than just a taste, and even then it is far less satisfying and does not last as long as when I drink directly from the donor.

Let me give you an example: I've spent the evening watching a movie with a friend and donor. As the evening ends, it's time to feed. My friend excuses himself to make the necessary arrangements, and when he returns we sit facing each other, knees touching. I reach for his hand and lightly caress his hand and forearm while meeting his eyes and speaking reassuringly. Taking the sterile single-edged razor, I make a small shallow cut along his arm. As the blood wells up in the wound, I place my mouth over the cut, sucking the blood into my mouth. I haven't taken more than just a taste. But I am satisfied with it because I have psychically fed from the contact as well.

It's all in the contact I have with the vessel (body) and the emotions I've created. The touching of our knees, my hand holding his, caressing his hand and his arm, locking on to his eyes—when I place my mouth over the wound and bring his blood into my mouth, I am not just ingesting his blood. I am breathing in his life force. The contact makes a more solid connection. Without this type of contact, I would need a greater quantity of blood for the same satisfaction.

If there is no connection or contact, then I need to take more blood. But when there is a connection like the bond my donor and I have, or that of a vampire who feeds from a spouse, then the amount taken is always far less; this is because the vampire is contact feeding from their donor's psi energies while feeding from their blood.

And those of us who use a more intimate area to feed from create stronger emotions that not only charge the blood, but also charge the emotions within the body, giving us a far more satisfying feed.

Sanguinarius said something to me at the annual get-together at Eagle's Mere this past year. She said that feeding didn't satisfy her as it did when she could have contact with her donor's body. Removing the blood by syringe and drinking from a cup didn't have the punch that being able to place her mouth over the wound did. And she couldn't last as long between feedings before the need would rise again.

Michelle Belanger has written that we are unconsciously taking energy from the people around us before we are awakened. But once we awaken, we learn to choose when and how we take the energy we need. So what I am saying is that, for whatever reason, we sanguine vampires have chosen to take the energy we need from the blood of living beings. Despite this choice, our bodies have never forgotten how to take it psychically as well. Through the bodily contact we have when sanguine feeding, we are also feeding psychically from our donor, drawing energy in as we drink the blood. And this deeper connection is what enables us to survive on the small amount that we take.

Definitions

ShadowLore: A network that encompasses individuals from a variety of backgrounds and belief systems—including vampires, witches, Therians, and Otherkin. ShadowLore was one of several nonsectarian, nonhierarchical networks founded as an alternative to the more structured houses and organizations within the vampire community.

Sanguine vampire: A vampire who drinks blood. From the Latin word *sanguis*, meaning "blood," a sanguine believes that he or she requires blood to satisfy some physical or spiritual hunger. Many sanguine vampires feel that there is a physical constituent to the blood that they require in order to maintain their well-being. Others acknowledge that the blood they drink is simply a vehicle for vital energy.

Sanguinarius: The founder of www.sanguinarius.org, one of the longest-running resources for real vampires on the Internet. A blood-drinker, Sanguinarius did not at first accept the concept of psychic vampires, and some of her commentary lay at the heart of a schism that grew between the psychic and sanguine vampires in the community in the late nineties. Sanguinarius herself has done much in recent years to heal this split, encouraging communication and cooperation between those who express their vampirism in different ways.

LadyBlak is a regular contributor to a wide number of online vampire resources, and her articles and opinion pieces have helped many gain a better understanding of the roles and responsibilities of both vampires and donors. An advocate of donor rights, LadyBlak also is the founder of the Holista Group, as well as an e-list devoted to the Kitra caste.

Being a Vampyre Donor

BY LADYBLAK

A vampyre is someone who has a condition of the physical body or simply a spiritual malady that causes them to need prana. This life energy must be obtained from outside energetic sources in order for the vampyre to sustain physical and/or spiritual health. The amount of energy needed and the methods used for acquiring it are quite personal to the individual. Just as methods vary, vampyres also can take energy from a variety of sources, although typically they seek out willing, consensual donors. Usually these donors are people with an abundance of energy, and it might come as a surprise to some that some vampyres can also serve in the role of donor. In this essay, I will be discussing these vampyres, sometimes known as Kitra, who serve within the community as donors. I myself identify as Kitra, and as such I have engaged in vampyric exchanges as both vampyre and donor. As a result, I have a unique perspective on the role of donors, as well as on the problems one can encounter in a vampyric relationship.

Having a personal donor you trust is a blessing to a vampyre. It is a wonderful, empowering addition to one's life that can bring health, friendship, companionship, and freedom from worry of ridicule and revulsion. I have heard donors referred to in times of need as an "oasis." That is a pretty powerful thing. Donors should be cherished for the gifts they are willing to give us, not just in sanguine or pranic form, but in the areas of companionship and acceptance. They should never be abused or used for anything they do not freely offer. A lot of us might not have the release or feelings of health and balance we enjoy if not for these exceptional individuals.

When a relationship begins between a donor and a vampyre, specific ground rules should be laid out. These could even take the form of a contract made in writing or at least verbally, with terms that each partner understands. There should be clear language used, so that misunderstandings and hurt feelings will not arise later. If the relationship is purely pranic, and both partners agree to this, there should be no pressure later from the vampyre for it to become sanguine; similarly, if the relationship includes sexual exchange, that should be clearly understood at the beginning.

A very good example of that which should be considered is in the Donor Bill of Rights (see page 131). This document gives some sage guidance about some of the questions both parties involved in a vampyric exchange should discuss before taking their interaction any further. I wish that in the beginning I had had this document to refer to. I believe that a mature discussion at the outset is the best way to ensure a smoother relationship later. All expectations should be calmly and maturely discussed, and each person needs to keep the other informed frequently and quickly about any changes having to do with their agreement.

In any relationship, I believe there are times when we are aware of warning signs that things might be going in a direction with which we are not comfortable, times when dependencies and misunderstandings begin to develop. It is the responsibility of both the donor and the vampyre to keep up good communication and to be as honest as possible about what they are feeling. If things change within the relationship, these feelings need to be discussed immediately. I have had experience with this kind of communication not being as upfront or as clear as it could have been. I look back on such experiences and see now where things went off track for me or my partner. At the time, I either ignored what was happening or felt that I could handle it and stubbornly continued on. At least such experiences have taught me what some of the warning signs can be when a vampyre/donor relationship begins to go bad.

In my last such experience, I was acting as the donor to another vampyre. One of the first signs of trouble in this vampyre/donor relationship occurred when he "tapped" me without asking first. This was a very long-distance draw, and he didn't think I would feel it. I felt him draw from me unasked, and I confronted him about it. I opened the idea of a joint energy exchange that might be beneficial to the both of us—suggesting that, since I had too much energy in the evenings, he could take then, since he was able to draw from far away. I had overlooked the first red light: that he took without asking. Things were nice for a while, and we both benefited.

After about two weeks, he messaged me to tell me that he loved me. I told him that it made me uncomfortable that he said such things, since romance was not supposed to be a part of our interaction. Still, we didn't stop the exchanges. When he began to take more deeply, also without asking, I didn't say anything. Again, this should have been discussed, immediately and without delay. But I was enjoying the exchanges, too, and ignored much that in hindsight should have been clear indicators of where this was heading. As time went on, I became tired. I finally did tell my partner that I needed to slow things down and have him back off. He began, as in the beginning, trying to "tap" me without asking, hoping I wouldn't notice. He would do this even after I expressly told him I was ill. I tried to withdraw further from the con-nection between us, seeking to block him.

That was when I found out how deeply this relationship had changed for him. He sent "I love you" messages to me constantly, and told me that I had changed his life, that I was responsible for everything from his renewed zest for life to his weight loss and freedom from migraines. He told me that he would do anything to get me back into his life as his donor. I stayed away, until one evening when I was so energized that I was extremely uncomfortable. I went to him for help, and he took the energy away. I felt better and he felt happy, but the very next day I was struck with the realization that this had become a very sick, dependent relationship for both parties.

At this point, I had to seek outside help to bring our interaction to an end. Had I heeded some of the signs I saw in the beginning, it wouldn't have become what it did. This is why I believe that a long conversation before and during a donor/vamp relationship is very important. It is no guarantee that feelings will not be hurt and misunderstandings won't happen, but it will help to state the intentions of both partners so that there is at the least a foundation on which each can feel respected.

Donors can be very affected by their role with the vampyre to whom they are donating. Most donor types are very compassionate, nurturing individuals. They embrace a role that allows them to give to others in many areas of their lives. Giving themselves to a vampyre is a very intimate and loving thing for a donor, bonding them to the one to whom they donate in a very deep, meaningful way. It is easy to adopt the caregiver role, feeling almost like a mother to the one being provided for. This has happened to me on a few occasions. I found myself giving my vampyre unasked-for advice, thinking that I had the right or duty to be involved in other areas of that person's life in addition to the vampyric exchanges that we had. I had to remind myself that I was their vessel—not a parent, girlfriend, sister, or any of these other roles. I was a friend, but I had become confused about the bond we had formed due to the intimacy of the exchanges. At times, I found myself feeling bitter or left out when the donors would seemingly have me in their lives only in the capacity of a battery.

Would I have wanted to become something more? In truth, no. I am not, and was not at the time, in a position to be anything more than what I was. Still, my feelings got hurt—all for lack of clear lines being drawn at the outset. Communion is not sex; it is not a wedding, and it is not a guarantee of relationships evolving later or turning romantic. When these things begin to happen between a vampyre and donor, and the feelings are kept hidden or are assumed to be shared back, all sorts of hurt and trouble can occur. Not just for the partners involved, but if it all spins out of control, also for the community. And the daysides of both parties can be affected as well.

Much of the time, one or both parties have romantic relationships outside of the exchange. Whenever possible, I suggest that people involved in a vampyric exchange engage in full disclosure with their significant others about their donors, so that there is no possibility of misunderstanding. However, sometimes romantic partners do not know about the vampyre and donor relationship. In these cases, both sides must be discreet and mindful of the other's situation, and respect their privacy and right to secrecy. Both should understand that at no time should either commit an act that would in any way draw attention that might bring discord or trouble to any area of family or dayside life for their partner.

When I was the one with a donor, especially a sanguine donor, I saw my own warning signs. I was elated to have a sanguine donor who I could trust and who was very free with the gifts of his blood to me. I felt like a kid in a candy store. From the beginning, our communion in this way was pleasurable and empowering for me. I felt better, more healthy, and energized. People even commented to me there was something different about how I looked, that there was a light in my eyes. For me, it was almost as if I were on a new vitamin supplement. It was almost intoxicating. That should have been my first sign of danger. It did intoxicate me. I began to crave the experience and the feeling I got when feeding. At times the experience seemed to react with me chemically in such a way that I felt entranced. I looked forward more to the feeding than to the person. I began to walk on eggshells, hoping not to upset or alienate my partner so that my source wouldn't go away. I tolerated a lot of things I was uncomfortable with in order to keep my "fix." Once the donor relationship ended, I realized how deep the "addiction" went.

At the time, my needs felt like very physical cravings. In hindsight, I can say that the withdrawal, as it seemed to be, also included a psychological feeling of need: both for the closeness of the bond and for the feeling of health and even peace I got from the exchanges.

When I look back on the sanguine experiences, I can see how it would have benefited me to not have been in romantic relationship with my donors. I used the relationship as a tool or bargaining chip; I used their feelings for me as a means of manipulation. Also, had I applied more effort to learning control methods or meditation, and even some of the psychic feeding methods, which I use now as a supplement, I wouldn't have found myself so dependent. Having other methods of obtaining energy at my disposal would have also made the times without a donor easier on me. I have since looked into meditation and ambient feeding as supplemental techniques. I infrequently get a sanguine craving, possibly once or twice a month, but they are less intense than they used to be.

Being able to review past donor relationships, whether I was the Kitra or the one doing the feeding, has been invaluable to me in making choices about my future vampyre/donor relationships. I feel that trusting one's intuition;

looking for the subtle and sometimes not-so-subtle warning signs; clear, frequent, and honest communication; and not being solely dependent on one source can all make a big difference.

Definitions

Kitra: According to Lady Eden of the Court of Lightning Bay, this term is derived from an Aramaic word that means "knot" or "binding tie." Used widely throughout both the Sanguinarium and the OSV, Kitra originally referred to a donor, vampire or otherwise. In some early groups, Kitra were perceived as being subordinate to "real" vampires, and they were often treated as second-class citizens within the vampire community. Through the work of individuals such as LadyBlak, Kitra have come to occupy a place equal to that of any vampire. In general, they are seen as a type of vampire in their own right.

Vampires as donors: Not all vampires have the same level of need. Additionally, there seem to be several key ways that certain vampires interact with energy. These differences lie at the heart of the Kheprian caste system, which divides vampires into three general types. These types, or castes, have been adopted by some—but by no means all—groups within the greater vampire community. Vampires of the Priest caste have the highest energetic need, but also exhibit a potent ability to harness and direct energy. This makes them ideal for directing the energy of ritual—hence the connection with priests. Vampires of the Warrior caste have a strong connection to primal earth energies, and seem only to need energy from other people on occasion to supplement this connection. They seem to gravitate toward feeding off the energy generated from physical or verbal confrontations—hence the connection with warriors. Vampires of the Counselor caste have a level of need that falls midway between Warrior and Priest. In this way, they are vampiric, but they seem to have an even greater need to connect with the energy of others, sharing and moving this energy in a dynamic fashion. As strange as it may seem, this type of vampire seems to benefit both from feeding and being fed upon, and achieving a balance of both give and take is essential to their well-being. For a long time within the vampire community, individuals of this sort were not accepted as "real" vampires and were often relegated to the rank of donor or "black swan"—someone who is not a vampire but who enjoys the companionship of vampires.

Tapping: A kind of slang term for the act of connecting energetically to a donor, usually over a long distance. The act of feeding, especially psychically, tends to create strong energetic bonds between the vampire and donor. These bonds are commonly referred to within the community as "links," and many vampires harness them to connect with former donors over long distances. Some psychic vampires will maintain a donor pool, making arrangements with past feeding partners so they can tap into their energy from a distance when the need arises. Less ethical vampires will maintain these connections and tap into their donors without making prior arrangements. Understandably, most donors find such behavior rude and intrusive.

Communion: An alternative term to describe the process of vampiric feeding. The term *feeding* is seen by some to perpetuate negative, predatory stereotypes, and so alternative descriptors are sometimes used. *Communion* emphasizes both the sacred aspect that the interaction holds for many people and the unified interaction of vampire and donor. Another, less poetic term that underscores the potentially symbiotic interaction of vampire and donor is *energy exchange*.

Dayside: In several groups within the community, a vampire's life is divided into a "nightside" and a "dayside." The dayside refers to the vampire's mundane identity, as well as any roles or responsibilities connected with that identity. A vampire's nightside self is the identity that is freely and openly vampiric. The vampire's nightside identity can also be seen as a magickal identity. Some vampires seek to integrate these two halves of their existence, achieving a type of balance commonly referred to as "twilight." This distinction between dual aspects of a vampire's nature, as well as the concept of "twilight," owe at least some inspiration to the teachings of the Temple of the Vampire.

Ravena Lee has established herself within the vampire community through her informative articles published on numerous websites. Ravena is a native of Canada, and is involved long distance with the California-based House Lost Haven.

Choosing and Working with Donors

by Ravena Lee of House Lost Haven

For those who identify themselves as vampires, a donor is often the key to general health and comfort. Without the blood and/or energy from a donor, a vampire's quality of life might suffer. Because of the crucial role the donor plays for the vampire, it is important that the donor is respected. Donors should not be referred to as "food" or "cattle." Vampires who refer to donors in this manner really do not deserve a donor.

Donors can sustain themselves on the things required by all human beings; they are self-sufficient in that they do not require blood and/or energy to maintain the feeling of good health. A vampire with a superiority complex is only a fool filled with stupid self-importance. Whatever it is that the vampire lacks—and needs from a donor—represents a form of weakness on the vampire's part. It is the vampire who is in need. For those who use their abilities as a way to justify their superiority, I'm afraid they are sadly mistaken. Any ability a vamp can claim may also be claimed by a non-vamp.

The vampires who act superior to donors or others are mostly those caught up in playing out the myths and stereotypes of vampirism. They enjoy the role. Being a vampire does not make one special, or more intelligent or attractive, or otherwise charming. Vampires with a superiority complex usually travel in groups and meet at various gatherings to congratulate themselves on being princes and princesses of darkness. Hopefully, anyone on a high horse has quite gracefully dismounted by now. Let go of the delusions of grandeur. A donor should be treated with respect. Save the "food" and "cattle" comments for your Cheerios or your steak.

Choosing a Donor

Even though donors are in short supply, it is important to exercise a certain degree of pickiness when choosing one. It is tempting to not be fussy when there aren't plenty of donors. However, a donor chosen unwisely can bring many problems that are often not compensated for by what the donor has to offer. It is a very good idea not to compromise on certain standards. Consider the qualities below when evaluating a donor. (Note also that a donor should be just as fussy when choosing a vampire to donate to.)

Trustworthy

A donor is likely to be exposed to highly personal aspects of a vampire's life. In the interest of keeping your private life private (and your vampirism secret if applicable), it is best not to give any trust before it is reasonably earned. Although most of us have probably experienced a betrayal of trust in the past, caution in this area can help to minimize these unfortunate situations. Do not give trust too soon or hand it out to anyone and everyone.

Open-minded

This is a given, since not everyone in society is going to be open-minded enough to accept that vampirism could possibly exist, let alone be willing to donate. Just make sure the donor's mind isn't open at both ends.

Honest

Honesty is essential. A donor should be honest and forthcoming if they have done anything that may have compromised the safety of their blood. For example, if they've had unprotected sex, regardless of whether or not their partner appeared "clean," they should be up-front about it. The only time this rule wouldn't apply is if the donor is in a monogamous, steady relationship in which neither partner has *any* sexual contact outside of the relationship. For those who are polyamorous, all parties who are involved would count as being in the relationship, and it is essential that they are not straying outside of the boundaries of the committed polyamorous relationship. This, of course, assumes that all parties involved in the committed relationship have been tested for HIV and other blood-borne diseases prior to getting into that relationship.

"Testing" means having actual blood taken and sent to a lab to be tested for various blood-borne diseases. It's amazing how many people often assume that a "clean"-looking person is disease-free. Practicing proper hygiene and showering daily does not prevent the spread of things like HIV and hepatitis. If a donor has done something that increases the risk of getting an STD or is infected with any blood-borne disease, then they should refrain from donating blood to a vampire until they have been tested again. Keep in mind that sometimes medical professionals advise people to be tested again for certain diseases in six months, since the viruses don't always show up in the early stages—but of course the diseases can *still* be transmitted. The "I feel fine" method of testing is not acceptable. Get real lab work done.

That being said, someone's sex life is often a delicate issue as it involves private matters. Depending on the pre-established arrangements, a donor can just simply inform the vampire that they won't be donating. They can add that it is for health or safety reasons, or they can choose to be more up-front about their reasons. What the vampire is told really depends on the comfort level and nature of the vamp-donor relationship. The point of all this, at the very least, is not to get information about your donor's less-than-wise sex life, but to make sure that the donor will do the responsible thing and not donate if they have done something that increases the risk. The *whys* should not be that important in this case. What is most important is that the donor has realized the activities they've engaged in have increased the risk of disease, and that they choose not to donate so that you, the vampire, are not put at risk.

It is absolutely essential that you discuss all of this with your donor beforehand, so if something comes up later you will be reasonably assured they will not continue to donate to you if they have done something to increase their risk of acquiring a blood-borne disease. Make it clear that their explanations will not be necessary, and that a simple statement from them will end the matter. Making a promise not to hound them or get angry when they aren't comfortable with stating the reason for not donating would be a good idea. If they want to state reasons, it's up to them. But be clear that the goal is to protect you from disease, nothing more. This also goes both ways—if the vampire has done something to increase their risk of disease, then they need to refrain from taking blood, at the least. Be sure that you both are well educated about STDs and blood-borne diseases. Don't assume you know everything; there are countless myths out there that people take as fact. Get information from a reliable source, such as the Centers for Disease Control and Prevention (the CDC) in the United States.

Honesty is essential for health reasons. But it's also necessary for any sort of genuine relationship. Being honest about expectations and concerns and anything pertaining to the vamp-donor relationship is the key to a positive association.

Understanding

Understanding in any relationship is a good thing. Take the time to make certain that you and the donor understand one another. Misunderstandings only cause problems. In order to understand you, a donor does not have to relate firsthand with the sensation of feeling out of control with a blood craving. The "you don't understand me" bitching and moaning should be reserved for certain teens and the more angsty Goths. Instead, explain, clarify, and communicate. Understanding is possible even if someone can't walk around in your shoes. The understanding may not be perfect, of course, but nothing in this world is.

Adult

Make sure your donor has reached the age of majority in your state, province, or country. There are many laws pertaining to what adults can and cannot do with a minor; rest assured that bloodletting falls under the "cannot do" legal category. There aren't only legal considerations, but ethical ones, too. A child is unlikely to be equipped to make an informed decision about whether or not to donate. They may be immature or just not emotionally ready to make such a decision.

Mature

Keep in mind that someone who has attained the age of legal adulthood does not necessarily possess the maturity of an adult. Make certain that any potential donor has the level of maturity required to handle all that encompasses being a donor.

Emotionally Balanced

Donors should be emotionally healthy. This does not mean that their lives should be problem-free or that they need to be happy-go-lucky types. They should, however, be able to deal with their problems in a healthy way. Someone who is mentally ill may not have the tools they need to be a successful, healthy donor. Moreover, depending on the type of mental illness they have, they may not even be in any real position to make sound and healthy decisions for themselves.

An emotionally unstable person can be very draining on energy and time, and can cause problems if you decide to end the vamp-donor relationship or not spend every waking spare moment with them, and so on. A whole lot of problems could arise—too many to list. Just keep in mind that an emotionally unstable person generally demands a huge amount of attention that is often above and beyond what most can give or are willing to give. Unstable people probably aren't equipped to deal with being a donor on an emotional level either. In fact, donating could even cause such individuals emotional harm.

A reasonably sane donor is a good thing, and any donor lost in la-la land should be avoided. Who knows how the vamp will be cast in the donor's la-la land world. Even if they cast the vamp as some divine god or goddess to be worshipped, it's not healthy (though it might be flattering). Those lost in la-la land don't really live in the real world, and it's best a donor lives in the real world so that they fully understand the need for discretion, blood tests, and good health—not to mention the responsibilities that most of us have in day-to-day life.

Method of Drawing Blood/Energy

Discuss the methods used to draw blood or energy. Drawing blood may be what causes the most concerns. For example, if the donor is terrified of knives, it is not recommended that a knife be used. Some won't mind a knife but can't deal with a needle. (Note: do not *ever* try to extract blood with a needle unless you have been medically trained—so no "my friend Joe taught me" qualifications.) The gentlest way to draw blood is with a lancet, but some vamps claim this does not yield enough blood. The truth is, most do not need a whole lot of blood, so making a few pokes with a lancet in quick succession in a small area can help address the problem.

Some people have a tolerance for pain; others don't like it. Whatever is chosen, the donor might be nervous, so it's important to go slow. It might be a good idea to let the donor do any cutting so they can set the pace. Obviously, the donor has to be comfortable with at least one method in order to donate to a strictly sanguinarian vampire. After trying one method, they may be okay with it or they may want to investigate one or more other options. *Never* coerce someone into donating. Most issues with methods are associated with the drawing of blood but that does not mean one ignores the donor's concerns over drawing energy. The issues likely to arise with energy drawing are usually about how much energy is taken and if physical contact (and what type) is required. And of course, no donor wants the experience to feel horrible.

As a late note on this subject, it is very important that you *control yourself* while feeding. If you are a newly awakened vampire, or if for whatever reason there's a risk of you losing control while feeding, make sure you keep a trusted person around who can be counted on to stop you and overpower you physically if it comes down to that. One of the very worst things a vampire can do is to lose control while feeding, and harm a donor. The trusted person needs to be in the same house or room as you are, and not "just a phone call away." People who have lost control rarely stop and think they should call so-and-so to come and help. It's not only the donor's safety that is at risk here. If you harm a donor, there could be some very serious legal implications, including criminal charges. Not to mention, you will have completely destroyed the trust the donor placed in you.

Working with a Donor

If a donor has been chosen wisely, it shouldn't be too difficult to work with them. Keeping things peaceful and agreeable for both parties is one of the key elements to maintaining good relations.

Communication

Communication involves a sender of a message and a receiver of a message. Effective communication depends not only on the sender conveying their precise meaning correctly, but also on the receiver getting the message that the sender intended. If the receiver does not know what the sender really means, then communication is not effective. It doesn't matter how brilliant the sender is; the whole point of effective communication is that the receiver not only gets the message, but fully understands it in the way the sender intended. The receiver has the responsibility to ask questions if they do not understand the message, and the sender has the responsibility for making the message as clear as possible. If senders and receivers are mindful of what makes communication effective, many negative experiences caused by poor communication can be avoided.

The nature of the vamp-donor relationship should be discussed so that both parties are on the same page regarding expectations. Will the relationship have a romantic element? Will it be based on friendship? Will it be more like a business arrangement? Attachments can form on either side that may or may not be wanted. In order to avoid unnecessary hurt, it's important to be upfront about what the vamp-donor relationship will entail. It's not appropriate to pretend an interest, romantic or otherwise, in order to get someone to be a donor. Leading someone on should not be part of a respectful relationship.

Drawing Lines

Each party should be forthcoming about what their boundaries are. Determining how involved both will be in each other's life is essential. Is the other person going to sit down with the family for dinner? Can either show up unannounced? Can they call at three AM? Can they call at work? How much time will be spent with each other? Obviously, it will be very difficult to cultivate a trusting relationship if the vampire only spends time with the donor to donate and do nothing else.

A relationship that is strictly business might allow for fewer emotional entanglements, but a friendship might work better because it is on a personal level. It's harder for someone to betray trust if they are personally involved with someone, rather than saying "It's just business." This of course remains a personal choice of the vampire and the donor involved. It's important the donor feels appreciated and gets some kind of fulfillment from the arrangement, whether it's a good friendship or a fruit basket once a month. What makes someone feel appreciated can vary, so make sure to ask. No matter what kind of relationship is established, avoid making the other person feel taken for granted. That being said, having a friendship does not mean one can impose on time you've put aside to spend with specific loved ones and such. In other words, a donor, or a vamp for that matter, should not cost the other person their other personal relationships. Balance is recommended, and priorities should be made clear from the very beginning. Obviously, a donor doesn't deserve to be the last person on your list when it comes to importance, but it's good to balance your relationship with them with the other relationships you maintain.

Checkpoints

Always make the time to take stock of the vamp-donor relationship. Is everything still realistic and healthy? Sometimes people change, and their views may or may not be the same as before. This is another area where effective communication comes into play. Converse regularly to make certain both of you are still on the same page.

Also, monitor the donor continually to check for signs of emotional problems, mental illness, or health problems. Monitor yourself as well, because vampires are certainly not immune to these issues. Sometimes people don't start off in la-la land, but end up there later on for various reasons. It's important to look for these signs, because they often indicate that trust is eroding. Health is a big issue. People who are ill physically or mentally probably are better off not donating until they are well again. As previously mentioned, both parties need to be honest if they have done something that could compromise the other's health. Regular lab tests every six months, or more often if agreed upon, should be routine.

Obsession and Addiction

It's not unheard of for a vampire to get addicted to not only blood/energy, but to the donor's emotional qualities as well. If the vamp-donor relationship ends, the vampire may experience withdrawal symptoms not unlike those experienced by a drug addict who stops taking a drug. As a result, the vampire can become obsessed with the donor. Of course, this also applies vice versa. The donor may get addicted to the feeling of being fed from and become obsessive over the vampire. Problems arise when the vamp-donor relationship ends in these cases, because it's difficult to let go. It is essential to monitor the relationship for signs that something ugly is developing with regards to obsession and addiction. Being aware of this potential complication allows both parties to watch out for it, and take steps to stop it before it escalates into something problematic.

Continued Discretion

Maintaining discretion is necessary for a positive vamp-donor relationship. How much discretion is up to those involved. A public vampire may not require quite as much discretion as a vampire who has not revealed themselves openly in a public way. Discretion goes both ways, of course.

Conclusion

With all of the information above, you should have some things to think about. Anything mentioned here isn't the "bible" of vamp-donor relationships, as individual dynamics vary within relationships. These are just some commonsense observations that may or may not help you choose a donor and maintain a mutually fulfilling relationship or arrangement with a donor.

DEFINITIONS

Polyamory: The practice, common among certain Pagan and alternative groups, of maintaining committed relationships with more than one partner, or maintaining a committed relationship that nevertheless leaves open the option to interact romantically or sexually with others outside of the relationship, often upon the approval of the primary partner. Many ideals of the practice of polyamory are eloquently portrayed in the fiction of author Robert Heinlein. Individuals who practice polyamory are described as being polyamorous, as opposed to monogamous.

HIV/AIDS: Several vampire scholars, including David J. Skal, author of *The Monster Show*, have convincingly argued that resurgence of the vampire in popular culture during the 1980s was tied directly to anxieties concerning the AIDS pandemic. From this perspective, fictional vampirism can be seen at once as being a metaphor for the contraction and spread of AIDS through the blood, but also a wish fulfillment of maintaining life and youth in the face of such contagion. It has also been argued that part of the appeal of bloodplay, at least for some individuals, arises from the very risks that this practice poses. Arguing against this last assertion is the fact that nearly all sanguine vampires adhere to strict safety practices, both in the process of acquiring blood from a donor and in ensuring that donor's freedom from any blood-borne illnesses.

Lancet: Lancets are small devices designed to draw a minute amount of blood for medical testing. The lancets sold commercially at pharmacies are used by diabetics to test their blood sugar levels. These lancets come in sterile packaging and are designed for one use and one use only. Because of the design of a lancet, it is very difficult to cause deep or dangerous wounds when using them, yet they easily draw several large drops of blood. As one of the safest and most hygienic methods for drawing blood, diabetic lancets are used by a number of blood-drinkers within the vampire community. The use of lancets also eloquently expresses how little blood is actually involved in most sanguine feedings.

SECTION
-FOUR-

The Vampire Community

Eclecta is a thirty-two-year-old eclectic spiritualist who lives in Atlanta. One of the five founding members of the Atlanta Vampire Alliance (AVA), she still finds time to be a mother to her two children and a friend to those who need one in the vampire community. When time allows, she serves as a global moderator for the online vampire community Sanguinox, better known as Nox, and she was formerly a co-branch head of ShadowLore for her area. She has helped to develop the widely distributed Vampire and Energy Work Research Survey, *which seeks to compile hard data concerning the community and its demographics. More of her work can be found on the AVA website, at www.atlantavampirealliance.com.*

Accepting Our Differences, Revealing Our Natures

BY ECLECTA OF HOUSE AVA

We are all different, unique, and eccentric in our own ways. We all also share similarities with others, whether these are physical characteristics, ideas about who we are, or the ways we feel about the things around us. Many of us feel we have to hide our true nature in order to protect ourselves from the pain that we know all too well comes from revealing too much about ourselves to the wrong people. Being called a freak, an oddball, a devil worshiper, crazy, or just plain weird—we all have heard such name-calling at one time or another.

Most of us have wished at times that we were someone else—someone normal, someone pink and fluffy, or athletic, or maybe something more. However, we aren't those people, and we don't do those things. To be something other than exactly who we are would mean only that we have denied who we are and have cast out a deep part of our inner being that is screaming for recognition.

As we go through life, more and more people are going to notice us, and if we do not learn to love ourselves for who we are, then how can we expect others to do so? A great many of us pride ourselves on our capacity to survive without needing anyone else. We are independent; we need no one. We dress in dark colors; we prefer night to day; we sometimes write dark, morbid poetry that documents the turmoil we feel in our hearts; and we are reclusive. Of course, not all of us do these things—some cannot, or do not, simply because they would rather blend in as best as they can, rather than have to answer any questions about why they are as they are . . .

Being different from society's norms can be hard on us. Feeling you are valued as less than others because you don't do things like everyone else, being told you're abnormal, or serving as the brunt of some derogatory remark—it's no secret that all of this takes a toll. But what can we do?

Revealing too much about yourself to others can unilaterally undermine potential friendships or relationships you may otherwise have, if that person to whom you reveal yourself is not ready to accept you for who you are. That's precisely the reason why so many of us remain secretive about so many aspects of our lives.

To ensure you don't divulge too much about your inner nature—which may be misunderstood by those to whom you'd like to reveal yourself—it is imperative that you first come to terms with accepting who you are.

Accepting yourself as you are can be harder than it sounds. A great many of us seem to struggle with issues that are ethical, spiritual, emotional, and physical. With each of these struggles, we must find the right combination that will unlock who we are meant to be. Your physical self will suffer as a direct result of neglecting other areas of your life. Deciding what is right or wrong—and making decisions without thinking about the consequences—can end up generating feelings of guilt. The choices you make could also lead you to depression or worse. These links to our greater consciousness should be understood and nurtured so that we can truly achieve inner peace.

Our parents or caregivers taught us ethics early on, but many of us later in life challenge certain things we were taught. If you were told as a small child that you must be good for Santa Claus to visit, as most of us were, you trusted the person who told you because you didn't know any better. When you found out that Santa Claus isn't real, you may have felt betrayed by that little white lie. Small instances like this can lead to other questions, such as those about ethics, religion, or many other topics. If someone we trusted let us believe in Santa, perhaps they would also lead us to believe in other things that aren't real. Take religion, as another example. If we are told to believe in Jesus Christ, but we never see him or hear him speak to us in a voice loud enough for us to hear, we may question whether he is really there. When we ask others for proof, and they tell us it is only a matter of faith, it may make us remember the innocent lie we were told as children about Santa. Such seemingly innocent events can perhaps cause us to doubt many things in our lives that we were taught through the years.

Part of accepting ourselves is learning who we really are and having a good understanding of why we do what we do. No one can force us to believe exactly as they do; this is a journey we must endure on our own. Our emotional state can cause us to need additional means to cope with the situations around us. If we pull energy from other sources, we may feel that what we're doing is wrong. We may justify what we are doing at first, but eventually, if we don't understand enough about ourselves and what we're doing, we may be left feeling that we have violated our code of ethics.

It is sometimes a long process to examine ourselves. Relaxation is the key to being able to find your true self. You may want to take a trip alone to collect your thoughts, take long walks, or perhaps study yoga. You may also want to write down the questions you seek to answer about yourself and re-read them several times a day. It may take weeks, months, or years to get the answers you seek, however.

Once you've answered the questions you had, and then accepted yourself, you should think twice about revealing your nature to others. While it is nice to share a part of yourself with others, many of those with whom we want to share simply do not have the capacity to understand who we are because they do not even know themselves. Our community as a whole is often misunderstood.

Putting trust in another being about your true self leaves you in a vulnerable position. As we grow up from childhood, we are often left with the knowledge of just how cruel others can be. This knowledge leaves us longing for someone to understand and accept us for the people we have accepted ourselves to be, but our memories of past experiences may frighten us about outing our inner selves to others. You should take the utmost care when choosing the people to whom you will reveal your true self.

The main reason most of us don't publicly announce that which makes us different is because some people would think us insane, or believe us to be devil-worshipers, or worse. It's no secret that mainstream society no longer believes in anything metaphysical. Therefore, revealing yourself to someone who is only going to question your sanity can be an unpleasant prospect.

Those who are open-minded about, say, pagan beliefs or ghosts may be more receptive than others. Yet there is no sure way to know who will accept you and who won't. Ask yourself questions about the various undesirable outcomes before you reveal anything.

Some of us spend years trying to find a way to explain who we are to our family and friends. Others decide that they never want to have to explain who they are to anyone. If you do choose to take a chance and decide to open up to family or friends, you should do so knowing that if you are rejected it might cause a rift in your relationship from that point on. Deciding whether or not to take that risk is a careful decision only you can make. It is important to take the necessary time to choose wisely. Weighing your options can be helpful; always keep in mind that once you have said something, you can't simply take it back. Paying attention to subtle clues about the person you wish to confide in may save your feelings later.

Accepting and revealing yourself to everyone you know or meet is not necessary. If you take the time to find others like yourself, you may not feel the yearning to be so open with others. Often, the feelings that keep you on edge, wondering if you should tell others about who you are, dissipate once you find someone who can truly understand how you feel—because they feel that way, too.

Rev. Vicutus is one of the more eloquent occultists who has adopted the vampire as a magickal identity. The archetype of the vampire, in its more Promethean aspect, lies at the heart of his formal occult organization, Ordo Sekhemu, a fully developed mystery tradition devoted to empowering the Self.

To the Seeker in Membership

BY REV. VICUTUS, ORDO SEKHEMU

*O*ccultism means the science of things hidden—not unbelievable things, but root things, both in our own human selves and in Universal nature. And what is hidden can be known to the trained seer. There is nothing strange or weird in this; it is merely a step further than the average man has gone.

What is the Pathway? The Pathway is you yourself. Therefore the call from the Teacher comes to you: "Awake, my Brethren, awake to the god within yourself: not outside, not in me, but in you—the Master Supreme." Where is the fountainhead of your understanding? Where arises the flame of your intelligence? What is the wellspring of love within you? Where is the sum of compassion and pity and self-forgetfulness? All within you. There is the Path.

Self-conquest, self-discipline, self-study (the study of the Higher Self), self-evolution, self-growth: *there* is the teaching. Expand your human consciousness so that it may become the consciousness of the god within you.

There is Truth in the Universe. That Truth can be had, and the way to have it is by willpower and perseverance in following the Path. There is but one fundamental Truth in the Universe, simply because there is but one Boundless All. No matter in what age, with what language or which figures of speech, in each and in every case the essentials of the teachings of the great sages and seers were the same, because the Truth is one.

The Archaic Doctrine, the wisdom-religion of mankind, the secret Doctrine of the ages: this is the Lost Word, which is a system of teaching, a wisdom, the existence of which still remains as an echo in the hearts of all good and true and intuitive men and women.

There is an inner god in every human being. When a person finds his, he will enjoy communion with the divinities, and will understand the Universe in which he lives and moves, and of which he is an inseparable part. Receiving his wisdom means the broadening of man's consciousness, the deepening of his being, the evocation of his latent intellectual powers, and self-acquaintance with his soul, so to speak—call it whatever you like. It also means becoming self-consciously at one with the All. Aspire. Be. But also look within.

Occultism is the science of things unseen and seen. Man, know thyself—for thy Self is a divine being, rooted in the Universe of which the human being is an extension, so to speak. Therefore, by looking within, by following the roots of your own inner spiritual being, you come to understand naturally the mysteries of the Invisible.

Everyone is capable of developing this inner consciousness in their heart. We are all brothers and sisters in this. And we should treat each other as such. For the first law of our nature is that we are creatures of beauty.

Sphynxcat is what many people in the community would call an "elder,"
although she is the least likely person to tell you so. Widely known for
her vampire resource Sphynxcat's Real Vampires Support Page, Sphynx has
made a point of remaining unconnected to any specific group, council, or
other organization, in order to better provide a fair and neutral perspec-
tive on the community as a whole.

Joining a House, Church,
or Other Organization

BY SPHYNXCAT

How do you find a house or other group to join? First, decide which philosophical or faith-based path you wish to follow. Whether it's a "church," "house," or some other organization or group, you have to decide what will work best for you. (For the rest of this article, I will use the term "group" to refer to any of the above types of organizations.) Second, ask around. Ask vampires you know, either online or offline, or ask in vampire-friendly establishments. Run a web search if you need to. Most groups are fairly well-advertised within the online vampire community, in posts about the group or in the profiles of a group's members or representatives.

Some questions you need to ask at this stage are:

- What is the path or philosophy they follow? Does it mesh with yours?
- What are the requirements for joining?
- What is the most common age range? Are there age limits or minimums?
- Are they primarily psi-vamps? Blood vamps? Or doesn't it matter to them?
- If you are not in that group's area, do they accept non-local members?

Approaching the House

If the group is online, check out their website to see if they have any membership information and requirements. (Most websites will have a link of this nature, even if it's just to a page that says, "Sorry, we're not accepting any new applicants at this time.") Read the requirements before applying for membership—if they expect frequent in-person attendance at events and meetings, and you're several states away, then it's probably not a good match.

Read the application carefully. Are you comfortable with the level of personally identifying information it asks for, such as a photocopy of your driver's license or state ID, your real name, and offline contact information for you and possibly your spouse or partner? Or perhaps the group wants even more detail, such as the name of the place you work. A request for proof of age *is* reasonable, but how much do they want besides that, and how much information are you willing to give out?

If and when your application gets a positive response, then you can start investigating the group more thoroughly. Make certain that you ask anything you want to ask in order to ensure the group is the right one for you. Ask questions on various issues to get an idea of the group's philosophy toward fellow vamps and toward non-vamps of all types. To determine if you'll fit in, you need to interview the group as much as the group needs to interview you.

Some questions you should be asking:

- How is their hierarchy arranged? Is there room for promotion/advancement? If so, how?
- How often are meetings held? Is attendance expected? If so, how often?
- Are attendance requirements enforced? Why or why not?
- How active are the elders outside of the house and in the community? What do they do?
- How busy are the elders?
- Are all more experienced members approachable for questions from new members?
- How formal is the group? Is specific etiquette required at all times, or is it fairly easygoing?
- What other groups is this group affiliated with, if any?
- What are the group's stated goals?

- What group(s) or individual(s) don't like this group? Why?
- What group(s) or individual(s) does this group not like? Why?

Judging the House

In order to tell if a group is a good one, talk to current and past members. Get their opinions on the group. If ex-members would not rejoin the group if given the opportunity, ask why not—it may be a simple personality or path/philosophy conflict, or it could be something more serious.

Just because a group seems to be in "good standing" in other places does not mean that's always the case—some things can be hidden under the surface of what outsiders see, and are only known by people who have been in the group and have seen it for themselves.

If you are local, ask to meet group members at events and talk with them. Observe how they interact with other members of the house. Find out whether these events are official events (and how formal) or unofficial "get-togethers" that happen for whatever reason.

Some questions you should be asking are:

- How much drama is there?
- How close-knit are the members?
- How many current members are there?
- Has the membership been growing or decreasing? If it's been decreasing, why?
- How are lower-ranking members (if any) treated within the group and at group events?
- How are non-vamps treated?
- How much respect is considered to be owed to the elder(s) versus respect freely given?
- How rigid, structured, or loose are the group's policies?
- How rigid, structured, or loose is the social structure?
- How relaxed or formal is the interaction between members?

Also use the Isaac Bonewits Cult Danger Evaluation Frame as a guide for your questions and observations. Don't be swayed by talk and promises often set up by con artists. There are good things out there, but there are dangers and pitfalls as well.

Definitions

House: A term for a group of vampires who share similar practices and beliefs. A house is essentially a vampire coven; the term *house* was presented as an alternative to the Wiccan term *coven* in the *Vampyre Almanac*. Most vampire houses have a name and a distinctive symbol that in some way embody their core ideals. Individuals involved in a specific vampire house tend to live near one another. It is not uncommon for the core of the group to share an actual house, which serves as the meeting place and social hub for the members. Geographic proximity is not required for a house to exist, however; there are a number of vampire houses whose central hub is a webpage on the Internet.

Isaac Bonewits Cult Danger Evaluation Frame: Developed by renowned Pagan author and Druid elder Isaac Bonewits, this survey first appeared in the 1979 edition of his seminal work Real Magic. The framework is designed to help individuals assess the threat of any group with which they may become involved. The Evaluation Frame surveys key factors of the group dynamic and its sway over its members, including internal control, external control, recruiting, and sexual favoritism. Widely circulated throughout the Internet, an updated version of the Evaluation Frame is also hosted on Bonewits' own website, www.neopagan.net.

Sylverë ap Leanan is one of many members of the vampire community who blends an affinity for faeries and the fey with her identity as a vampire. Her chosen surname, Leanan, is a direct reference to the Irish Leanan Sídhe, a type of vampiric faerie believed to inspire poets and artists, but also to feed upon their life force as the poets and artists create great works.

American Vampires—A Rant

BY SYLVERË AP LEANAN

Why do vampires in this country insist on forming "courts," "covens," and "houses" that take on the trappings of feudalism? If we were European, Asian, or Indian, it might make more sense. Those regions have long histories of caste-based societies, complete with all the problems associated with such societies.

But we're Americans. Our nation was founded on the principle that all are equal in the eyes of our Creator and should be acknowledged as such by those around us. We waged a revolution to establish this philosophy as a fact and emerged victorious. Over the centuries, we have fought other battles, both military and civil, to expand the reaches of democracy so that all humans everywhere might enjoy the rights and responsibilities of this way of life. In some areas, we have made tremendous strides. In others, the battle continues, but we persevere, confident that our cause is just and that we will prevail.

Yet, in clubs and on the Internet, we revert to the very societal structure from which our countrymen struggled to free us. Is it a need for a sense of community? I don't think so. There are plenty of people, vampire and non-vampire alike, who do not feel the need to be addressed as "Elder" or "Lord" or "Mistress." There are egalitarian organizations everywhere that welcome all without the need to elevate an elite cadre over the masses. Surely, those who seek a sense of belonging can have their needs met by one or more of these groups.

Why do we persist in subjecting ourselves to an artificial hierarchy? Why do we continually adopt false titles that have no basis in merit and serve no purpose except to offer a flimsy excuse for the bearer to put on airs and degrade others? Oh, I've heard all the standard lines about honoring those who serve our community and offering titles as a sign of respect.

Those excuses are simply not good enough. I know plenty of people who have worked long and hard over the years to better the community. They hold no titles and do not care to have any. So, recognizing achievement cannot be the underlying purpose of adopting a title. Are the titles hereditary? Of course not, because we abolished such counterfeit structures when we declared our independence. Why then do we do it?

Is it so we can feel powerful? We have long felt ourselves to be outcasts, have felt the need to hide our true selves from the eyes of the world—is this irrational drive to adopt an even more discriminatory order a product of our need to feel special? Why do we need to justify our collective existence by establishing a system of recognition that oppresses others as we have felt ourselves to be oppressed? Where is our pride? How does subjugating each other equate to unity? How can bigotry and snobbery ever generate harmony among us?

How many times have we heard the call to "unite the vampire nation" under this council or that order? How many of those groups have fallen by the wayside or degenerated into harmful cults? If it is unity we seek, how can we ever achieve it by allowing our peers to subjugate and tyrannize us while we prattle on about how our so-called leaders bring honor to us by upholding the "old ways"? Honor is not a prize to be won nor a gift to be given. It is something we know to be true about ourselves. No one can bestow it where it does not already exist, and only we can take it from ourselves. There is no honor in assuming the façade of an outdated power structure. To say otherwise is to belittle and demean the warriors who have fought and bled and died to give us the freedom to choose for ourselves who is worthy of our respect and admiration. It is those brave soldiers who are truly noble. It is those who cherish their liberty, bought with the coin of sweat, blood, and tears, and use it to lift up all whom they meet who are the most honorable among us. Those who give selflessly and ask for nothing—it is they who display integrity.

> *We hold these truths to be self-evident, that all men are created equal,*
> *that they are endowed by their Creator with certain unalienable Rights,*
> *that among these are Life, Liberty and the pursuit of Happiness.*

No pretentious title will ever hold the significance, contain the splendor, or bear the majesty of the philosophy that gave rise to those words. None ever could.

DEFINITIONS

Court: An old Sanguinarium term that describes a gathering of vampires from a variety of different houses. A court represented a network of groups and individuals who resided in a specific geographic location. Courts often meet monthly for the members of a local community to socialize, interact, and learn. Many courts employ guest speakers, present workshops, or feature rituals. Although the Sanguinarium no longer really exists, a number of courts founded during the peak years of the Sanguinarium still exist, including the Court of Gotham in New York and the Court of Lightning Bay in Tampa, Florida.

The Sanguinarium: A vampire organization founded by Father Sebastian in the late 1990s. The Sanguinarium, also called the Vampyre Connection, was originally established for lifestylers and was based primarily in the New York City club scene. The network was the first to organize vampires into houses and courts. As it grew, the Sanguinarium expanded to include real vampires in addition to vampire lifestylers, accepting sanguinarians and psychic vampires alike. The Sanguinarium is best known for its publication *The Vampyre Almanac*, printed versions of which appeared in 1998 and 2000. The Sanguinarium also established and promoted the vampire code of ethics, the Black Veil.

Raven Kaldera is a self-described shapeshifter who is active in a number of magickal communities—with the exception of the vampire community. Author of The Ethical Psychic Vampire *and many other works, Kaldera is the parent of a vampiric child and approaches vampirism from both a Pagan and a shamanic perspective.*

Avoiding the Vampire Community

BY RAVEN KALDERA

I am not now, and never have been, a member of any vampire community. (I have, however, been a member of communities—generally Pagan spiritual ones—in which vampirism was accepted and discussed.) I peered into the vampire community a few times, but I was put off by several things. First, the general spooky attitude bothered me. There seemed to be a great deal of posturing and posing, and a lot of melodrama. People seemed to be in love with the fictional vampire à la Anne Rice; there was strong pressure to prove your vampiric nature by adhering to certain stereotypical behaviors, styles, and aesthetics. For that matter, the overriding aesthetic was overdone Byronic (they call it Gothic, but it's really Byronic). While there's nothing wrong with liking a certain look, it wasn't something that I was interested in doing.

Probably the most disturbing thing, however, was the use of the fictional vampire stereotype as a model for excusing bad behavior. Far too many were in love with evil, or at least with amorality. Saying that "it was just their vampire nature" was an all too easy excuse for any sort of nastiness. A therapist friend of mine pointed out that in vampire fiction, vampires are rewarded with power by remaining eternally static, by never growing and changing, which of course is the exact opposite of reality. But it can be very seductive to immature people who want power without work or responsibility.

I was interested in asking questions like: Where did this come from? How can it be controlled? How do we handle questions of ethics? How do we wrestle with the black impulses and put them in their place? How do we integrate this into a life that doesn't center around just getting our needs met? Even more importantly, can this ambivalent gift be redeemed and used to help people? No one seemed interested in talking about that. I suppose I was interested in exploring how to get one's vampirism under control to the point where it was not the overriding issue in one's life, and they were heavily invested in it being the overriding issue, for good or ill. What they saw as power and importance, I saw as immaturity and lack of ethics. What they saw as being a Romantic predator, I saw as being a mosquito. There was a terrible dearth, in general, of common sense.

Maybe I just found a bad community; I don't know. Maybe it was just the loudest voices there—and those who didn't feel that way were shouted down. Either way, it put me off, and I went my own way. When I wrote *The Ethical Psychic Vampire*, I didn't write it for any vampire community. I wrote it for vampires who aren't interested in that word as an identity, who will be slow to accept the idea, and who may be unconscious and desperately in need of help before they alienate everyone around them. I actually figured that the sort of folk that I'd met briefly in the vampire communities wouldn't think much of the book, as it emphasizes discipline and ethics and hard work and redemption.

Since then, I've been more interested in talking about vampirism—specifically, psychic vampirism—with communities of people who know nothing about any of this. The target audience I'm most interested in are energy workers, especially healer types. They, more than anyone, are often given false and negative data about psychic vampires, and I want them to have a more balanced and realistic view.

The Internet does seem to me to have crystallized and brought together many small communities, but I think (as an occasional observer) that it has also managed to homogenize the idea of what a vampire is to the point where it has quietly driven a lot of people away.

In terms of the schism between blood-drinkers and psychic vampires: on the one hand, the blood-drinkers do have a point in that they are more at risk socially. Someone claiming to be a psychic vampire is dismissed as a probably harmless loony, but someone who drinks blood can be wrongly seen as a psychopath. So their issues are different, as are their support needs. On the other hand, there are people who belong to both camps. As long as there is a schism, it passes through their bodies and hearts, so there will always be a bond to draw the two together.

I think the whole situation would be helped by a good dose of common sense, which would start out with both sides honestly asking, "What is it that we want to gain from community in the first place?" and then comparing those answers. If I've done anything to help the situation—and I don't think that I have, really—it's to be careful to add disclaimers when I speak at workshops on psychic vampirism, educating briefly about the different sorts of vampirism and how they cross over, without putting anyone down.

Sanguinarius has run the website www.sanguinarius.org since the mid-nineties, educating people on issues of vampirism and safety. Since its inception, her site has distinguished itself as one of the most reliable sources of information on sanguine vampirism on the Internet. A blood-drinker, Sanguinarius was originally hotly opposed to the idea of psychic vampires. She was one of the main voices in the bitter split between the psychic and sanguine communities. Since that time, she has worked to repair the rift, accepting a more general view of what comprises "vampire culture."

Vampire Lifestyle and Culture

BY SANGUINARIUS

In the vampire community, there are a number of those who are both real vampires and into the lifestyle and culture. Granted, many "vampyres" or "vampyre lifestylers" are not real vampires, and many real vampires are not "vampyres" or "vampyre lifestylers." But the way I see it, all real vampires do live a vampiric lifestyle to some extent or other.

Since we have no culture of our own, historically speaking, we are inventing it for ourselves. What we are doing is similar, in a way, to what the African Americans have done. Ripped from their cultures and homelands, displaced in this country as slaves, African Americans had no real cultural heritage in this country. Instead, over time, they have created a new identity and culture. This consists of drawing what they can from the existing knowledge base of African cultures, and also developing their own culture, lifestyle, and community based on what they have, as they go along.

In our case, the only "existing cultural heritage" or knowledge base that could be said to exist are the social/cultural aspects of vampiric fiction, at least those few fictional works that are adaptable to real-life situations. But, just as cultures evolve and grow, and just as African Americans are not limited to the traditional elements of their past, we are free to evolve and grow, and to adapt our culture to meet our needs.

The way I look at it, rightly or wrongly, is that we vampires, having no actual common cultural past, traditions, or social structure—and therefore, no identity as a people—are creating our own identity out of group/cultural/social necessity. Many non-vampires are going to be attracted to this. Many non-vampires have initiated this cultural evolution, but we can continue it with or without them.

They drew on such things as fiction to form the basis of the "lifestyle." But the baby has been born—and it is now growing, finding out about itself, and becoming its own person. Eventually, it will no longer need to be reliant upon the "mommy," the fictional aspects from which it was born.

We, in turn, can adapt with them and influence the culture that is ours as well. I believe that is only as it should be.

Unity. Cultural identity. Social conventions and structures. Traditions. Think of this all as a social gold mine. Everybody else has their culture/lifestyle/social system. Why can't we?

Furthermore, it's not mandatory to exist within the boundaries of a certain culture to be considered of that . . . "ethnic" (if that's the proper term) persuasion. Example: an old boss of mine was Jewish by background and family tradition. But he himself was Episcopalian and did not adhere to traditional Jewish culture. Yet he was still Jewish.

Another example: imagine someone who is a solitary practitioner of Wicca and is not connected to others who practice it. This person makes up many of the rituals, is not connected to a coven, and has no traditions (though Wiccans do)—yet she or he is still a Wiccan.

I don't consider myself a vampyre or vampyre lifestyler, but I am a part of the vampire culture. I live a vampiric lifestyle, but not necessarily a vampyre lifestyle, unless you consider the term very blandly and very loosely—or make no distinction between the terms *vampire* and *vampyre*.

"Culture" is so much bigger and more expansive than mere lifestyle. Lifestyle is a stepping stone toward culture. I am for the development of vampiric culture. We have a right to our own cultural identity.

Definitions

Lifestylers: A term for individuals who enjoy the fashion, aesthetics, and identity of the vampire. Lifestylers are not necessarily vampiric by nature, a fact that has caused some friction between this aspect of the community and those who consider themselves real vampires based upon their energetic needs. Lifestylers are in love with the vampire archetype, and many of them in recent years have adopted the vampire not just in terms of fashion, but as a potent magickal identity.

SECTION
-FIVE-

Codes of Behavior

Belfazaar Ashantison, known as Zaar to most of his friends, is one of the few vampires who stuck things out through Hurricane Katrina to help maintain the community in southern Louisiana. Actively involved in the founding and maintenance of several vampire houses over the years, Zaar continues to support the community in his beloved home of New Orleans.

The Donor Bill of Rights

BY BELFAZAAR ASHANTISON

This bill of rights is used to promote the continued safety of donors' most precious of gifts to us, their life essence. It is suggested that this contract be signed by both the vampire and the donor on a thirty, sixty, or ninety-day trial basis. After this, the contract can be signed again for an extended period of time, which can be either the same as the original term, or six months to one year. When the contract expires, the two parties can discuss whether or not changes should be made, including what will and will not be allowed.

✠   ✠

1) As a donor, I know that it is through my personal sacrifice that the vampire's needs are met. It is my loving nature that allows this relationship to continue. It is my right to decline to feed the vampire for any reason.

2) As a donor to a vampiric being, it is my right to know that I am in a vampiric/donor relationship that will be mutually beneficial both to me and to the vampire to whom I am donating my life essence.

3) I am the essence provider. It is for me to decide whether or not I am able to give of my essence to the vampire I am with. I must be allotted time to heal and regain my essence in order to better support my vampiric partner.

4) At no time should my wounds not be allowed to heal.

5) At no time should I feel stressed out about giving of my essence. If at any time I feel stressed, I have the right to back away from the feed, without being threatened or feeling threatened by my vampiric partner.

6) Should I feel threatened in any way, shape, or form, I have the right to seek guidance and counsel from other donors and leaders of the vampire community.

7) As a donor to a vampiric individual, I have the right to know that my position as lover, friend, family, or roommate should not be jeopardized if I do not want to give of my essence. To put it in slang terms: "It should not cost me my ass to be a donor."

8) As a donor, I should also respect the needs of the vampire and try to learn more about his or her feeding habits in order to help stabilize his or her imbalances in energy.

9) As a donor in a vampire/donor relationship, I realize that though I have many necessary rights, I must also take care not to abuse the person to whom I am donating my essence. These same rights afforded me in this bill of rights should also be extended to the vampire I am donating to.

10) Ultimately, it is my right to know that I will be safe in all aspects of the vampire/donor relationship. Should I ever feel that my safety is jeopardized, I have the right to walk away clear and free.

Ultimately, it is both the donor's and the vampire's responsibility to ensure that neither party is abused. It is the donor's and the vampire's personal responsibility to leave any vampire/donor relationship that either side feels is abusive in any respect. We cannot be abused unless we allow ourselves to be.

Alexander DuCoeur has been involved in the vampire community since its inception, albeit quietly. In the mid-nineties, he was a regular contributor to publications such as The Midnight Sun, *often writing under multiple pen names. In the late nineties, he ran a modest website that housed information on several vampire creation stories. However, he found that the online community was simply too public for his tastes. He makes a brief reappearance for this collection, fully intent on dissolving into the shadows once again.*

The Sanguine Creed
BY ALEXANDER DUCOEUR

This is the creed for those who must feed upon life. Do not forget these words, for they separate the gods from the monsters.

✴   ✴

Respect the blood:
It can bring life or death.

Honor the blood:
It is our weakness and our strength.

Celebrate the blood:
It is our sacred, precious gift.

Sylverë ap Leanan is one of those "elders" in the community who has been around for many years, but who often fades in and out of activity. Throughout her years of involvement in the community, she has been a part of Tir Nan Og, the Vampire/Donor Alliance, the Global Vampire Network, and, most recently, Lost Haven's initiative for widespread communication between diverse groups within the community.

Ethical Principles for the Vampire Community

BY SYLVERË AP LEANAN

This document was written in response to feedback and input from a number of community leaders involved in a networking group called the GVN, or Global Vampire Nation, founded shortly after the start of the new millennium. Although the GVN has since ceased to be an active group, the principles covered in this document remain relevant to the community at large.

Preamble

We recognize the intrinsic value of everyone, regardless of age, sexual orientation, color, spiritual philosophy, or gender. We do not adhere to or promote any particular religious or political creed. We strive to create an atmosphere in which individuals are not only free to create their own meanings, values, and convictions, but are, in fact, expected to do so. However, it is shortsighted to tell someone to think for himself or herself without also providing some tools for building. To that end, we have created this document.

Respect

If we want others to respect us, we must be willing to offer them the same respect. Our beliefs evolve from our own experiences, so there is no one set of "rules" that is right for everyone. We won't always agree with each other, and there's nothing wrong with that. We promote fair treatment of others and keeping our minds open to their views. It violates our principles to accept or encourage arrogance and conceit. We will not grant respect to those who prove themselves unworthy of it.

Honesty

Each of us is responsible for his or her own words and actions. We must be honest with ourselves and those with whom we come into contact. If we lie, we show disrespect to others. We will not tolerate those who lie to us or about us, because this demonstrates that they do not respect us as individuals.

Integrity

"No man is an island." By the same token, no member of our community—whether vampire, donor, or enthusiastic advocate—is isolated from the rest. What each of us does reflects not only on ourselves, but on the rest of the community as well. We discourage gossip, both the spreading of rumors and listening to them. We encourage everyone to be himself or herself. We believe that adopting a phony persona robs us of the opportunity to form genuine, lasting bonds with others. We encourage more experienced members of the community to help those who come seeking knowledge. However, we recognize the existence of sensationalistic media and its threat to our safety and that of our loved ones. We expect those members of our community who appear in public—whether through print, film, radio, or the Internet—to conduct themselves in a responsible manner.

Safety

We, vampires and donors alike, are committed to protecting the safety of ourselves and our families. We will make every effort to educate ourselves on safe feeding methods, including but not limited to basic anatomy, first aid, and prevention of HIV and other diseases.

We will not put ourselves or loved ones at risk by:

- feeding from those who carry a disease, whether it is HIV or a common cold
- allowing others to feed from us if our health is in any way compromised

- feeding from anyone who is intoxicated or otherwise unable to give informed consent
- failing to practice safer sex or feeding from those who do not practice safer sex
- feeding from someone whose psychological health may be harmed by the experience
- failing to screen donors carefully, taking into account both physical and mental health
- drawing unfavorable attention to ourselves by either flaunting what we are in an inappropriate setting or exposing ourselves to those who actively seek to exploit us for their personal gain

Michelle Belanger has become known for her work on both The Psychic Vampire Codex *and* The Black Veil. The Black Veil *has become one of the most widely recognized codes of behavior used within the worldwide vampire community. It has been referenced in numerous documentaries as well as on an episode of the television series* CSI.

The Black Veil, 2002 Revision

BY MICHELLE BELANGER

The Black Veil is a commonsense set of ethical guidelines originally developed for the Sanguinarium and the OSV. In the years since its original publication, it has been adopted by a number of groups in the greater vampire community. In addition, it is supported by a number of independent houses, including my own House Kheperu. An early version of the guidelines was drafted by Father Sebastian in the late nineties and appeared in the first edition of *The Vampyre Almanac*. In 2000, through a collaborative effort, I worked with Sebastian to revise the original Black Veil into the "Thirteen Rules of Community." As a result of further community feedback, the guidelines were revised again in October 2002 to produce the document reprinted here. This is the document I continue to support in my work with House Kheperu and the greater vampire community.

✖   ✖

Discretion

Respect yourself and present yourself so that others also respect you. Take care in who you reveal yourself to. Explain what you are—not to shock, but to teach and to inform. Do not flaunt what you are, and know that whether you want them to or not, your actions will reflect upon the rest of the community.

Share your nature only with those with the wisdom to understand and accept it, and learn to recognize these people.

Diversity

Among us there are many different practices and many points of view. No single one of us has all the answers to who and what we are. Respect each person's individual choices and beliefs. Learn about them and share what you know. Our diversity is our strength, and we should not allow misunderstanding to weaken our community. *Find the path that is right for you and uphold this freedom for others.*

Control

Do not allow your darkness to consume you. You are more than just your hunger, and you can exercise conscious control. Do not be reckless. Always act with a mind toward safety. Never feed because you think this makes you powerful; feed because this is what you must do. *Be true to your nature, but never use it as an excuse to endanger those around you.*

Elders

Give respect to those who have earned it. Anyone can claim a title, but a true leader will prove himself or herself through dedication, hard work, and great deeds. Even so, leaders should be guides and not dictators. Look to them as examples, but always decide for yourself what you must do. *Respect the person, not the position, and understand that your choices are always your own.*

Behavior

Know that there are repercussions to every action, and that you alone are responsible for your decisions. Educate yourself about risky behaviors, then always act with wisdom and common sense. Do not allow others to abuse you, but also do not selfishly abuse. *Respect the rights of others and treat them as you would be treated.*

Donors

Feeding should occur between consenting adults. Allow donors to make an informed decision before they give of themselves to you. Do not take rapaciously from others, but seek to have an exchange that is pleasant and beneficial for all. *Respect the life that you feed upon and do not abuse those who provide for you.*

Community

Reach out to others in your community. Exchange ideas, information, and support. Be hospitable to others, and appreciate hospitality when it is extended to you. Do not engage in illegal activity, for this can endanger us all. *Seek to nurture our community and support all those who do the same.*

DEFINITIONS

Vampyre Almanac: A publication of the Sanguinarium that included vampire book reviews, folklore, interviews, and a business directory. The *Almanac* also included some articles and a definition of terms, although it was limited primarily to the terms in use in the New York vampire scene. An edition of the *Almanac* was published in 1998 and a second one in 2000. Although there has been talk of producing another edition, none has been forthcoming.

OSV: "Ordo Strigoi Vii," or the "Order of Living Vampirism." The OSV is one of the latest permutations of the Sanguinarium. When Sanguinarium founder Father Sebastian realized there was growing interest in magick within the greater vampire community, he sought to transform the Sanguinarium into an occult order. Blending elements from chaos magick, LaVeyan Satanism, and the Kheprian tradition, the OSV claims to achieve personal power through a blending of dayside (mundane) and nightside (vampiric) aspects. The key teachings of the OSV were established in the 2004 release *V* and were later elaborated on in *The Sanguinomicon*. Both are currently restricted publications, available only to members.

Madame X has been involved in the vampire subculture on both sides of the Atlantic. She is one of the contributing authors to V: the Book of the Strigoi Vii, *and she is founder of her own group, House of the Dreaming. A longtime member of the New York City vampyre scene, Madame X is a strong proponent of the elegant, courtly vision of the community. Those views are underscored in her offering here.*

Community Etiquette

BY MADAME X OF HOUSE OF THE DREAMING

When participating in vampyre community gatherings like Quabals, rituals, havens, as well as when preparing formal letters of communication, whether online or offline, you may find this code of conduct and manners to be very helpful. These guidelines may vary from dominion to dominion and house to house, but in most cases it has become a tradition within our subculture, especially among old-school groups of vampyres. Adhering to simple lines of community etiquette reflects a certain form of elegance or *bella figura*, leaving a lasting impression without being exaggerated, creating a bonding respect which unifies our community. How others perceive us is very important, and our actions must always at least appear to be the "right" thing to do. Moreover, behaving appropriately—especially out of loyalty to family members, friends, hosts, or associates—establishes and reaffirms our integrity and credibility.

Standards of Behavior

Regardless of your advancement within the community, live as an example to others by reaching out and exchanging ideas, information, and support. Be hospitable and appreciative not only to your housemates but also to others, respecting their rights in a supportive, nurturing way. Mind your manners, both in verbal and written communication. Your words and actions should reflect your character since your character will certainly be judged by them. Honor and personal pride are critical in our culture; consequently, never insult the honor or personal pride of fellow community members, their families, covens, or clans. Do not selfishly abuse, but also do not allow others to abuse you.

Most of us are reserved people, and as a rule we disapprove of loud or demonstrative behavior (except in very informal situations). Traditionally, a certain amount of deference is maintained towards elders and women. Doors are held open, and the right of passage deferred to elders and women alike.

There should be no "play fighting" or "role playing" in public places or community gatherings. This type of behavior is frowned upon and, as such, should be kept private, as should the chewing of gum and the use of personal items such as combs and toothpicks.

It is recommended that Ramkht and Kitra attend events escorted by at least one Mradu. Traditionally, Mradu walk on the left of the Ramkht/Kitra. While the Ramkht or Kitra may have the right of passage (if women or elders), it is customary that the Mradu open doors and lead when entering a narrow hallway, staircase, or when exiting an elevator. It may be considered hostile for a Ramkht to attend a haven or private gathering escorted by a team of Mradu. Mradu should make a point of offering their protective services to the host or presiding elder of the gathering.

Know that there are repercussions to every action, and that you alone are responsible for your decisions.

Communication Skills

A very important factor is the art of effective communication. It is important to communicate to the level of understanding of those around us. Poor social interaction skills, whether verbal or written, cyber or in person, will certainly reflect badly on you.

Introductions

It is recommended that at large official functions, guests be announced as they arrive, unless otherwise requested. The formal announcement should be title, nightside name, and place of residence. Interpersonal introductions, however, may include title, name, household, mentor, and place of residence, thus establishing social standing, identity, and points of reference leading to further conversation. Expect to discuss your background and interests in order to establish your individuality and credibility. Do not however, feel pressured to reveal any personal dayside information. Try not to become too friendly too soon; formality is frequently encouraged.

When introducing two people to each other, you may want to remember precedence—the order in which people are addressed, greeted, introduced, referred, seated, and served. Women have precedence over men and elders over the young; if there are two individuals of the same social standing, defer to the one with seniority. When making introductions, there are three things to remember:

1) Observe order of precedence.
2) Stand.
3) Say the most distinguished person's preferred nightside name and title first, while looking at him or her; and then follow suit with the next in line.

If you are not introduced, it is appropriate that you introduce yourself. It is considered rude to interrupt an embrace or private conversation, so wait for an opening. It is always recommended that you approach openly facing others; a silent approach from behind can be perceived as hostile. Avoid acronyms and abbreviations when you are giving your title or family affiliation.

Never reveal your nature to those who will not understand, keeping in mind that it is equally precarious to discuss someone else's nature, practices, or confidences.

Forms of Address

It is considered proper and a sign of respect to address individuals according to their formal titles. Conversely, it is discouraged to use these same titles in normal dayside society, such as at work or among dayside family; such use of titles may lead to minor embarrassment or more extreme breaches of the Black Veil.

Certainly we do not wish to foster or encourage any type of elitist behavior, only to recognize achievement. Some individuals prefer to abstain from formal community titles and that too should be respected, keeping in mind that it is not the title but the individual that is prized.

The following are some traditional forms of address: "Brother" or "Sister" (generally between members of the same order or household); "Sir" or "Madame" (titles generally used by Calmae or higher); "Lord" or "Lady;" "Magister" or "Magistra" (tiles generally reserved for community elders); "Father" or "Mother" (normally Fangsmiths); "Reverend" (Kharrus or Priest/Priestess); and "Matriarch" or "Patriarch" (elders who founded and maintain a household or family).

Regardless of formal titles, the terms "Sir" and "Madame" are perfectly acceptable during conversation.

In-Person Greetings

The embrace or the exchange of a hearty hug is commonly used as the standard gesture of open welcome; many, however, employ a solid handshake. As a certain amount of deference is maintained towards women in our community, it is customary for a gentleman to kiss the back of a lady's hand, in lieu of the simple handshake. Many pagan groups use "Merry meet" and "Blessed be" as standard greetings.

Household/order-specific and often secret in-person greetings have been established by many groups to designate members of the family apart from others. They can be as simple as a formalized bow or hug, or as complex as a lengthy dialogue. Households and regional groups are encouraged to design their own specialized greeting, symbolizing each group's individuality and traditions. This type of greeting, depending on its level of secrecy, can either be introduced to you when you first arrive at a gathering, after your official initiation ceremony into an order, or only after you attain a certain level of respect with an order.

Travelers' Protocol

When entering a new city, show proper respect by familiarizing yourself with the local community and seeking out the household elders. Remember that our community is diverse, and every city has different traditions, views, and hierarchies. Most communities are very cautious, so making a positive impression is the best way to be respected and accepted.

The custom of bringing tribute or a gift to the host of a private gathering, haven, or cabal is customary, particularly for first-time attendees or out-of-town guests. Similarly, a host may choose to recognize the guest with a small token of friendship. Simple gifts reflecting the nature, interests, background, skill, or efforts of the guest or host to the community are usually the most appreciated; however, a bottle of good wine is always a fine substitute. Although an exchange of gifts is a nice opening statement, indicating interest in building a relationship, costly overwhelming gifts can have a negative impact. Simple tokens are the key.

When seeking out the local havens, it is only by respecting the owners and all patrons, as well as by demonstrating discreet behavior, that you can effectively promote a positive image of yourself and our community. Settling private disputes openly or engaging in any unlawful practices will reflect badly upon you and can endanger all of us.

Hospitality Guidelines

1) A good host should be gracious, welcoming, and attentive. He or she should be prepared to see to the needs of the guests, in consideration of their position in the community, by planning for their comfort and entertainment.

2) Hosting often includes providing adequate directions and meeting the guests at a halfway point, or sending a trusted envoy to meet the guests, escorting them to the haven or gathering place.

3) It may be considered hostile to insist your guest come alone and to suggest wearing a blindfold when taking them to the haven location. Hosts must consider the secrecy of their haven prior to the invitation, opting instead to meet at a different, less covert location.

4) Some hosts might like to determine their guests' preference, and prepare a screened donor or escort for the guest of honor.

5) A host may feel the need to meet with the guest(s) privately before the gathering to bring them up to date on the local state of affairs or regional traditions. It should be important for the host to ensure that the guest will not be caught at a disadvantage.

6) A host should never hesitate to call the gathering to a close; a polite way to do so is to suggest "last call" or "one last nightcap" and to put the liquor away.

7) Overnight accommodations and travel fatigue should be kept at the forefront of the mind when first inviting an out-of-town guest. A good host will offer their home, plan accommodations with a trusted family member, or at the very least be able to recommend a nearby hotel.

8) It is the host's responsibility to see that any inebriated guests are taken home safely by the host or a trusted family member, or offered accommodations in the host's home.

Appreciation Guidelines

1) A good guest is enthusiastic, congenial, natural, and considerate, treating other guests and hosts, as well as their property, with thoughtfulness and respect.

2) In many communities, it is considered impolite to decline an invitation to a private family affair, or an invitation to visit a private residence without a legitimate reason (short notice, illness, death in the family, unavoidable trip). Conversely, it is frowned upon to request an invitation to, or appear uninvited at, any private gathering.

3) It is the responsibility of guests to familiarize themselves, in advance, with local customs and traditions. Respecting these traditions is a great sign of esteem to the host and the host's community.

4) A good guest should be punctual, never more than fifteen minutes late for any engagement.

5) Never travel hungry; "feeding" on another's territory can be considered ill-mannered to the local denizens. A good guest should feed only upon invitation by the host. Never feed in public; this should be conducted privately.

6) If you have been invited to a dinner gathering, it is important that you discuss any dietary restrictions you may have. It is perfectly acceptable to suggest bringing your own dish prepared to your needs to a small private affair; however, you might have to decline an invitation to a formal public dinner.

7) When dining, it is recommended that you show respect by waiting for the elder, or the host, to start their meal before you start yours. Common table manners are applicable: it is considered rude to season

food before tasting it, eat gluttonously, speak in mid-chew, reach over someone else, yawn, or walk away from the table before the host or elder does. Avoid messy finger foods unless you are at a very casual gathering.

8) Do not drink until a toast is offered by the host, or until you are given the invitation to begin.

9) It is considered rude for a guest to become deliberately intoxicated at a private affair. Guests should refrain from any kind of belligerent, insulting or argumentative behavior, as it will embarrass the hosts, soil your image, and spoil the evening for all others.

10) It is impolite to extend the duration of your stay past the host's invitation, and it is also impolite to ask the host to extend the invitation to someone else; if you cannot attend because of a third party, indicate such, and the host may extend the invite without your direct prompting.

11) Official household gatherings, affairs in private homes, or overnight stays require a return invitation; conversely, invitations to functions at which one pays to attend carry no return obligations. Even if you refused a private gathering invitation, you are still expected to return the invitation (not necessarily in kind) in the not-too-distant future, as the host has demonstrated the intent to entertain you.

12) When a party is given in someone's honor, the guest of honor should be the first to leave. It is customary for the honoree to send tribute or a gift to the host before or after the party; a public verbal thank-you is encouraged, and a follow-up phone call or correspondence the next day is always welcome.

Dress Codes

Many times your invitations will include a dress code request. This dress code should be adhered to, or else you may pay extra at the door, embarrass yourself and the host, or not be allowed in at all. Appropriate attire is always expected; whether wearing formal or casual attire, everyone will feel more at ease with guests who show the same degree of attention to appearance. Traditionally, your attire will be perceived as a reflection of your creativity, social standing, and relative success. It is always recommended, when attending social community functions, that you wear any jewelry that may help identify you as a friend or member of the community, or that identifies your affiliation—i.e., the BloodLines pin, the bladed ankh, or your household insignia. Below is an explanatory list of common dress codes.

Casual

This is the most relaxed attire. T-shirts, jeans, sneakers, caps, and shorts are welcome. This is the perfect attire for an outdoor or high-activity event or gathering.

All-Black Minimum

Requires that even if you wear casual attire, you choose the color black. All-black minimum implies that you should wear more stylish or scene-oriented attire than just casual; this generally implies no baseball caps or casual shorts.

Semiformal

Suggests that men wear a dark suit or sport shirt and black slacks at minimum. Women wear dresses or black dress slacks. Do not wear T-shirts, jeans, or sneakers.

Goth / Industrial / Fetish

Recommends that you wear attire that reflects the Gothic, industrial, or fetish aesthetic. Passionate colors with long sweeping lines, laces, buckles, rivets, platforms, or pointy shoes and daring designs are some ideas to incorporate. Individuality is the key, regardless of gender.

Dress to Impress

Suggests that you dress up, leaving room to be either conservative or fabulous. Elegant dresses for women and dark outfits or suits for men are recommended. This can also be referred to as *cocktail attire*.

Black Tie or Formal

Implies a tuxedo with a soft shirt and a bow tie with a jacket. Women usually wear long dresses, but a short or cocktail-length dress is acceptable.

White Tie

This is the most formal evening wear, and suggests white tie, wing collar, tailcoat, and top hat. This is perfect attire for official diplomatic occasions and private balls. For a woman, white tie indicates that a long formal gown should be worn, and gloves and fans are invited. Think "Victorian."

Masque / Fantasy / Cyber

This is the perfect time to explore your creativity. Masques, bold colors, feathers, wings, and glow-in-the-dark piping are just some ideas. Think Mardi Gras, Tolkien, and Giger.

The words *optional* and *invited* can follow dress-code descriptions; this means you do not have to adhere to the dress code, but it gives you an idea of what to aim for and what the majority of the guests will be wearing. You can certainly bring it up or down a notch, but it is always recommended that you do not stray too far from the invitation. Sometimes there is no dress code remark—when in doubt, ask your host.

Conflict Management

Despite our most focused efforts to follow community rules of etiquette and standard protocol, there will unfortunately always be miscommunications and misinterpretations that lead to conflict between individuals and households that can become community-wide issues. Regardless of our nature, orientation, practices, and interests, the community at large is our extended family; we must respect the ideologies, traditions, and values of each other.

It is vital that differences be settled quietly among one another, seeking out an elder's mediation when there is no other solution. Before challenging another of your kind, always contact and obtain the support of your mentor. Elders are the cornerstones of our society, and we must heed their counsel; failure to do so may have serious repercussions. When a community member faces punishment for actions he believes he did not commit, he may request a tribunal of elders. Any exiled or excommunicated individual is not permitted to join another family; if another household accepts this individual, it may invite undesired hostility from the family that initiated the exile, as well as from others.

Struggles between families are unfortunate inevitabilities of our community, but it is possible for different families to coexist, even in the same territory, as long as there is mutual respect for others' traditions.

Do not make any community dispute public, and do not allow such disputes to cause strife. Similarly, it is inappropriate to make any personal issues a community matter or to force others into any situation by making them take sides.

There should always be an effort made to present stability and unity, even when things are less than perfect.

Closing Notes

It is certainly not expected that every community member behave in exactly the same way, as we must account for individual personalities and backgrounds. Yet I do hope you find these recommended guidelines to be a good reference, and I welcome any suggestions or additions to this essay.

I would like to thank Father Todd of House Sahjaza, Michelle Belanger of House Kheperu, Lord Stefan of House Phoenix Resurrectus, Bholanath of the Dreaming, and, of course, Emily Post, for their own writings on standards of behavior.

DEFINITIONS

Haven: A home or place of business owned or operated by vampires. A haven is typically open to the community as a gathering place for social interaction, ritual, workshops, and sometimes for the performance of art related to the community. Some of the better-known havens—such as Mother in New York and the Fang Club—have been nightclubs.

Quabal: Also spelled *Qabal*. A term developed in the Sanguinarium to denote a special vampire gathering, a Quabal is often a club night with a specific vampire theme that caters directly to the vampire community. Although a Quabal may be held in a nightclub, it often features a workshop or ritual for the vampiric participants. Quabals are not limited to clubs, however, and can also be hosted at an individual's home in the style of a nineteenth-century salon.

Fangsmith: While there is certainly an element within the community that resists and rails against it, there is a good deal of crossover between the aesthetics of real vampires and the aesthetics established by the vampire archetype. Perhaps the most enduring—and striking—of these aesthetics is the vampire's fangs. References to fangs are few and far between in vampire folklore. Likewise, the early vampires of literature are sometimes described as having sharp teeth, but these rarely take the form of the familiar fangs. It was not until the vampire made it to the silver screen that the fierce twin eyeteeth became traditional vampiric mainstays. Now, thanks to Barnabas Collins and the Hammer films of the sixties and seventies, no vampire is complete without a set of elongated canines. For lifestylers and others who want to go out clubbing in the height of vampire chic, fangs are an absolute must, and the need for high-quality, movie-worthy fangs created a job description unique to the vampire subculture: the fangsmith. Often trained as a dental assistant, the fangsmith uses dental acrylic and other tools to create custom pairs of removable fangs for eager members of the community. Not all members of the vampire subculture own or wear fangs. Many think they are showy, fake, and rather silly. But few can deny how interconnected the symbol of the fangs has become with the vampire archetype. Consider that all one has to do to turn an ordinary drawing of a person into a drawing of a vampire is to add in two pointed canines protruding from the lips.

Kitra/Counselor: Originally used in the Sanguinarium system to denote a donor, Kitra later became the third part of the three-part caste or road system adapted from House Kheperu. The road of the Kitra represents a major deviation in the Sanguinarium and OSV traditions from their Kheprian inspiration, as Kitra serve as altars in OSV ritual. This is a conscious echo of LaVeyan Satanist rites, in which a naked woman often serves as the altar. The integration of LaVeyan overtones is part of the OSV's identity as a left-hand path tradition. Despite the variations, OSV Kitra retain some qualities attributed to the original Counselor caste of House Kheperu, serving to connect, cycle, and refine energy for magickal workings.

Mradu/Warrior: A caste or road within the Sanguinarium and OSV traditions. In ritual, Mradu act as guardians. Energetically, they ground and stabilize energy. The term *Mradu* first appeared in the 1998 *Vampyre Almanac* and is defined as a "vampyre scholar." Later, the Mradu were changed to more closely resemble the Warrior caste of House Kheperu. In the Kheprian tradition, Warriors are one of three roles in feeding and ritual based upon the preferential flow of an individual's energy. Unlike Kitra and Counselor, Mradu and Warrior are interchangeable.

Ramkht/Priest: One of three roads within the Sanguinarium and OSV traditions. Ramkht were originally defined as "vampyre artists" in the 1998 *Vampyre Almanac*, but as the Sanguinarium adopted more Kheprian material, they came to be equated with the Kheprian Priest caste. In the OSV tradition, Ramkht run rituals and serve in leadership positions. A number of groups were influenced by the Strigoi Vii material and thus retain these terms.

Kharrus: A term generally used to refer to a vampyre elder. Often, a Kharrus is someone who has been ordained to run ritual. In the early days of the Sanguinarium, a movement was begun to develop a special vampyre language. This initiative gave rise to words such as *Mradu*, *Ramkht*, and *Kitra*. *Kharrus* is a relatively late addition, and its use is not quite as widespread as certain other terms. The collection of words that originated in the Sanguinarium tradition is often described as being part of the Elorathian tongue. *Elorath*, another word created for the early Sanguinarium, has held several meanings over the years. Although some ambivalence remains concerning its precise origin and definition, Elorath is, in general, used to refer to the overall spirit of the vampyre community. It is occasionally invoked in ritual, and those who use it in their rites perceive it as a kind of personification of the vampyre current of thought. The word is used primarily among those who follow the teachings of the Sanguinarium or OSV, but some instances have appeared outside of these organizations.

LadyBlak has been involved in the online vampire community from its earliest beginnings, and her articles and words of wisdom can be found on a wide variety of vampire forums and websites. As a vampire who identifies as a Kitra, someone who needs both to feed and to be fed from, she possesses a special insight into the relationship between vampire and donor. This is her manifesto.

I Am a Vampyre

BY LADYBLAK

I am a vampyre. I have realized through my awakening that energy is my need. Obtaining it requires the gift given from others around me. It is either something that comes from the Divine, or God/gods, or it is simply within us and cycles through us to others, then back to us again. But whatever one thinks about energy or life force, I feel it is a sacred thing. It is not to be taken lightly, for it carries with it a part of the one that is offering. I owe it to them to care for that which they share with me so deeply.

I am a vampyre. I feel the bond that grows between those I have shared with and those who share with me. I do not use this bond to control or to make them dependent on me. We are sharing a common unique relationship. Each is allowed safety and honor in that relationship, and respect for their important part of it.

I know that sometimes feelings will develop that are beyond what our relationship is about. At that time, I owe my donors honesty and I need to respect them enough to be honest about these things, so that they and I can make decisions to go forward or to part ways. At no time is it okay to lead them along, playing with their emotions so that I might feed. That is a selfish act, as is emotional blackmail or leaking information they have shared with me to anyone. Trust is part of our sacred bond.

I am a vampyre. My donors are under my care. It is up to me to teach them to protect themselves at events, and around others who might mean them harm. At no time will I place them in situations that would cause them fear, danger, or compromise. I also acknowledge that I have to stand back at times and not save them from things they put themselves into. To allow my donors to see me as their sole savior or protector only allows for dependency and drama within the community. It is my responsibility to bring any such attention-seeking to their attention and to suggest corrective actions. I am not their parent, nor am I their guardian in all areas of their life.

As one who senses the energy of others, it is up to me to not take from a donor who is weary or vulnerable. I must cultivate self-restraint.

I am a vampyre. I know that I was created this way for a purpose, one of good work and benefit to myself and others. I will carry myself with honor and remember my own place in this world. I will not despise or loathe what I am, nor use it to make others feel small or less than me. We are all important in the world. I will protect my body and seek out those who have the same respect for their own, as I know they will understand the importance of good health and of transmitting good energy versus mere feeding. I will be cautious about what I expose myself to, spiritually and physically, because I know this affects those I interact with.

I am a vampyre. I will not seek out personal attention that will cast negative light on my fellow vampyres or on the community as a whole. I realize that when I tell someone who and what I am, I make myself the voice of many who did not ask me to represent them. I will carry myself with honor, respect, power, and humility.

I realize that each person's spiritual path is intimately their own to walk. I can lend an ear, but I should never try to convert or argue with others or attempt to change their path.

I am a vampyre. I am in control of my will and my actions. I will not blame my vampyrism for treating people unfairly, taking what is not mine, or being callous to others around me. Vampyrism is not an excuse to run roughly over other people. I will not pass poor choices off as merely a "part of my nature." I am a strong being with a strong mind. I make my own decisions, good or bad, and I learn from them.

SECTION
- SIX -

Vampire Traditions

Within the vampire community, there are many different ways in which individuals embrace their identities as vampires. For the vampire Rev. Vicutus, vampirism is not merely a quirk or condition. It is the fundamental part of a potent spiritual identity. Earnest, eloquent, and highly educated in a variety of ceremonial and esoteric traditions, Rev. Vicutus is an excellent example of that portion of the community that embraces vampirism as part of an occult revelation.

Rev. Vicutus: Founder of Ordo Sekhemu

reetings. I am the Vampyre Vicutus. Although we are born with the vampyric gift and can date our inner selves far into history, I wish to maintain focused on this lifetime so that you may better understand me as the person I am in the now. At first glance, I am quiet and may appear somewhat shy until we begin to speak. Then my essence begins to flow, and you'll know that I am no better than you—only different.

I am expressive with my hands and fluent in my writing. I don't really like to speak unless the mood is right and your presence has made me feel comfortable. Your smile means everything to me, and my sweet embrace is my gift to you. Allow me to Braille your body with my eyes so that I may see the real you.

In these writings, I do not wish to gain favor nor create opposition. I do it for myself, and my intention is to bring understanding to those who wish to know the real me.

Thoughts on the Past

I was brought up as a gifted child, though I wasn't raised as one. I dropped out of school a long time ago, while still in elementary school, although my body continued to attend classes every day. My mind was elsewhere. I took it upon myself to wear a mask simply to fit into the school setting, and I learned what I could from the teacher.

At first, this was very difficult because I couldn't understand their for-matted thoughts in particular content areas. After much analyzing in my sec-ond-grade class, I began to comprehend my teacher's techniques and realized that I had to step down to the integral group level. Then I became as the entire class—one and the same. The individual me remained hidden. Masked. All potential of my undiscovered self seemed held to the ransom of their expectations.

Whenever I finished my work, I would be put aside and given more work. My teachers' idea of a challenge was to time me on activities. Little did they realize that depth and complexity were the key to my academic success, rather than allowing me to finish by the clock. Is it any wonder that they were so amazed when my will to cooperate was lost?

I spent the rest of my class life in deep, meaningful thoughts of the world, the greater universe, and all that lies beyond the unknown. What makes the world work—how and why? By what known law and by what unknown mechanics could it be possible for such action to take place, or even be con-sidered to occur by a much greater Force?

My mind was filled with a longing for answers—so many questions and yet no one to answer them. Whenever such an "odd" question arose, I was given a ridiculous answer to shut me up, or I was told to be quiet. How dare they not allow me to ask? Are we not in constant search of who we are? Are we not the sum of our experiences? Are we not the sum of what we know? How can I grow when the beautiful flower is not watered?

I spent my time writing poetry and articles based on my ponderings. Whenever my expression seemed perplexed, I was often asked, "What's wrong?" Rather than having to explain myself, for I knew no one would truly understand, I would simply dismiss the pests with the shrug of my shoulders and make as if it were nothing at all.

At such a young age, I had no living role models. All the great thinkers were dead. Some had died thousands of years before my birth, and others are yet to be born. Was I to be amongst them? Was I to die as well? O! No, I don't want to die without contributing something. But what?

The world changes quickly. Nothing stays the same. This change is fascinating, but most of all this change comes in different forms! What is the cause of such change? Scientists call it evolution. Clergymen call it progressive revelation. Occultists call it magick. The idea of causing change by altering universal laws intrigued me. The idea of constructing and manifesting my thoughts was powerful!

We are of the world, although our consciousness is not. My only hope is to someday contribute something for humanity to make up for the destructive ideas humanity has left behind. Is it possible we can pave the way for our own salvation by our own charity?

Every day, I face having to conceal my identity, what I am. I do not belong; I never will. I wish there were others like me willing to share their ideas, their experiences. It upsets me that I cannot speak boldly the mysteries of what I know in my heart without knowing full sure. And when I do, it scares and threatens adults. Other children my age merely laugh after they are left frozen with confusion, amazement, and fear. I don't know how I know some things; I just do.

I don't like it. I am different, yet the same. My body is small, yet my mind is big. There are times when I use black humor to conceal my insecurities, frustrations, pain, or anger. Do they even understand my own affective issues? Do they know what is best for me? Will I ever know? This unknowing unsettles me. It is difficult to accept not being able to have an answer for something I feel I should know, something as trivial as this.

I do not like doing what is expected of me in class. The work is boring and it seems without direction, but I know it must be done for the sake of a grade. If only I had a quiet place to contemplate, for I find people frustrating and it drains me so. I have my own interests, no matter how irrelevant or out of the school environment they may seem. My interest—that is my direction. So I leave the rest behind and press forward on my own into the Valley of Search.

Thoughts on the Present

It is strange that I reflect upon linear time (past, present, and the soon-to-be future). This present shall quickly come to pass, and become my past just as everything else. And tomorrow's morrow will become the present, and so on as we leapfrog through the timeline. In all things I have come across, nothing intrigues me more than the study of the unknown—the realm of the invisible. The occult.

Occult. It seems such a frightening word. There are many negative connotations that go with this term, and it is a word so often misunderstood and uncommon in the use of everyday language. Occult is a study, an art, a science. As an aware being, I find a great delight in this field because it encompasses all the academia one could ever desire: reading, writing, depth, cultural diversity, language, complexity, deep and meaningful thoughts, philosophy, religion, metaphysics, discovery, expression, logic and reasoning, math, and faith. All such things move me entirely, and through this lifelong study one may hone certain skills and tap into those that may be dormant, if not latent.

Because the occult is so misunderstood, I feel a great kinship to that term. I wrote the word down once in the fourth grade on a crisp piece of white paper. I placed it in my pocket, took it home, kept it under my pillow when I slept, and took it to school the very next day. It meant nothing, really. But I kept it as a friend. Never for anyone's eyes but mine. I kept to myself, pondering the mysteries of life and its solutions.

I have constructed something around me. I have developed an essence. Apart from my being a vampyre, this essence may also be felt even by those who are insensitive to any form of subtle energy. I'm not quite sure what to call this essence. Perhaps it is the projection my personality upon others. Perhaps it is the "real" me.

There is a great loneliness here, in my heart. I have many brethren close and dear to me, so companionship and friendship are not an issue. It is something far deeper and subtler: I feel so alone, without anyone to truly comprehend my soul. I feel longing—a need, a want I can neither explain nor identify. I walk with no sense of logical direction. I eat with no sense of acquired taste. At times I feel nothing nor a care for what happens, yet I feel everything with a heavy blow. The world aches yet moves me here and there to shake and awaken the minds of man. The stars shine yet reach endlessly, as I do for nothing that's there. I want to cry for me and my loneliness, yet I treasure it with all my heart, for it separates me from you. I don't seek answers, only understanding. Only recently have I truly begun to comprehend how one cause affects the other, thus representing what we are or how we feel at different levels, some far more intrinsic than others, few much more meta-cosmic.

I see patterns. They take shape and often take on a form all their own. This reminds me of what I, during my childhood, understood to be an imaginary friend, which is truly nothing more than a mental construct of myself. At times it represented my mood, other times my good consciousness. There were instances when its voice spoke to me and seemed quite feminine, other moments when it was with great authority. Was I insane in my youth to visualize and respond to these delusions? Am I insane even now?

I have always noticed patterns in life. The results of actions develop an outcome, thus making it and everything that surrounds us predictable. This sentence formula may be applied to social interactions, inter/intrapersonal communication, mathematical equations, or any logical reasoning. Nevertheless, my Higher Self has guided me and continues to steer me along this unpaved road to discovery.

The road to discovery is an endless journey. The future holds no promises; you create it as you go along. One must maintain a clear focus and visualize the goal, and then make it realized. This is the key to your future: assess your current setting, conduct a self-diagnosis, plan what you will, implement your plan of action, and evaluate the outcome of your actions. Much can be accomplished with the power of your will and faith in Self.

Being a Vampyre

I do not wish to exaggerate vampyric abilities, nor am I obsessed with a desire to elaborate on occult truths. There are many, many sources of such information online, just as there are many vampyres in the world who are willing to delve into their ego, making themselves gods above all others. And there are those who care for nothing but themselves and indulge in self-gratification through the manipulation of pronounced energies. Instead, allow me to bring you into my light and my darkness as a spiritual vampyre.

I am in constant search, forever endeavoring to fulfill the need of my soul through exploration and discovery. There is a pain in me that is subtle and deep, yet it purifies me from the world. It molds me into a passionate being, and often enough I feel that I transcend beyond a conventional mentality into a universal oneness.

As a vampyre, I am cycled energy—a medium of exchange for healing, giving, and taking. It is my personal path of spiritual evolution to separate, change, and reintegrate through Nature's laws and by the powers of divine influence. I am beautiful. A creature of beauty, I am. I see with Grigorian eyes, in constant watch and carefully noting the simplest things. Project an image of your thoughts to me, share and make known your darkest secrets. Allow me to alleviate your pain. Consider me an angel on earth, fallen from glory only for you.

There is a passion in me, soft and deep. I walk amongst you as a member of society, but I am not of you. I feel what you feel; I see the visions in your mind, and I hear a faint whisper of the world's loudness.

Everything passes so quickly, and to me it seems as though it were a mere instant of time. My heart beats loud and fast. At times, too softly. If only you could feel it and tell me I still live. A great energy surrounds us. It fills everything that lives.

May I share a twisted philosophy with you? It is not my belief, but I would like to share this sinful thought: vampyres are humans with the souls of fallen angels. We prey upon humanity to bring fear into their lives; in doing so, they acknowledge a known evil and seek the guidance of their faith, thus bringing them closer to God. Vampyres seek redemption through the absorption of others. By delivering souls to God, the vampyre in turn saves his own.

If only you could see through my eyes. The world is lovely, and every being bears a special light that represents a manifestation of the Greater Realm. Common folk are not like us nor are we like them, but they have their place and serve a purpose, just as we endeavor to advance spiritually. Their time will come accordingly and then shall they take their seats as members of the elect—this is important to remember. Often, a vampyre becomes agitated and looks down upon others when patience has been expanded. One should realize that in the end we all return to the Source.

Being an Elder

"Titles mean nothing. It's what you do with it that counts." I heard this once at a gathering several years ago. And this phrase holds so much truth and has stayed with me since. I am not better than anyone else. I am just as different, just as unique, and just as special. There is the responsibility to ensure an even flow in the House, within its members, and with those who cross our path. Often enough, I become a father figure to my beloved brethren, and therein lies much pressure. Always the strong one, I must be. It pains me that I am not able to socialize and interact too much with my children, for I must maintain an objective view at all times—never favoring one more than the other. Always clear-minded, ready to act as judge, jury, and advocate.

But who shall be there for me when I need to be held, when I am saddened? Who can I turn to when I am weak? Don't look at me when I am in such a state, for I shall bring you down into the abyss of my dark heart. You will feel true sorrow and know detachment. Pain purifies, my love.

I was once dark and rancid, never caring for anything but myself. I was hurt and wanted the world to feel my suffering. I was tormented and wanted revenge. I had my vengeance and wanted more. Without love, hate and anger become a ceaseless cycle. One must learn to approach all things with love, even when it hurts us the most. I have learned to follow my heart and make no attempt to impress. Be yourself, and everything shall fall into place.

DEFINITIONS

Grigori: The so-called "Watcher Angels," whose story is told in the extra-biblical *Book of Enoch*. The leader of the Watchers was Shemyaza, and he encouraged two hundred angels to descend from heaven on Mount Hermon in order to live and marry among men. The children begotten of the unions between the Watchers and mortal women were giants, described as "men of renown." They are also called Nephilim, and their very existence is, at least in the *Book of Enoch*, given as the reason for the Great Flood. Within certain aspects of the vampire community, the myth of the Watcher Angels has become an eloquent metaphor for the descent of spirit into matter for the exploration and enjoyment of mortal flesh.

Ordo Sekhemu represents an initiatory system in the tradition of the ancient mystery schools. The group blends aspects of hermeticism, ceremonial magick, Gnosticism, and Luciferianism with the self-empowering image of the vampire. Founded by the vampire Rev. Vicutus, Ordo Sekhemu remains one of the most serious and scholarly left-hand path occult traditions at work within the modern vampire community.

Rev. Vicutus: The Philosophy of Ordo Sekhemu

We must look within rather than "without," for true faith resides in Self and not in the edifices in which artifacts are found. And how many times must this be mentioned, and why agree to it and yet continue to be a hypocrite unto oneself? We all carry a portion of the Divine within ourselves, for the true Temple lies within and not without. There need never be an institution to serve as mediator between you and the Creator of all that was, is, and ever shall be.

Of this institution I refer to the Great Mother Church who rides the beast of the Apocalypse as a whore dressed in scarlet. And of the mediator, I refer to the unction one has with the God of Many Names to include the Divine Mother of the Ages.

Ignorance is the only real evil left. And from this ignorance stems fear. True darkness is living in the shadows of ignorance—and many "holy" men walk with their eyes open, but yet see nothing. Being spiritual and being holy are two different things.

Living in darkness is termed the "left-hand Path." As with this, one finds responsibility in Self rather than in a deity (*Id est Deo*). By this is said "As I will it, so shall it be." Here the power of one's will is used to cause change in the laws of the universe, which are composed of rhythm, harmony, and symmetry. This "change" is termed magick. And magick is a most laudable science, for it deals with all the mental, spiritual, and physical faculties of absolute Self, through which the Divine is found within. By these faculties, it may very well serve as the mediation of the Most High.

The "right-hand Path" is based on faith upon a deity rather than Self. In this, all hope is bestowed onto a given deity such as "God." By this is said "Thy will be done." Here all hope is given to one's god, and the only form of magick used is prayer, which acts as an invisible force that eventually causes change in Nature's laws.

Every human being has the potential to construct the magickal temple within themselves. From the moment of conception, a special spark ignites. This miracle of life is proof that a divine seed is planted within our soul, and it may be discarded and never realized, or it may be wielded as a metallurgist wields a sword. This spirit seed requires nourishment, and by this, one must practice all the qualities of virtue—for it is by goodwill and acts of charities that we will be judged, not only by Higher Powers but by the laws of society as well.

And let it be known that all acts of goodness are manifestations of our Higher Self. Should this be witnessed, then it is our Spiritual Self that feeds from onlookers who may say, "Yes, he is a 'just' man for I have seen him act in such a manner." And if we be good unto the world and if our acts are not witnessed by people, then know that the spirits watch and are forever tracking our lives from beginning to end, and back to the beginning when we must be reborn. So charity is not just the beginning, but also the end.

Every religion has a philosophy. To follow those teachings will eventually "save the soul" from ignorance, but to follow only one religion and believe it is the only "true" religion is walking blindly. How can one accept Christ as Savior, yet be a hypocrite by not accepting the teachings of other prophets? The teachings and the roots of diverse religion stem from one common seed, which is generated from within the soul. And salvation is "coming to Being"—*Xeper*—or to become "aware"—*Khepra*—of our potential to reach spiritual enlightenment: *Nehas-t*.

Be that as it may, all religions have shared this school of thought, so how can one be better than the next? If asked "What religion do you follow?" or

"What is your Path?" I simply respond: "I follow the 'Old Way.'" Because it is from this ancient design that all things came about.

Introduction to Sekhrian Consciousness

Three major realms are our primary focus, with many minor realms in between and throughout: the world of man, the realm of the Spirit (the astral realm), and the Greater Realm.

The world of man is a physical place bound by Nature's laws. Anything that defies the laws of Nature in this world has metaphysical origins and invisible properties understood only slightly by science and by those of faith.

Man is a sentient being made up of mind, body, and spirit. The spiritual evolution of man varies greatly, depending on the opening of his own consciousness. The ancient Egyptians used the symbol of the scarab to represent the spiritual life cycle as life, death, and rebirth. Life is a journey of exploration and self-discovery. Death is the end of ignorance and signifies a new beginning of acceptance and tolerance—therefore, death is our reward for living. The rebirth stage of development involves the understanding of one's higher consciousness. Others view these stages of spiritual development as a physical process of living, dying, and incarnation. The Egyptians used the spreading of the scarab's wings to symbolize this Awakening—the opening of one's consciousness.

An Awakened one creates their own Temple once their Inner Self channels the powers of universal consciousness. One's innermost Self is an emanation of the Divine (containing absolute attributes) while the corporeal shell and its faculties are a reflection of creative principles of the Divine.

Occult is a term meaning "hidden" or "secret." When approaching such a subject, it is generally understood that the topic is based on the invisible realm and its metaphysical properties. Because one's inner Sanctum is concealed, it is recognized as one's inner Darkness. This is the hidden or secret Temple found within you. It is not found in edifices created by hand, but resides in the very soul and germinates when appropriate, as is Nature's law of growth. One's Temple can only be seen through the manifestation of their works and felt by the power of their essence.

The Sekhrian Consciousness involves the student of magick connecting the inner Sanctum to the Divine Source. Through one's inner Darkness, the aspirant journeys through spheres of transcendence to achieve divine power (*Sekhemu*) and Become (*Xeper*) part of the Isolated Intelligence. This is the development of divine endarkment known as the Sekhrian Consciousness.

The World of Man

Let there be Light! The world of man is a world of the visible. Magickally speaking, it is neither "heaven" nor "hell," but rather the manifestations of the superior and supernal realms of cosmic consciousness. Man develops his own faith, and since faith is a power of the soul, it segregates the faithful from the lost.

One's development of faith determines one's spiritual placement in this realm. To the Sekhrian, change and evolution of the Self implies death and destruction of the "old" self as one moves from the lower to higher states of consciousness and becomes reborn. This "Resurrection" is significant in magick because the student has moved towards inner Darkness by looking within his own soul (the inner Sanctum) to discover the Divine.

Nehas-t, meaning "Resurrection" or "spiritual Awakening," is the manifestation of divine endarkment significant in this school of thought. The Sekhrian occultist discovers how to broaden the consciousness to erect their own Temple of Power. In magick, we become creators of our own system; thus, the Sekhrians create their own Temple and connect to the Divine Source through themselves. Since movement is towards the emanation and glory of the Isolated Intelligence, it is understood that Sekhrians move against the "static" of the inner Logos to become one with the profound Darkness at its center. This is the core of Luciferianism; thus, the Aeon of Sekh represents the divine Power of Illumination through endarkment. Darkness resides in the heart of Sekhemu and within the minds of its Inner Circle members. The expression of inner Darkness is imprinted into one's sanctum.

Opposites in life bear their effects. For every inner, an outer; and every light bears its shadow. The Sekhrian realizes that in the World of Man he is consciously employing invisible powers to produce visible effects throughout the natural course of life. The scholar of Inner Darkness is opposed by Inner Light. Whereas both aspects are microcosmic, it is an earthly battle that rages between the opposites of Self. Hence, we become masters of both dark and white lights. As a principle, Sekhrians endeavor to balance their spiritual work with their mundane lifestyle. The continuous balance of the two forces is understood as Absolutism—being both positive and negative.

The radiance of Inner Light is the crystallization of one's Inner Darkness. Magickally, an enlightened individual becomes visible to the World of Man as the outer glow mirrors the inner. One's personality is endowed with a dual consciousness—that which lies within and extends throughout.

Faith in Self is absolute. It is a seed that germinates and sprouts as sanctioned by Nature's Law of Growth. As with any living form, it may be nourished or withered by neglect. Such is the nature of faith. As a microcosmic quality, faith is an interior force that radiates into the outer and thus shines forth as illumination. This brilliant beauty given off by the Luminant is understood thus by the Sekhrian: by being wrapped in Darkness we find the Light. The Sekhrian creates their own place that is not a place, in a time that is without time. Being out of time with the physical world creates isolation. Through this solitude one finds endarkment—the Light of Being, for the Darkness abideth forever.

The world of man continues to expand and constrict. The known universe is bound by Nature's laws, and as Man continues to aspire toward spiritual perfection and taps into the power of his being, then so will his mind become One with the cosmic consciousness. In the work, the Sekhrian channels the divine Power of Isolate Intelligence. As the Dark Angel brings more of the positive aspect into himself, the world begins to shun him, causing friction against the aspirant. The challenge here is to endeavor toward balance not only spiritually, but to overcome the negative forces the world projects into one's life.

Sekhrians must have a burning desire to face and conquer the lower self and regain the glory of becoming One with the Higher Self when dealing with the macrocosmic influences of the visible realm. The Illuminating Sekhrian realizes that the world of man is the antithesis of the Self. As the Self represents inner Darkness by way of inner Light—Darkness is more powerful than Light—then so it is contradicted by outer Light and outer Darkness. This is the paradox that

Nature has mysteriously bestowed upon the physical plane of existence to balance the spiritual with the mundane.

O! Damn you, stupid priests who spread lies and deceive the masses with your forked tongues, that by which faith has only redeemed the souls of men towards personal salvation! Those who have fallen short of their own glory of Nehas-t have slipped into outer Darkness, also known as the shadows of ignorance. In the visible realm, the outer is distance from one's inner Source. Distance from Self is distance from profound insight, which motivates a desire to practice spiritual discipline.

Realm of Spirit (Astral Realm)

Let there be Darkness! The realm of the Spirit is a realm of the invisible. Magickally speaking, it contains two polar opposites wherein the thoughts and actions of the physical realm become manifest.

The polar aspects of the astral have been widely accepted as "heaven" and "hell." Both spiritual places correspond with the distance associated with the Divine, the Greater Realm. The highest level of the astral is heaven and its proximity is closest to the Source. It is a place nearest the Universal Love source, and is warm due to the amount of heat (+) produced by the radiance of the Great Energy.

The lowest level of the astral is commonly understood as hell. Hell is also a spiritual place and bears the opposite effects of heaven. Due to its being the farthest distance from the Greater Realm, hell receives less—or no—radiance from the Divine and is therefore often perceived as cold (−) and loveless. In mainstream Christian thought, hell is a spiritual place where the soul suffers due to the absence of God's love.

In contrast, the realm of the Spirit doesn't separate these aspects of higher and lower levels of the astral regions. The Spirit realm may be perceived as a great "filter" that combines both aspects throughout its entirety, with specks of both qualities dispersed throughout the regions. In this perspective, "distance" from the Source is intrapersonal proximity rather than obvious distance from the Greater Realm.

Human will and thought have great impact upon the realm of the astral. Thoughts and actions carried out by human beings become manifest. The nature of thought and action takes its place appropriately in the astral planes. Malicious intentions and harmful doings form into "shadows" or phantoms and manifest themselves in the lowest regions as hybrid creatures constructed by men, often innocently by children. Such hybrid creatures are in the form of animals, demonic in appearance, with the essence of what is commonly interpreted as fear, disease, hate, anger, and perversity. These creatures have no life of their own except what is given to them by their creator. These "mental constructs" feed off fear and all the negative qualities and happenings of man.

Perhaps the most intense and most feared mental construct designed by the human race is the image of Satan as a devil ruling over all demons in hell. This Satanic construct has gained a tremendous amount of psychic energy over the millennia; it actually governs over people's lives as an idea of torment. Hence, only those who believe in possession become possessed. These types of people believe in such influences so strongly that they lose faith in Self. The stronger the fear toward such "evil" constructs, the more readily one opens to its invitation.

Mental constructs appear not only astrally, but in the physical realm as well. One may project an image through visualization, often enough and with intense enough emotion to produce shadows or phantoms. Children have been known to produce such effects when left scared in the dark. The amount of fear is so intense that the mind projects shadowy images of one's innermost demon—fear. Therefore, fear is the only real evil.

Like attracts like. People with malicious intentions tend to draw malicious forces, while people filled with sincerity attract goodness. The highest region of the astral (closest intrapersonal proximity to the Divine) encompasses goodness, warmth, and positivity directed by the person who surrounds themself with peace of mind, harmony, and removal of self-iniquity.

Not all mental/astral constructs are the product of fear, evil, or goodness. One who has a firm understanding of how these products take their form may design their own construct to suit this purpose. The power of the mind, with creative imagination and reason, may accomplish much through faith in Self. The mystic may design such a construct and use it to fend off or spiritually neutralize an enemy or Power who is against him. One's construct acts as an astral extension of oneself, which is why the creation will tend to "feel" like its creator, since the mental link carries with it the essence of the creator's personality.

Such constructs are also designed by groups, Orders, lodges, and so forth. The image of Baphomet was designed by Eliphas Lévi, and combines man, woman, and beast. Sekhrians use the image of Sekhmet, the lioness-goddess form, to represent the spiritual attributes of Sekhemu. Sekhmet is also the combination of human and beast. These egregores are designed as a focal point of power. They are referred to as *Animus Mundi* (Spirit of the World) and become a reservoir of spiritual strength, containing within it all the love, dedication, and devotion of most Inner Circle members and outside followers of Sekhmet to ward off any spiritual attack or to heighten one's magickal intention. In doing so, the Animus then acts as a tool in one's spiritual workings rather than a deity of worship. Very much as with the Satan construct, Sekhmet has gained a tremendous amount of psychic energy by those who have fed it to keep her alive.

However, people involved in working with Animus Mundi should understand that the work is solely subjective, and the egregore is simply a tool used to accomplish magickal tasks. Creating and working with such constructs allows one to explore the imagination, power of mind, and use of will. However, the true mystic doesn't require such tools, as the use of one's faith and power of Self readily connects to the Divine, by which all things may be accomplished.

The realm of the astral also bears within it not merely the manifestations of the physical realm but also the qualities or ideas of one's consciousness. For example, the act of wholeheartedly praying to saints or to the idea of what saints represent forms into the qualities of a consciousness or being. A dead saint is not physically living in the astral regions, but rather a symbol of what that saint represents may be found there. Another example of the qualities of one's consciousness is the creation of one's true identity. Like most "monkeys" in society, such people swing about their social lives wearing masks and concealing their innermost selves. This repressed phobia of allowing others to view them as what they truly are takes its form, while there are those who willfully project their known identity and set themselves as gods in the astral regions by creating thought forms to serve their intentions, malicious or benevolent.

The Greater Realm

Let there BE! As there was, there is, just as there always shall be. The Universe is a mental product of an Omnipotent Mind, and because it was created mentally, it therefore is mental, and can be manipulated by our own minds —which raises the age-old question: "Is our mind greater than the universe?"

The Mental Universe is not the ALL, and neither are we. Rather, all things contained within this vast universe are mere creations and act as extensions of the Great Being.

Each Awakened individual has discovered the Divine within, and each Awakened individual has it within their capacity to discover the Divine intelligence, which is regarded as an inborn quickness of understanding inspired by Providence. All such individuals are components of a greater piece, and each of us is acting in accordance to our design and free will to fulfill our soon-to-be-discovered purpose. All beings possess the potential for acquiring wisdom; and the higher that one rises upon the scale of knowledge, then the nearer one's approach to the mental likeness of the Creator. Thus, the Illumined individual is formed out of the vastness of Darkness, which is the occult learning of the Illuminati.

The outer reflects the inner. We all carry within us the divine spark that makes us as gods, and we are empowered to manipulate Nature's laws for the benefit of the whole. The world of man and everything within its limits is created out of the pure love energy. Not love as regarded by humanity—with emotions and fascinations that bind us to earthly understanding of the human condition—but the infinite and eternal embracing creative energy that emanates from the ALL, resonating throughout every element with respect to the laws that govern them.

To the Hermeticists, rhythm, harmony, and symmetry are parts of a fundamental template placed over any design in creation. Every action has its reaction (rhythm), every chord has its vibration (harmony), and every vibration has its due proportion between its parts (symmetry). Chaos was the state of the material universe before its creation, before the mental template brought order from its primitive state. The minds of men demonstrate such an effect as seen in their progressive revelation from primal to intellectual, and from intelligence evolving to the noetic.

The ways of the world are horizontal because time is linear, but the minds of men receive providence from the higher Planes; therefore, the Greater Realm is not subjected to man's concept of time—of a past, present, and future. There is only the Now. The Now simply IS. The Greater Realm directly reflects the mental manifestations of THE ONE. Thoughts become, whereas upon the earthly Planes one's mental will requires a measure of time to manifest, because the material Plane is subject to the linear concept of existence and is bound to its physical laws. As creatures of the flesh, we always have time at our side. However, our mental consciousness is designed to surpass dimensions where the Law of No Time applies. The Masters of Life know this, and although they are subjected to the causation of the higher Planes, they are nonetheless able to rule upon the material Planes.

The Source and Its environment are incomprehensible. The state of the Isolate Intelligence is beyond words. Only by studying the laws of Nature and the Principles of such laws are we able to grasp the mechanics of the Greater Realm. It is generally accepted by all forms of religious study that there is ONE Supreme Being. Even more so, it is commonly accepted that the ONE Supreme Being works as a triumvirate, identified in the Christian mainstream as the Father, Son, and Holy Spirit. The Three are one and the same, making up the Supreme Being known as THE ALL. In various schools of thought, the concept of three is applied through magickal applications such as: separation, change, and reintegration; life, death, and rebirth; Creator, God, and Goddess; and so forth. Even Nature's own laws work in accordance with the Godhead through principles we cannot see, but through the wonders of cause and effect we witness the manifestations of such principles.

The majority of the world's inhabitants are familiar with the idea of Father, Son, and Holy Spirit. So this portion of my essay will reflect this concept for the reader's understanding—that even though the Trinity is composed of three distinct and separate entities, they are still considered one unit serving three distinct and separate functions. For example, the Father says "Let there be Light." The Son brings forth the Light, and the Holy Spirit makes the Light visible. This is the principle of causation and effect, by which it is learned that nothing happens by mere chance, and that the orderly chain of events flows from the creative energy of THE ALL.

The flowing energy emanating from THE ALL demonstrates that everything is in motion. Throughout the innumerable Planes, nothing is at rest, no matter how quiet. The principles of vibration are constantly in effect. The higher the vibration, the higher the placement on the harmonic scale. Every Plane (a level of development) operates at a different degree of vibration. The greater the vibration, the greater is the mental power of the species inhabiting that Plane. All such beings are but degrees on a scale operating at different frequency (rates of vibration), yet everything has its existence within the Omnipotent Mind of THE ALL.

There are innumerable degrees rippling away from the Source, the anode being nearest the Source, and its cathode distant from it. The principle of polarity is not so much a contrast between good and evil; rather, it reveals the various degrees between the poles of the same state. The mental "objects" are identical in nature, but different in degree. This is how the Illuminated Intelligences are classified—differing in their degree of polarity. The higher along the polar scale, then the nearer to the Divine and closer to the Mind of THE ALL. Thus, the intelligence of such beings is more illumined than that of those drifting farthest from the Source.

To the occultist, the symbolism of the fallen angels is that of the selfish soul losing its spiritual balance on the spiritual Planes. The "fall" represents the striving for spiritual power, and it falls back as it had previously risen. Hence the saying, "What is an angel but a demon waiting to fall? And what is a demon but an angel waiting to ascend?" And even to such souls, the opportunity for a return is always given, for the Creator is all-merciful and all-loving.

Definitions

Xeper: A power-word employed by the Temple of Set. The *x* is actually a Greek letter, so the term should be pronounced "kheper" although it is often mistakenly pronounced "zeper" instead. The term is taken from the ancient Egyptian word *kheperu*, which means "to transform" or "to become." In Setian philosophy, *xeper* is a reminder to constantly Become.

Egregore: Derived from the Greek word for *watcher*, an egregore is a spirit construct. Egregores can be created intentionally, but they can also be the unintentional side effects of powerful workings. Many occultists believe that an egregore is formed out of a magickal group's combined intent and will. The egregore can be looked upon as the literal spirit of the group, and when intentionally invoked, this spirit adds further power, identity, and cohesion to the group.

Animus Mundi: Latin, literally meaning "Spirit of the World."

Luciferianism: This is a tradition, influenced by Gnostic beliefs, that reveres Lucifer not as the Devil, but in his guise as Lightbringer. "Gnostic" is a blanket term for a number of early Christian sects that were declared heretical by the church. Most Gnostics made a sharp distinction between the world of flesh and the world of spirit, seeing each of us as a holy spirit trapped in the base world of matter. They saw the physical world as evil. Several Gnostic sects went so far as to suggest that the Creator of the physical world was also evil. This put a new twist on the Garden of Eden story in Genesis, where God the Father was seen as an oppressive principle, while the Serpent, believed to be a guise of Lucifer, was seen as a liberator. Revering knowledge as a path to spiritual freedom, these sects of Gnostics looked upon Lucifer not as a tempter or corruptor, but as a guiding spirit whose purpose was to set poor humanity free. Modern traditions of Luciferianism, while not all rooted in the traditions of Gnosticism, approach Lucifer in much the same way.

Nehas-t: Derived from an ancient Egyptian term that means "awakening" or "spiritual enlightenment," *Nehas-t* is the buzzword of Ordo Sekhemu in much the same way that *xeper* is used by the Temple of Set. Ordo Sekhemu is among a number of occult-oriented vampire houses that derive inspiration from ancient Egyptian sources. Perhaps the most obvious influence can be seen in the use of the ankh. This symbol represented eternal life to the ancient Egyptians—and for a large portion of the vampire community, variations of the Egyptian ankh are worn to show one's affiliation with that community. In this way, wearing the ankh parallels the use of the pentagram among Pagans and Wiccans. It is important to note that the Egyptian element in vampire beliefs owes less to orthodox Kemeticism and more to the romanticized ideal of Egypt as the de facto source of ancient wisdom.

Madame X is an elegant and creative soul who was active in the New York City-based Court of Gotham when the idea of high-society vampirism was at its peak. For her, the social, aesthetic, and courtly aspects of the vampyre are inextricably linked with its spiritual meaning. As someone for whom the vampyre is both a lifestyle and a life vision, Madame X eloquently represents those aspects of the community that mix fashion with their spiritual pursuits.

Madame X: Lady of the Dreaming

Call me Madame X. This name is a synergy of inspirations: my time spent in Europe, a painting by John Singer Sargent, a play by Alexandre Bisson, a 1929 movie, and my own last name. I first used the alias Madame X as a pen name for my more controversial poetry, and later found that as I intended to work closer with the vampyre community, I would need an alias to protect my dayside identity.

I was born at the end of the world, or so it was thought for thousands of years. I still consider the southern crags of Western Europe to be my home. It was in Europe that I began my formal studies, both mystical and didactic. Despite being brought up as a Roman Catholic, I always had pagan tendencies. My godfather and first mentor was a vampyric ceremonial magician whose dissident circle of friends included renowned laureate writer Antonio Pessoa. When I was very young, I found a book that discussed palmistry and numerology. I was eight years old, and since the kids had already stoned me (in a very biblical sense) for being a witch anyway, it just seemed right to learn the Craft. As a child, I read many mystery books; from there I turned to unexplained phenomena, which led to the paranormal and mysticism. I read my first books on the occult and demonic possessions when I was eleven. I was positively fascinated with dream interpretation, ESP, and mind-over-matter techniques. By the time I was in high school, I was performing séances and practicing hypnosis.

Despite invitations from Ivy League schools, I opted for a more subdued path, deciding to pursue a degree in earth sciences at Montclair State University in northern New Jersey, where I also delved into the darker realms of philosophy and paganism. It was then that I began to understand the relevance of Christian symbolism, and in my quest I barely escaped a nunnery—only to reaffirm my true calling to a very diverse acceptance of spirituality. I started reading books about ritual, applied magic, and lunar influences, realizing that not only had I known these things for many years but I had been unknowingly using them . . . It has been an interesting realization. After my godfather's death, I continued my studies in the United States with other mentors, delving into Eastern approaches like yoga and T'ai Chi, which helped me better understand and work with energy/prana/chi. I accept many principles endorsed by New Age and Wicca, but I also find many of their beliefs restrictive and . . . fluffy. I don't believe in the traditional "good" and "evil," but simply in natural forces of creation and destruction. In order to understand "the light," I believe one must also understand "the shadows" and the ebb and flow of life.

It is difficult to say what first attracted me to the vampyre community. Perhaps it was the lust for the dark aesthetic, followed by an immeasurable feeling of acceptance and belonging. For an intelligent person like myself, the idea of being a vampyre was at first very unreasonable. It was easier to explain my nature as being that of a natural-born witch. Witchcraft is an art, a science if you will. But vampyrism was far more difficult to accept. As time passed, I tested and retested new knowledge against old information long stored away; the result was my awakening to my true identity, which transmuted my reality. The most difficult part of the awakening process is acceptance, particularly after being in denial for so long. Having been a solitary practitioner for so many years while surrounded by mystical individuals—and being repeatedly solicited to teach, demonstrate, and counsel others—I was compelled to finally step forth.

I evolved into an eclectic spiritualist and consider myself something of a chaos magician; as such, my views on metaphysics and vampyrism are sacred and diverse. I believe in the balance of nature, science, prayer, ritual, intent, individual and group energy, energy transference and manipulation, the rebirth of the soul, enlightenment through focused meditation, the vibration quotient, the here and now, a hereafter, quantum forces, magic, miracles, extrasensory precognition, telepathy, telekinesis, prophesy, destiny and the ability to alter it, love, and the fine line between myth and reality. Knowing that the vampyric nature is not easily explained, I feel that the desire to decipher it opens portals to a kaleidoscope of personal ideologies—transcending an insatiable love for life, spheres of spiritual awakenings, and transformations into the completion of the self, where the journey itself is the ultimate key.

Travel is one of my passions; perhaps it's the gypsy in my blood. Aside from traveling extensively within the continental United States, I have spent some time in Mexico, Brazil, Venezuela, Canada, England, the Netherlands, Portugal, Spain, France, Italy, and the Transylvanian haunts of Romania. I am quite the polyglot. As such, I really enjoy reading and writing. I was fortunate to be selected to read my original poetry at a 1998 United Nations–sponsored reception aimed towards strengthening relations between Turkey and Greece.

I have been considered a Muse to aspiring artists, through the Rift Arts Forum, a creationists' not-for-profit guild, for years offering an outpouring of cultural and art-related happenings. If you delve into such events, perhaps you have met me in some dimly lit café, heard my lyrical words on the radio or on the cable TV programs *Vampyre Dreams* and *Vampyre Lounge*, or read my work in *Vampyre Magazine*. In the past, I have choreographed and enacted several fetish-themed performance art pieces in Savannah, Georgia; performed at the orphans' charity and at the New Jersey Renaissance Faire; have volunteered as literary panel mediator for the AIDS charity "GothCon," held in New Orleans and Atlanta; and have taken an active role at the "Endless Night" gatherings held in New Orleans and New York.

Constantly inspired by a desire to motivate others through my own path of self-discovery and evolution, I took part in the conception of several regional vampyre societies, including the Iron Garden, the Court of Lazarus, Black Atlantis, and Black Oaks. When mystical Savannah became my new home, with idyllic surroundings freeing my mind and time for travel and more introspective pursuits, I set my passions on the completion of *V* and *The Sanguinomicon*, vampyre subculture books no longer in print. These controversial books presented a collection of philosophies, traditions, and techniques designed to challenge and inspire this rapidly growing subculture. They focused on community conduct, spirituality and energy work, and provided an excellent compendium summarizing vampyre folklore throughout the world.

Although I have maintained a positive interaction online, my more real endeavors are in real life. I choose to interact with individuals, organizations and communities in person. I have been the promoter for Savannah's own Pagan Pride Day—a very successful event, of three years running, for the local pagan community; it attracts individuals of many paths under one roof for socializing and deeper understanding. As Kharrus, or priestess, of the Strigoi Vii, I am available to the community to preside over naming ceremonies, vows of wedlock, initiations, ascensions, and any such rites of passage. I am also the Head of the Georgia Chapter of Bloodlines International, a social organization that brings together witches, vampyres, Therians, and Otherkin. I dream of a united community in which diversity is accepted.

Of nostalgic value: I was at the first vampyre balls at the Bank in Manhattan and at the Trocadero in Philadelphia. I attended the inception of Long Black Veil at Mother's. I was also there for the final club nights and eventual closure of the famous vampyre hangouts in the New York area: the Cat Club, the Mission, Robots, the Bank, Mother's, the Pipeline, and the Edge. Their influence will never be forgotten.

Yet after all this, my most important accomplishment is that I am the founder and Matriarch of House of the Dreaming, my nightside family. House of the Dreaming is a group of particularly chosen individuals who share a common philosophy: "One Honor, One Family, One Dream." We are unified by a strict code of integrity and honor. We pride ourselves on the quality of our membership and on our introspective evolution toward the greater good. Many of my Family's written articles, including my own, which broach different topics of interest to the community, are on my Family's website: www.houseofthedreaming.org.

The House of the Dreaming developed within and around the Court of Gotham when devotion to the vampyre as a personal aesthetic was part and parcel of the vampiric path. Under the guidance of the gracious Madame X, the House of the Dreaming retained much of this courtly aesthetic while also striving to apply its standards of beauty and elegance to a dark spiritual path.

Madame X: The House of the Dreaming

We are One Family, One Honor, One Dream. Come to us not to find yourself but to better understand yourself.

Creed of the Dreaming

We are a collective of individuals:

A collection of dreams and dreamers.

The diversity of our views is our strength.

We come together to learn the truths of our existence and of the universe that we live in.

We share the same Dream:

The dream of family,

The dream of diversity accepted,

The dream of a transcendental nation, and

The dream of life eternal.

We believe that truth comes from understanding.

The truth is our sword and our shield.

We believe in being true to our own selves and that this truth will set us free.

We believe dreams become reality for those who chose to make them so.

We have chosen to live out our dreams and make them real.

We live in a world of dreams and a world of dreams lives within us.

Our Dreams have borne us our Household and our Household is our Dreams.

A Transcendental Nation

Our claim is no small thing. We dare to transcend normalcy, our inner duality, and the common criterion for humanity. We transcend the physical, our dreams, and even death itself. We claim an evolved spiritual consciousness, a perception of life independent from the material world, and an intuitive understanding of our selves and the universe, emanating from an intrinsic— albeit unknown—center. We claim an ancient divine hegemony, personal experiences beyond the simple scope of humanity, and an innate knowledge of transcendental truths.

Unlike individuals who take it upon themselves to choose a religion, a political platform, or a philosophy of their liking, we are chosen by our transcendental nature, like it or not. Although we can opt to deny or dismiss our instinctual propensities, the seed grows within us—unfurling its enormous wings like a rousing dragon pervading every aspect of our life, commanding us to sate its hunger for recognition and acceptance. Spirituality, metaphysics, ontology, and thanatology are considered transcendental. So is our effulgent nature, mystic and preternatural, which is undeniable, transcending the empirical and scientific, being knowable only through intuitive self-discovery. But unlike any religion or philosophy, we are connected to our transcendental nature, and to each other, by a resilient spiritual tether of recognition stronger than blood, linking us together as a family.

Unlike gods, angels, or demons, infinite in their magnitude, we claim only a certain level of transcendence—our spirit purposeful, guided, guiding, dedicated to its own expansion, readied to disseminate our innate truths as the right time presents itself. We are discordant creatures, spiritual individuals who much prefer to meditate introspectively, alone or in the company of a few chosen others, than to attend frequent public organized religious masses. We do share a passionate appreciation for the divine, and the extraordinary, knowing that our reality originates from a central core within, which is ultimately linked to our ancient heritage.

Whether we are the next evolution of mankind or not, we have long coexisted beside the greater majority—those who do not share our spark of kinship—and regardless of the years of persecution and the many other efforts to wipe out our intuitive memory, we know that our nation will continue to blossom as long as we remain steadfast in support of our traditions, continuing to honor intuition and acumen above all. We may be romantic idealists, but we have no illusions of utopia. We live in a world where everything is judged by its appearance; our presence naturally commands attention, being more mysterious, daring, and dramatic than the bland majority. We are intense, bold, unpredictable, and audacious—speaking softly and sparsely yet poignantly. We live in a world where the meek fade away and the greedy thrive, and perhaps that is why so many of us are perceived as eccentric rebels. We are the outcasts, the loners, the isolationists, but in the right setting, we are sociable, gregarious creatures who delight in the gestalt of like minds. While we may be disillusioned by society and disinterested in politics, we share a terrific enthusiasm for the razor's edge of life experiences. Similarly, we may choose to withdraw from elections and from competition, but make no mistake: our predatory instincts are insatiable. And like the noble predator, we carry ourselves with confidence and elegance, perhaps even an air of regal arrogance. But unlike the predator, we understand the requirements of civilization, the propriety of demeanor, and the principles of honor.

We, the Dreaming, are only a small tribe of a much larger Transcendental Nation, scattered over the world, individuals of all ages and educational backgrounds hailing from many continents, from many races, from many genetic stocks, and from many religious backgrounds. The nightkind archetypes we identify with are a form of creative alienation that assists us with our introspective self-assessment, with our community interaction, and with tapping into our transcendental dream potential. You may see the vampyre, the wolf, the elf, or the magi. Yet you are looking at the dreamer, the nonconformist dissident, the transcendental thinker, and the wielder of mysticism.

Twilight Within—Unlocking Our True Nature

House of the Dreaming dares us to discover ourselves and explore our true nature, that inner part of us that is beyond personality, thought, or spirit—that eternal, unchanging core of essence inside all of us, dreaming ancient dreams.

Over time we have learned the art of deceiving everyone around us, even those who mean the most to us. We seem to be accepted and loved for those parts of us that we have chosen to share, yet we fear how others would feel if they really knew us, what would happen if we stripped away our dayside personality. Certainly, our explorations need not involve anyone else; they are personal, private investigations.

It may not be easy to acknowledge that we are very different from how we present ourselves; similarly, neither are we the people our parents and society have insisted we be. Within every one of us are dueling oppositions: light versus dark impulses, instinct versus conscience, desire versus duty, and reason versus imagination. We can deny those unacceptable sides of our nature, but we risk being at the mercy of their powerful, primitive demands. Our inner nature is not exclusively made up of savage predatory impulses, but also of all those aspects that our dayside personality cannot accept; these may include awkwardness, insecurity, submissiveness, and tenderness. For what to one may be strength is weakness to another. Knowing this, we can see the need to understand and accept our true nature, finding ways of dealing with the conflicting contradictions of our dual or even multiple selves. House of the Dreaming appreciates this innate struggle, but before we continue on our quest we must commit our character to the Veil of the Waking Dream; for as we delve further into our inner selves, we will be faced with serious internal conflict, where such bastions of the Veil—like loyalty, fortitude, resolve and compassion—must become our only guides.

A good deal of psychic energy is utilized to sustain our dayside personality. The more divided we are within ourselves, the more energy is necessary to keep away the threat of losing that façade. Achieving twilight within means meshing the conscious dayside personality with our denied innate instincts. Once we achieve inner twilight, we no longer need to misappropriate our precious energy. Discovering, acknowledging, and accepting our true nature will not only enhance our self-awareness, increase our inner balance, and let us become more self-assured—we will also become more respectful and less critical of others as we realize our own personal meaning. Undivided, we will be better prepared to face the challenges of the world around us, while reaching for higher goals. As children of both darkness and light, achieving twilight within can be the most empowering triumph of our lifetime.

To do this, we need some essential tools, as ours is not an easy quest. First, we must develop suspendability, putting aside our preconceptions of who we are, who we are supposed to be, and what is reasonable sanity. We need to be aware of our first instinctual thought and initial inclination in any given situation. We need to suspend subjective judgments of our actions, as they serve only to deceive ourselves and lead us astray from our quest. Second, we must leave behind aspects of our ego that can only serve as impediments, such as preconceptions of mastery and control; certainly, we do not know everything nor can we control everything. In this creative alienation exercise, where we dare to look beyond our dayside identity, finding our twilight within, we realize that, as different as we may be, we are an intrinsic part of an intricate universal web. Regardless of which individual point we select to touch, it affects and reverberates throughout the whole. To succeed in our quest, we must surrender, accept, and befriend our innate nature. Third, and perhaps most important, we must continually remind ourselves that although every unthinkable aspect of our inner nature must be identified and reckoned with, we do not need to act upon each and every one of them. Allow the Veil of the Waking Dream to guide you.

Before we dare to pursue any kind of Dragon work (utilizing our extrasensory gifts), we must come to terms with our true selves and the solidity of our character. Knowledge is power, but power corrupts. Therefore, have a firm understanding of who you are and where you stand within yourself.

It is important to know what influences our dayside identity—the initial defining of who we are that took place before we were even born. Should we believe in spiritual reincarnation, then a myriad of factors come into play: parental sexual fantasies during conception, death and rebirth trauma, innate nature, unfinished work, continued growth, quests. Touching on a more material plane, our first influences were our hereditary lineage implications, genetic predispositions or mutations, and unavoidable parental expectations. When we were children, our family's behavior was the most potent factor in our becoming, as it established the boundaries of who we were expected to be. It was our parents' reactions to our natural behavior that taught us what facets of ourselves were acceptable, and it became necessary to hide our natural, instinctual selves behind a façade of protection from disapproval, punishment, or humiliation. This early defense system supported the repression of our instinctual responses, recollections, and innate nature, creating a division between them and what is acceptable, expected, and appropriate.

We all have used fantasy to compensate for all those expressions that were taken away from us. It was our games of make-believe and role-play that allowed us to express those inner parts of our being that we were not allowed to explore elsewhere. Many of us seldom had this opportunity aside from the fantasy games of early childhood, while some of us were actually able to continue our explorations into our teen years or early adulthood with role-playing games of marvelous superheroes and villainous antiheroes. Although we are something very different than what we played in those fantasy games, we understand that they were a creative exploration of different facets of ourselves.

Giving wings to our fantastic creative impulses—whether with games and music, or on paper or canvas—is for many of us the only way to express those latent parts of our true self. We are opening the gates to imagination, and expressing it through the only available and permissible outlets of music, artwork, and fiction. Without the world of fantasy to turn to, we could certainly be prone to turn the tide on the levels of acceptability, indulging in debauchery, excess, violence, self-destruction, apathy, or ennui; there we may become irretrievably lost, unable to renounce our newfound ways. Some of us exist in the even dimmer half-world of self-deception, denial, and people-pleasing, which often also results in an irretrievable loss. The few of us who have emerged from the other side know how close to the void we have been, how close this false self was to becoming the only reality we knew, and how truly fortunate we are to have found one another today.

Our dreams are one of the many roads toward discovering the denied aspects of our nature. In the privacy of our dreams, we often see clearer reflections of our true selves, revealing aspects that we buried deep inside. In our dreams, dark figures offer us small opportunities to claim those lost pieces of our inner being, often offering us useful tools to disarm current perspectives or situations, as long as we are willing to listen. Certainly, encounters with our inner self are better left to the dream world than to times of stress or duress, when we need control more than ever. Yet it is during those very times when we are more prone to lose reason, being truly beside ourselves in thought, word, and deed, as if possessed by some demon. Circumstances generating high anxiety, disorientation, and stress provide perfect introspective opportunities during which we can opt to make lasting changes in the way we acknowledge and process our inner identities.

Spiritual journeys such as meditation, ritual, journeying, fasting, chanting, isolation, sensory deprivation, corporeal stimulation, and Tantric work can evoke substantial revelations about who we are. The key lies in the interpretation of these often symbolic visages of indefinite times and places that often challenge the preconceptions of morality, reason, and reality. A place of twilight, magic, and illusion, our true nature is unlikely to present itself in a straightforward manner.

Past-life regression work can also be extremely useful, as any result of such explorations casts a definite light on another facet of us, regardless of whether or not it reveals a certifiable past life. Such procedures as hypnosis, self-hypnosis, the Christos method, archetype contemplation, Ouija board consultation, and astral plane retrieval may help unlock those deep unconscious energies that lie beneath our observable threshold of perception, or in some cases will process thoughts from varied perspectives.

Whichever approach, or combination of approaches, we choose to take as a means to discover and accept our true selves—if it is worth doing, it is worth doing well. Cultivate patience, discipline, and perseverance. Keeping good records and always checking our sources is vital, as is the ability to temper our serious desire with humor and a good dose of *joie de vivre*.

DEFINITIONS

Dragon: A term that has come to refer to a vampire's inner nature, the source of magickal power. The Dragon is equated with personal power but also with hunger and the dark side. Some traditions use the term in a manner that equates it to the Jungian shadow, the dark side of the psyche that, if properly harnessed, yields a great deal of psychic energy. The Dragon also serves as an alternate term for "the beast," a term for a vampire's darker, more primal nature that was popularized by the roleplaying game *Vampire: The Masquerade*.

If you passed Gabrielx on the street, you would never take him for a vampire. With a baseball cap worn backwards over his thatch of strawberry-blond hair, he is the perfect antithesis to the fashion mavens who populate the New York City clubs. Gabriel's take on vampirism is utterly in keeping with his personal appearance: practical, ordinary, and unapologetic. Because of this, Gabe is here to represent those for whom vampirism is less a fashion statement and more just a simple part of who they are.

Gabrielx: At the Crux of East and West

I am the founder of House Lost Haven. I've been practicing energy manipulation since the age of nine. At age seven, I was introduced into the martial arts and spent every free moment in the dojo. At age nine, I was introduced to Qi Gong healing techniques by a T'ai Chi master in Rocklin, California. Qi Gong is a Chinese self-healing art defined as the skill of attracting vital energy. With it I learned to manipulate and modify the *qi*, or chi, traveling through my body to affect ailments in a positive way.

After spending ample amounts of time in Qi Gong training, I spent time learning different techniques from instructors who were taking *Wing chun* as well as T'ai Chi and playing with something I'd later find out to be defined as the *jings*. Jings are proper postures that use the internal chi not only of the practitioner but of the attacker. One of the most popular jings, which takes a wonderful amount of time to understand, is *Fa-jing*, which is most commonly seen in Bruce Lee's one-inch punch; this combines structure with a quick release of energy into an opponent.

As time moved on, I found myself intertwined with Asian culture and belief structures that didn't deny the existence of such things as vital energies and the ability to use them. Between the ages of nine and eighteen, I was told on two distinct separate occasions that I was an energy vampire. Not comprehending this term either time, I allowed it to flow out of my thoughts. Early in 1999, I found myself looking up, for some odd reason, information about energy vampires on the psychic vampire exchange website. This is when I began to ask questions and noticed things matched up. My constantly altering moods and constantly altering vital energetic levels were soon leveled out after I practiced some of the techniques given to me. This process began to open my mind up to other possibilities with my chi that I had never really thought of before. Later, I would also be attuned to master over a study of three years in Usui Reiki that helped amplify my healing skills.

In mid-1999, I finally ran into someone else who was also an energy vampire. As soon as I walked in the door, it was as if a block of energy just hit me in the face and for some odd reason I knew right away. We caught up later, and he showed me exactly what I was feeling and how to properly use the techniques I had been trying to learn on my own.

This was the first time I had ever really intertwined energy with another person as a nonphysical contact or very close tapping. It was awesome to me, and it was as if I had found a missing puzzle piece that locked me right into a comfortable groove.

At this time, I was also invited to join a house that was not so local to me by a friend whom I had met earlier. This connected me with another local energy-taker who helped me along my path. Going through the process of being taught in a long-distance house made me realize the importance of face-to-face teaching. So I kept on good terms with the house and separated with the other local member to form a local group in which we could teach and learn from others with more or less experience. We wished to generate a family-like atmosphere for learning, playing, and acquiring new skills.

To this end, we created a group known as Valesco, from the Latin for "strength" and "growth." It was our philosophy that learning about others gave us strength through understanding the ways in which others think—which in turn gave growth without prejudice to those we may not have once understood. In return, this gave us strength yet once again, creating a circle.

About a year or a year and a half later, Valesco merged with another house from central California. This merger gave way to our houses and members combining with one another to create a deeply set-in family structure with one another. As many of us had children, and were getting a bit aged, our focus started to lean toward family-oriented events as much as possible. It was within this structure that Valesco found true strength within itself and became a cornerstone for some of the newly awakened individuals in our area.

Then we ran into a problem. We ran a very small website that was geared to our local area only. It was a private site, set up for all of us just to communicate back and forth. The key problem was with the word *local*. We soon came to understand that there were a growing number of people online searching for knowledge who were lost in their path. Wanting to reach out to these people or allow them to reach out to us, we decided in 2002 to create the website known as Lost Haven. Lost Haven was to be geared to Internet users around the world, as well as to local users. Lost Haven started making its way—until 2003, when we had a server crash and lost all of our archives and everything we had online. We now understand the importance of backups.

We continued to operate within a larger area locally, keeping to ourselves and being private. However, in 2004 we decided to revive our website and join the online community more fully than we had before. For the first time ever, we agreed to open our membership status to the whole world instead of just to locals—meaning that we would welcome other households or groups into our ranks, merging with a few houses around the globe and creating relationships with other houses.

In 2004, after serious consideration, we merged Valesco into the name House Lost Haven, and made it an addition to the 2005 rebirth of Lost Haven.

House Lost Haven had done what it set out to do. It has opened its doors not only to local members, but it has also welcomed in people from all walks of life and with all sorts of knowledge all across the world. Valesco, the same now as House Lost Haven, carries with it a reputation for bringing in solitary practitioners who are normally not known to associate with groups or houses, and who are truly of the lone-wolf variety. We're a family made up of other lone wolves. The house thrives on its diversity and our ability to work together within that diversity. Well, we get along most of the time. Family is family, after all.

Lost Haven is one of the many vampire organizations that is more of a family circle than a spiritual society. Because of the very nature of vampirism, many of its members follow their own spiritual paths; the group gets together to share a sense of community and to be an open place for new ideas. Under the guidance of Gabrielx, Lost Haven has been striving to ensure that other vampires can set aside their differences of belief in order to focus on being more productive in a community of equals who help one another explore themselves.

Lost Haven: A Community of Helpers

We don't adhere in House Lost Haven to a religious structure or a set path of belief. We attempt to cater to most everyone's beliefs and religions as long as each individual can accept our basic codes of conduct within the house and toward others. One of those codes is to accept others for who they truly are.

In 2005, House Lost Haven decided to become more involved with the community and wanted to give something back. It was at this time that we started our child recovery project, assisting missing children. We came to realize that when a child runs away or is kidnapped, the police rarely put many hours into the recovery of the child, while the families who may have no knowledge of tracing individuals or tracking down children sit at home and cry. We adopted a donation-based system that poor families could afford. When the child is located, the family member is usually brought to the scene in order to call the police and bring the child back into their custody or place them in a youth correctional facility, a decision that is purely up to the parent.

Our abuse-assistance program helps abused women get away from their abusers. Depending on the circumstances, abused women are normally picked up, taken to a safe house, and given options. Our primary option, which we try to strongly encourage, is counseling.

Despite the nature of the things that we do, we are usually a pretty private family. However, we are very friendly and easygoing. If you have any questions, please feel free to stop by our website, www.losthaven.org. Send an e-mail, or stop by our chat channel and introduce yourself.

I personally attempt to gear my thoughts about the metaphysical to a near-grounded mentality that I believe was instilled in me during martial arts practice. The near-grounded aspect of my mentality helps me to allow room for new discoveries in the world of which I may not be aware.

It is also my belief that a student will always teach a teacher something new. In that, we will always be students of one another.

Eclecta is an articulate and energetic member of the vampire commu-
nity who has had a particularly challenging path: she discovered and
explored her vampirism while growing up in the traditionally conserva-
tive American South. A vampire in the Bible Belt, Eclecta is someone who
understands the struggle for acceptance and personal meaning, and her
work within the community reflects that. Together with her group, the
Atlanta Vampire Alliance, Eclecta has been working to collect accurate
demographics of the vampire community so we can all better understand
who we are and what that means.

Eclecta: Finding a Path in the South

Imagine being different from everyone you know: never fitting in anywhere, being in a crowded room yet being alone, having "friends" you
have nothing in common with, wandering around the depths of your
mind knowing that those around you will never understand the thoughts and
ideas that reside there. Picture yourself hiding in the place that you know will
comfort you: the darkness. It doesn't have to be a sad, depressing, morbid
place that engulfs you. It is only the place you know and call home.

It lurks in the shadows of your mind and lets your imagination empower
you to the point where you know you don't have all the answers—but yet it
lets you know that you are safer there. Among those who also call it home,
you are able to find a release, some answers, and much-needed friendships
that you have never had before.

What do you do now? Do you submerge yourself into the darkness,
trusting that it cannot possibly be worse than the light? Or do you take caution and proceed slowly? Or do you choose to run?

Take my hand and walk with me as I tell you my story. Bleed with me, and engulf yourself in my life, my existence.

Now that I have your attention, let me state that I'm not really that melodramatic. I'm actually rather plain, simple, and perhaps a bit blunt.

I am thirty-two years old. I awakened at the age of fourteen, although I wasn't aware at the time what it was I was going through. My life up until this time was quite normal by most standards. I was in band, choir, and even cheerleading. I searched for somewhere to fit in, but I was never quite able to find my niche. My parents were supportive, encouraging me to do whatever it would take to make me happy—yet happiness seemed so far away.

I did well in school, had a few close friends, and was on the honor roll so often that teachers began to expect more of me than they did other students. I got along well with most of my classmates. It was in the summer of 1989 that I really began to awaken, just shortly after my fourteenth birthday.

Looking back now, I recall feeling misunderstood and often frustrated, as most teenagers do.

Let me back up a few years first. My family always thought children needed a healthy dose of Christianity when they were growing up, at least until they were capable of gaining enough knowledge on their own to make an educated decision about what precisely they would claim as their own set of beliefs.

There is one Sunday in particular that I remember well. I had recently found a chapter in the Bible and was asking some rather odd questions for a twelve-year-old after Sunday school. It was the book of Revelation—chapter 13, if I am not mistaken—that told how the beast would rise from the sea.

Fascinated by the story, I confronted the pastor of the church after his lengthy sermon that afternoon. "So this beast," I asked, "what makes him come from the sea? Is he like the Loch Ness monster?" I can remember the pastor asking if I had read the rest of the book of Revelation, to which I replied, "Most of it." He began to explain that Revelation was the book that revealed what was in store for the world in the end times. So I kept on, asking then, "Where did God come from? Who made him? Are you sure God isn't a woman? How do you know for sure?" He told me I wasn't old enough to be asking such questions and that I should "go play with the other children."

Now, I don't know about you, but I thought I was pretty grown up when I was twelve, and I took his response to be very offensive. I immediately decided that I would not be returning to that or any church in the near future.

That night I sat up until about four AM, reading my old set of encyclopedias. I started out looking up beasts and somehow found references to information about Satan, witches, demons, and other topics that seemed by far more intriguing to me than church had ever been. I remember when I finally went to bed; I lay there thinking for at least another hour about why the church didn't tell you all the fascinating stuff. They seemed to focus on scare tactics; this stuff didn't seem too scary to me, and at least it was interesting!

School the next day was boring, and I remember going to my second period teacher Mrs. Pratt (not her real name), thinking surely a science teacher would know where God came from, and asking her the same questions I had asked the pastor. She said she didn't know, and when I asked her who would know, she suggested I ask my parents or my pastor. I did ask my parents that evening at dinner. My father laughed and said, "What even makes you think there is a God?" I was appalled! Why would they send me to church if there weren't even a God! What kind of sick joke was this? I suddenly remembered Santa Claus, the Easter bunny, and the tooth fairy. It all made sense now. It's about making someone else believe something in order to get them to go to bed earlier or do something you want them to do without much argument.

My father didn't ask me why I didn't return to church. I never told him why, though I'm sure he had already figured it out. I never went back, and no one ever questioned it, except the pastor who thought I was too young to know certain things about the Bible in which he so wholeheartedly believed.

Thus, I began my journey into the world of the occult. From that long Sunday night until now, I have always enjoyed that which others did not want to talk about, the things that others scorn, and the things that simply cannot be explained. It is my yearning for knowledge that leads me where I am today.

✱   ✱

During the summer of 1989, I began to crave blood. I had no idea at the time about anything pertaining to vampires. I didn't even associate it as such for quite some time. The mere sight of blood would send me into a frenzy, to the point where I would run away for fear of doing something that would freak out everyone who saw my reaction—not to mention myself! I had gory dreams of blood splattering all over me, and though I didn't know where the blood was coming from, I realized that, when consumed, it would empower me in a way that nothing else ever would. It became something of an obsession that summer. I read books about it, learned about how a drop of blood made its way throughout the entire body, and constantly thought about the taste of it. I wanted to feel it in my mouth so badly that I would chew my nails down so far that they bled, just so I could taste my own blood for a few moments.

Kate was a friend of mine who lived just down the road. She moved there only a few weeks after my obsession with blood began. She could drive and liked some of the same bands I did, making me comfortable enough to want to be around her despite my newfound fascination. We became good friends over the next month or so before school began.

She was at my house often and I at hers. We used to listen to big-hair bands, tease our hair to the point where it stood up, and then spray it with so much hairspray that it wouldn't even blow in the wind if a tornado came. We used to hang our brand-new blue jeans on the clothesline and have her dad shoot at them with his shotgun to give them the desired look of that time. Then we would bleach the jeans and wash and dry them four or five times. I felt closer to Kate than I had ever felt to any of my other friends, most likely because I spent night and day with her for over a month.

We rarely came out during the daytime since we were both pale and burned easily. We slept all day and stayed up all night, as though that were normal behavior. I don't remember ever being happier in my life, at least during my teenage years.

Shortly before school was to start, she had to leave to go back to Alabama. I didn't want her to go, so we made a blood pact to be best friends forever. That was the first time I ever tasted blood other than my own. I can't even begin to describe the way it made me feel. "Euphoric" would be putting it lightly. To say I felt invincible is a more accurate description. From that moment on, I began to try to figure out how to get other "blood sisters."

School started again. Kate had left, and I was now in ninth grade. I was still as curious as ever, but by this time I had started smoking, skipping school, and wearing black. I was Goth, by today's standards, in a little hick town whose residents did not know what Goth was then. I recall being asked on a regular basis if I worshipped the devil. That always made me laugh—though I am not sure why, unless perhaps I relished being different. It was no secret that I refused to go to church.

All of my school folders were decorated with pictures I thought cool back then, from *Metal Edge* magazine. I used to dye my hair with Kool-Aid in bright colors like orange and yellow. Or I would dye it jet black—actually, it was naturally blue-black. I was set on being different and expressing myself. I prided myself on listening to music that made my parents want to scream as loud as the songs I played. My only friends those days were the other kids everyone thought were as weird as me.

There were times during those years when I can recall deliberately seeking out high-energy places. I had no idea at the time, of course, that I was actually feeding on this energy. Friends sometimes noticed they were unusually tired after spending any amount of time with me. Empathy came naturally to me as well. Some of my friends through the years came to depend on the calming effect that I had on them. One friend, who was one of the Ritalin kids of those times, pointed this out to me.

It took me years to associate all of this for what it is, simply because there was not a great deal of information out there for me to compare it to.

I wrote sad, morbid, engrossing poems to document my inner turmoil. I ran away from home once because it seemed like the next best thing to do. I began to smoke pot, though back then I didn't realize that you were supposed to inhale and hold. Ha! I drank when I could find something to drink. Why did I do all this? I really have no idea, but I think it was because I wanted people to recognize I wasn't a child anymore. I got tired of hearing "You are too young for this or that," and I wanted to find my own place.

My mother was my tower of strength, and I know I was slowly driving her crazy. She was the one who never questioned why I was so eager to learn about ghosts, spirits, and Ouija boards. In fact, she was the one who showed me how to make and use a Ouija board. She told me about times before I was born when she used to play with one herself. My mother also encouraged me to learn all I could about everything so that I could eventually make decisions for myself. Granted, she never liked my hair colors, my music, or my choice to wear slashed-up jeans, but she was there for me when I needed her most.

I ended up graduating a year early because my grades were good, and I had that yearning thirst for knowledge that prompted me to take classes far ahead of the normal sequence.

By the time I was seventeen, I had been married, had a baby, and gotten divorced. I no longer had anything in common with anyone I had ever known who was my age. I felt a silent calling to leave the place where I grew up. That same calling led me to many places through the years and eventually to where I am now. It also took me to places where I met the people I would need, or those who would need me, for the next phase of my life. You could say I depend on this calling now to get me where I should be at the right time.

I went to nursing school and then joined the army. Due to their undying devotion, my parents were willing to keep my son while I did what was best for me. During this time, I was still fighting the urge that lived within me to consume blood. There were many sleepless nights. So many, in fact, that I reveled in being able to sleep from about four PM until around midnight, and then stay up until the same time the next day. Nighttime was when I felt most alive. Sleep was the last thing on my mind at night. The sunlight of daytime often leaves me feeling drowsy and lethargic, so I do avoid it.

When I was about twenty-one, I was learning to consciously psi-feed, although at that time I didn't have a name for what it was. I began to realize that I was able to manipulate energy around me in such a way that I could actually feel energy being pulled into me from another living body sitting near me. This curbed substantially the cravings I had for blood. The older you get, the harder it is to find someone to be your "blood sister," since everyone thinks it is silly by around age sixteen, or sometimes even younger.

✖   ✖

Déjà vu seems to be something I have always experienced; however, it began to get stronger as I learned to pull energy from other people. Its intensity and duration seemed to last longer the more energy I was able to consume.

Dreams began to come to me even during waking hours. Dreams of storms, blood, strength, life, and on occasion even death. I began to record them, but lost my journals—along with a great many other things that would come in handy now—when my house burned in 1996.

I did not find the online vampire community until 1999, and then I was so unsure and mistrustful of people that I was ashamed to admit the things I believed to be true. How could I convince, or why would I even try to convince, anyone that I could actually remember things that weren't from this lifetime? Why should they believe me? Living in the South most of my life taught me one thing in particular: if you aren't Christian, then you must worship the devil. But the devil never really comforted me either. I suppose he overlooked me because I never really believed in him either.

I also struggled with ethical questions. Was I doing something wrong? Was taking energy from someone else who did not know what you were doing wrong?

Finally, I decided I did not care what others thought about me or what I was doing or had done. I was determined to find others who could understand me, and I knew I could not do it being so paranoid. I engulfed myself heart and soul with the Internet vampire community in 2001. I never really looked back. I delved deeper and deeper, knowing that the only way I would ever fit in was to find these people and make myself known to them.

Eventually I did exactly that—found others. Fort Worth was the first place where I tried to find people like me. They either weren't there or were hiding so deeply that they couldn't be found. It was not until I was visiting my soon-to-be husband that I was actually able to actually feel what others called the "beacon" so strongly. Not knowing what to really look for, I just consciously became more aware of who and what was around me. I moved to Atlanta in the summer of 2002 and began again to actively seek others like myself.

It took me until 2003 to find anyone in person. I am sincerely glad I never stopped looking. Atlanta will be my home, I suspect, for a number of years, and I wouldn't have it any other way. The like-minded individuals I now surround myself with make me feel at peace. And finally, what means more to me than anything else is that I do feel that I fit in.

Atlanta calls to me more strongly than any other place where others seem to gather, such as New York or New Orleans. It is in Atlanta that I feel close kin relationships with those I know here. Our city may not have the popularity that other cities have, but I hope that will change one day.

On a trip to New Orleans in 2004, a good friend of mine, Kiera, and I were driving to Endless Night. We had both been considering joining a house, when we decided then and there, in a car, somewhere in the middle of Alabama, that what we should do was start our own house. We tossed that idea around for quite some time before putting the plan into action.

The Atlanta Vampire Alliance (AVA) was born in 2005. We have five founding members, six regular house members, and a couple of associates. No one in our house is more than or less than anyone else. We are all equals. We are not striving to be the biggest or the best, nor are we aiming to be the most popular or the most powerful.

Personally, I feel a pull to Atlanta, and I know that if I feel it, others may too. And those others will come, as I did, if they are meant to be part of AVA.

I used to wonder why some of the other houses called themselves families. It didn't make sense to me, at the time, although I could feel the kinship occasionally, with certain members. It had more of a distant-cousin kind of feel to it. Now I understand that I was not meant to join another house but to co-found AVA with those who share ideas and beliefs so similar to my own.

AVA is going to be part of my life now because I do finally feel those familial bonds. It is not something we as founding members are choosing to do as a temporary endeavor, but rather it's a lifelong commitment.

My life has drastically changed since those days almost seventeen years ago when I felt confused and misunderstood as a teenager. I have grown mentally and spiritually as a direct result of who I am, and finally I know who I am meant to be: myself.

The Atlanta Vampire Alliance is an organization dedicated to under-standing the vampire community as a whole. In the past few years, it has become well-known throughout the community for its exhaustive ques-tionnaires dedicated to compiling statistics about what vampires really believe as well as how vampirism affects each individual. Because it is dedicated to answers, the AVA is friendly but unaffiliated with all other vampire groups. The AVA remains the best example to date of an educa-tional group whose work can help outsiders take vampirism seriously.

Atlanta Vampire Alliance: Initiating Serious Studies

The mission of the Atlanta Vampire Alliance is to promote unity in the greater Atlanta community while being available to the newly awakened to encourage self-awareness and responsibility. We honor the traditions of history, respect, and discretion regarding community affairs, while advocating the safety and well-being of our members. Emphasizing research and supporting social gatherings, we highlight the importance of education and strength of involvement as a cohesive force in our area. By tak-ing an active role, we will serve not only ourselves but also our community and our city.

The Atlanta Vampire Alliance promotes itself as a neutral vampire commu-nity organization. We are not directly affiliated with any other house, order, or council, although we welcome associate members from many diverse areas of the online vampire community. The majority of our members share a similar background of solitary participation, and therefore, when drafting our fun-damental articles, we made a personal decision to avoid using a hierarchal or social-promotion system. While we respect others who choose to institute such a caste system, we remain steadfast in our chosen structure, allowing us to freely encourage camaraderie and proactive involvement within the vampire community. Despite the lack of common ritualistic protocols, our policies regarding those we do accept and the maturity of our applicants are taken very seriously. Our members enjoy equal status and voice regardless of the path, religion, or philosophy they hold. Further complementing this system, the five founding members of the AVA conduct business as a cooperative body, sharing a vision of responsibility, tolerance, and awareness among both the greater and local vampire communities. In addition to our participation in a varied spectrum of social activities, our energies are also directed toward the support of the local vampire populace and those who come to us seeking guidance. The majority of our work is conducted offline with regular monthly meetings. Aside from the strong offline presence, we host an expansive open forum to all who wish to join, regardless of location or affiliation. The topics of discussion in this forum range from psi/sang vampirism to occult magick to metaphysics to local issues.

The primary focus of the AVA is to expand the educational boundaries of our own community while improving the quality of the study of the vampiric condition among the non-vampiric population. Members of our house have been working on various educational and professional papers over the course of several years. Our base membership and associates encompass decades of involvement from all paths of the vampire community. It is from this collective of unique individuals that we draw our strength in the fields of occult, paranormal, parapsychological, phenomenological, psionics, and general underground community research. The AVA's research company released both the *Vampire & Energy Work Research Survey* and the *Advanced Vampirism & Energy Work Research Survey* in 2006, and is currently involved in other related studies of interest both to the community and to institutional researchers. Composed of hundreds of questions and covering a vast range of personal and community vampiric experiences, these studies are unique in their scope and purpose.

All who share a sincere interest in our research, forums, and community-hosted events are encouraged to participate. We extend an open hand to those of all houses, orders, or paths who visit our city, as we share a common vision of productive growth and organization within the community. For more information, please visit us at www.atlantavampirealliance.com.

SECTION
- SEVEN -

Other Views

Camille Thomas has been a practicing Wiccan since her very early teens. A dedicated scholar, she has completed a degree in computer science and is busy doing graduate work in business management. In between studies and moderating the House Kheperu forums, Camille finds time to teach magic and energy work to a number of students.

A Wiccan Perspective on Vampires
BY CAMILLE THOMAS

*M*any Wiccans have experienced the difficulty of dealing with the stigma attached to the word *witch*. It's challenging, particularly when you're alone and without the support of community, to attach yourself to a word that can have such negative connotations. I was thirteen when I first dedicated myself to Wicca—but couldn't bring myself to use the word *witch* in conversation with very many people until a number of years later. I was "Wiccan," occasionally "Pagan," and the magical practices that grew from that were part of my "spirituality." Even *magic* was almost a taboo word—shared only among the people who I felt understood where I was coming from.

I grew out of my hesitancy in using the word *witch* in my own life—though I am still continuously aware of the associations the word has outside the community. As time went on, it became more challenging to know if the word *Wiccan* were more appropriate. How do you say you are part of a belief system whose tenets and beliefs come from so diverse a field? I followed the Wiccan Rede and believed in the god and the goddess as both a representation of the duality of the universe and as vital forces. I respected the concept of the cycles of death and rebirth and attached myself to the symbolism I found in the first books I read by Cunningham and Starhawk. Still, I never followed British Traditional Wicca. I was never initiated through a lineal coven, and I can't trace the person I learned from back to Gerald Gardner.

I choose to use both the words *Wiccan* and *witch* because I find them to be the labels most appropriate to define myself. The meaning of the word *Wicca*, as the community I feel myself a part of understands it, fits with what I believe. The same is true of with the word *witch*—regardless of the hesitations I had when I first encountered the word. These are the words that have been chosen by the community to define what I am. *Vampire* also carries strong negative connotations. In common usage, it brings to mind images of evil blood-drinking undead and all manner of storybook villains.

But still, despite its negative connotations, it is the word that has been adopted by a community—or more accurately, a number of diverse communities. They feel that the term is the most appropriate, out of all the concepts they could draw together, to describe how they identify themselves. Virtually none of the people who call themselves vampires would claim to be immortal undead creatures who would catch flame in the sun, just as virtually no witch would identify with a green-warted woman poisoning fields and eating children. The idea holds the draw of an archetype, but that's as far as the literal interpretation of the word goes.

But what is the vampire community? In my view, it's actually more accurate to say that there are several different communities than it is to say that there is only one. The word *vampire*, much like the word *witch*, has been picked up and adopted by many different groups. Trying to lump them all together is akin to making the assumption that all Pagans follow Wiccan beliefs. To further complicate things, even within the subcategories there is a lot of diversity. For almost any statement made about the community, there will be someone who sits up and yells loudly that they disagree. It should be kept in mind that any statement made about the community is by necessity a generalization.

So how does one talk about (or have views on) a general community? On that topic I can only speak from my own perspective. That perspective has been shaped through the lens of my Wiccan beliefs and through my contacts with portions of the community.

My first experience with the vampire community occurred in high school. Even then I was open about my Wiccan beliefs, regardless of my inability to use the word *witch* in conversation. In that school system, I wasn't the only one practicing some form of magic. There were probably about a dozen students in my high school who followed some sort of magical religious system. There were four Wiccans in the school, including myself. We were remarkably serious about the whole thing. Even back then it was a magical, religious, and spiritual path for us.

There was another group of students a couple years ahead of us. In retrospect, they were much like many of the "vampires" you can find flooding message boards online—teens looking for attention, drinking blood without any regard for safety, and "cursing" people left and right for no real reason besides the desire to do something spooky. I never took that group seriously. My beliefs stemmed from a religious background, and I had no comprehension of what the purpose of their actions could be. Ever since I had begun practicing a magical and spiritual belief system, I had been fighting the stereotypes of either not being serious or being entirely insane. By these students' association with anything even vaguely related to me, they threatened the work I had done to show that I was serious. They were what I considered a bad example of following a magical belief system, and I tried my hardest to dismiss them and distance myself from this group of students.

Yet in doing so, I dismissed not only that group but also the entire idea of a vampire community. Because of those experiences, I considered myself justified in disliking anything related to vampires in a nonfictional sense. My first impressions were powerfully negative, and they combined well with my rather narrow view of things at the time. From the moment I heard of vampirism existing, I didn't want to take the community seriously—and was quickly able to find evidence to back up my prejudice. Part of this was that I was still having difficulty being open about my own religious beliefs. I did not want to deal with their association with magic and thus my beliefs. It was good to be able to draw a line there and say "I am not these people—these people are bad. I am not."

The statement *was* true for that group of students; if I met them today, I would likely shake my head and walk away. But when I spoke those words, I was referring to more than just that group—I was dismissing the entire belief system. This is a common occurrence in the Pagan community, most frequently aimed at Satanism. The legitimate desire to differentiate oneself in the public mind evolves into the vilification of an entire belief system—a generalization based on uninformed perceptions rather than genuine knowledge.

That experience continued to shape my view of the vampire community for many years. During that time in my exploration, I ran into a few miscellaneous texts and websites—I found the Black Veil and a smattering of other information. It didn't do much to change my views of the community—the scantily clad, fang-mouthed photos of vamps at clubs combined with the melodramatically dark language in the writings largely left me feeling no need to investigate any deeper.

After dismissing the first "vampire" group I ran into early in high school, it wasn't until after my second year of college that I seriously ran into vampires again. This time it was online, through an old occult personals site. I was looking for people to talk with about various traditions. Honestly, I was mostly bored. I ran into someone doing about the same thing, except this individual was claiming to be, of all things, a "psychic vampire." He made a few other claims that bothered me; he claimed his "house" was fairly influential in the "vampire community." I tend to be a bit skeptical of anyone making claims of influence over the Internet—they may be true, but more often they're not.

"Psychic vampire" was a term I had run into through Dion Fortune in her book *Psychic Self Defense*, and thus it carried in my mind many negative connotations. In that text, a psychic vampire is defined as a person who drains the life of other people maliciously, often stirring up drama and hard feelings in order to create situations they could draw from. I couldn't help but wonder why anyone would want to claim that as a belief system. As his story became in my mind less plausible, I became rather frustrated at the idea of people hiding behind the Internet and making ridiculous claims. Finally, this online contact claimed to have access to a library of some three thousand occult texts—and coming from someone who I was half convinced was just a decent role-player, that was enough to make me a little sick of the entire thing. Up to this point, everything he had claimed was either part of a belief/metaphysical practice or some sort of amorphous "community" idea. Now he was making physical claims—and physical claims are easy to prove or disprove.

Now, perhaps at this point it should be noted that I've got a little bit of an adventurous streak, and that I'm not necessarily the most safety-conscious person in the world. Tired of letting people hide behind the Internet to make ridiculous claims, I decided to tell this gentleman that I'd love to see his collection, if such a thing existed. He surprised me when he said that it could be arranged. Assuming that he was just attempting to call my bluff, I upped the stakes a bit: I decided to actually follow through on my challenge.

I set up a couple of safe-calls with friends and ventured out to meet the guy. We met at a Denny's restaurant a couple miles away from where he lived. We spoke for a bit, and despite my initial impressions, he seemed remarkably sensible, interesting, and not at all idiotic or terrifying. Feeling relatively safe and making a couple of phone calls about where I was going to be, I decided to follow him back to his home, where the books were supposedly located—at this point a little less sure of my conviction that the books didn't exist.

I spent the next three hours reading titles. The works ranged over a variety of subjects and branched out into a wide array of traditions. There were also more traditional (though related) works on a variety of subjects, including psychology, history, and biographies.

Later that evening, I was given a chance to meet the owner of those books—Michelle Belanger. She turned out to be one of the most knowledgeable and insightful occultists I have had the pleasure of meeting. I am more than a bit of an occult bookworm; I have a genuine passion for religious, spiritual, and occult subjects. Given the chance, I will speak on and listen to conversations about these subjects for as long as I can find a knowledgeable person to talk to. It's rare for me to have the chance to speak with someone who shares that passion with me and who has been self-educated on the matter.

After that experience, I repeatedly visited, eventually spending the majority of my summer vacation with Michelle and the other members of House Kheperu. The topics we spoke on at first had very little to do with psychic vampires. But as a core part of her beliefs, the subject came up eventually, and I ended up speaking with her at length about it. What I discovered was a belief system which, while I didn't necessarily agree with it, was comprehensible. I could understand how she came to have the belief system that she did, and why she felt it appropriate to use the phrase "vampire" to describe it.

From my encounter with Michelle and House Kheperu, I moved on to contact other members of the vampire community. I had a rare opportunity to have a prominent member of the community introduce me to people who had already gained her respect. The result was the opposite of my high school experience; instead of meeting the community through some of its worst members, I met it through some of its best. It wasn't until several years after I had met Michelle that I began to deal with the general community at large. When I did, it was with a much more educated perspective.

As I mentioned before, there is not one vampire community; there are several. There are the psychic, sanguine, and hybrid vampires who tend to make up what is sometimes called the "real vampire" community. A term also used at one point, though now not often seen, is *human living vampire*. Both these terms have fallen somewhat out of fashion, leaving the groups just calling themselves vampires. It could be argued that there are actually different communities for the sanguine and psychic vampires, but I would propose that there is sufficient overlap to consider them a single community with different overlapping aspects. When I hear the phrase *vampire community*, this is what comes to mind.

An almost entirely separate set of communities has formed around the various religious systems that have developed around the idea of the vampire as an archetype. These groups tend to be more insular and often do not acknowledge the psychic, sanguine, and hybrid communities as having any legitimacy at all. They may or may not believe in the idea or concept of a need for energy or blood. Anything said about these vampire religions is by necessity a generalization, but most of the groups I've run into tend to be attracted to vampirism both because of its power and because of the predatory aspects of the archetype. These belief systems tend to be strongly left-hand path, strongly honoring individual power. A number of them I have run into also tend to have fairly negative views on the "white light" magical communities, perceiving them as naive and foolishly idealistic.

The last community I am aware of that claims the vampire label is the lifestyle vampire community. These are people who are drawn to vampirism as an aesthetic and who choose to imitate it in their daily lives. Generally, this community has no interest in either the psychic/sanguine/hybrid community or vampire-archetype religions. There can be some overlap between this community and the other communities. There are individuals who are spiritually interested in vampirism who also follow a vampire lifestyle. However, most people in the other communities do not dress the part of the Hollywood vampire in their day-to-day lives.

Of these communities, a Wiccan is most likely to run into a psychic, sanguine, or hybrid vampire. Many of the people who are involved in these communities, particularly the psychic vampires, are also involved in various magical communities outside of vampirism. These vampires will frequently get involved in established magical groups comprising a wide array of beliefs. These include both beliefs traditionally considered to be "dark" such as Luciferianism, as well as more standard "white light" belief systems like Wicca.

Unfortunately, many vampires who become involved in outside groups, particularly "white light" groups, are very hesitant to mention their vampiric associations out of a fear of misunderstanding. While it would be nice to say that Wiccans and other magical practitioners are tolerant, this is not always the case. The stigma attached to the word *vampire*, as well as to the vampire community, is often more than groups are willing to deal with. While it is not always the case, there can be ostracism when someone is discovered to be a vampire, particularly in more "white light" groups, regardless of how ethical and serious they are with their practices.

In some parts of the vampire community, this closed-mindedness is viewed as hypocrisy and can lead to frustration. Vampires who identify themselves as having a need to take in energy or blood feel that they are being judged for something beyond their control. They are thrown into both the label and the community because of this need. To deny that they are vampires as the word is defined (as much as they may dislike the word) would be to lie. That identification ties them to a label and a community that they may or may not be comfortable with. There is sometimes frustration at the failure of a community whose members identify as witches not to look beyond the cover of the word *vampire* in order to attempt to understand the underlying beliefs before passing judgment. This frustration is particularly acute among the most serious and sincere segments of the community.

While the word *vampire* accounts for some of the prejudice against the community, it is not the only cause. The frustration within the community is aimed not only outwardly but also inwardly at segments of the community itself. Like all magical communities, the vampire community has a large number of individuals whose seriousness and stability is questionable. Because this is a young and often reclusive community, these loud and obnoxious voices are often some of the easiest to hear.

Discretion has always been a major tenet of the vampire community, and in many cases the people most willing to honor that tenet are the wisest voices in the community. Left with few voices from the intelligent sections of community, it is easy for various "experts" to make claims about the community as a whole—even with no knowledge of the subject. People no one has heard of, let alone support, have stepped up, claiming to speak for the community. Often they make radical and ridiculous claims regarding either their own practices or the practices of the community.

When Jonathon Sharkey began his gubernatorial campaign in Minnesota in 2006, there was no real voice that rose up from the community to challenge him, despite his rather shocking stances. In his choice to run in that election, he associated the vampire community with his beliefs. Many vampires were extremely unhappy with that association.

Perhaps what is even more disturbing about the silence of knowledgeable people within the community is that when someone comes to seek out information, it can be difficult for them to tell credible sources from dangerous ones. The problem here is most obvious in the case of sanguine vampires. I have read material from individuals claiming authority who say they are "traditional vampires" (a term I have seen used nowhere else). They "only take blood by biting the neck," and present this insanely dangerous practice as the way "real vampires" take blood. Unfortunately, if this information comes from a self-declared authority, there are people who will believe it is true.

With the psychic vampire community, misinformation can be far more insidious. Because what a psychic vampire manipulates is less tangible, judging which practices are "correct" is far more subjective. Still, cults arise when someone "embraces" herds of "children." While these groups are not very common, they often have the loudest voices and the most extravagant claims. Because of this, they can attract quite a bit of attention and develop followings.

Some of this is beginning to change. Just over the course of the past few years, a small number of people who are seriously involved with the community have begun to step forward and be more open about their beliefs. The realization that *someone* will speak for the community if none of the genuine people do has begun to sink in among community leaders. In short, the vampire community is being pushed to the same conclusion that a number of magical communities reached decades earlier.

I see many parallels between the development of the Pagan community and the vampire community. There are certainly differences, but there are also some notable similarities. The vampire community is dealing with the same influx of interested but uninformed individuals that the Wiccan community seems to have learned to deal with effectively. As I have watched the vampire community develop—something it is doing with remarkable speed—it has given me a better understanding of the development of communities and has allowed me to better understand the movement the Wiccan community has made over the years. I am hopeful that, as the vampire community continues to grow and mature, many of its most sincere and beneficial teachings will become prevalent, while the less desirable elements will either mature or become less common.

I have always been passionately interested in understanding the world. I view my pursuit of the occult as grasping at a portion of that understanding. I want to find the boundaries that shape reality—and my experiences have led me to believe that they are beyond the concepts encompassed by materialism. I want to understand what others believe and why, so that I can attempt to expand my own horizons. I want to know what is possible. Exploring that boundary of possibility is one of the reasons I find the vampire community so fascinating. I have found within it things that I perceive to be genuine. My experiences in the community have challenged my perceptions, and through that I've grown. Along with the connections I have made with people who associate with this community, that is why I have become as involved as I have with this community. I feel that there is something valuable here.

The Bakers—*James Mitchell Baker (aka Tau Heosphoros Iacchus) and Alexzandria Baker (aka Tau Peristera de Magdalene)—are currently High Priest and Priestess of Liberi Sanguinis Luciferi, an experimental entity best described as a "Luciferian, solar-phallic, blood and sex magick, Gnostic Voodoo, hippie, bohemian love cult"based in Athens, Georgia. Former long-standing members of the Ordo Templi Orientis, they have served the occult community in varying capacities for a combined three decades. For more information on the Bakers or Liberi Sanguinis Luciferi, visit www.solarphallic-cult.org.*

The Serpent's Kiss
On the Love / Hate Relationship between
Vampirism and Ceremonial Magick
BY ALEXZANDRIA AND JAMES BAKER

Aleister Crowley and the Legend of the Serpent's Kiss
He shaved his head, filed his teeth to stiletto-like points, believed in the devil, tried to enchant women by puncturing their throats with vampire-like "serpent's kisses," copulated with animals and dined on the dung of diseased prostitutes.

—John Symonds, *The Great Beast* (1973 edition, p. 224)

✖   ✖

Aleister Crowley has long been rumored in certain circles, including in the vampire subculture, to have been a vampire. (Crowley was even given his own entry in the annals of White Wolf's *Vampire: The Masquerade*.) Most sources touting this information cite Francis King's work as their source, while some go a step further and cite King's source: John Symonds. These rumors stem from the stories of Crowley's "serpent's kiss," which were, as in the quote above, greatly hyped by Symonds. So what was Symonds' source?

There is, to our knowledge, only one documented case of Crowley actually delivering a "serpent's kiss." The recipient was Miss Nancy Cunard. The book *A Magick Life: A Biography of Aleister Crowley*, by Martin Booth, mentions Crowley's meeting with Cunard, "whom he was said to have interrupted in mid-conversation with a request that he be permitted to give her a serpent's kiss. She acquiesced, whereupon Crowley bit her on the wrist. Later, she claimed the bite had given her blood poisoning" (p. 434). Another account, this one in *The Private World of St. John Terrapin* by Chapman Pincher, mentions St. John Terrapin witnessing Crowley giving Cunard the serpent's kiss. He states, "I saw him on one occasion seize the arm of a lady companion— the heiress Nancy Cunard, with whom he was friendly—and bite her wrist, drawing blood and a cry of pain" (Pincher, 1982, p. 165). There are numerous accounts of this incident, all more or less the same as the two quoted here and all listing Miss Cunard as the recipient; however, Nancy Cunard tells it differently in a memoir of Crowley, written at the request of Gerald Yorke:

> Still only just knowing Crowley, I don't remember what brought us together that particular day. Someone had given me a bottle of whiskey and, coming in from lunch and intending to go to a public meeting on Germany, I met Crowley in the hall and asked him to have a drink. We sat conversing for probably two hours, gently and [agreeably] drinking, and he talked and talked . . . It was then I began to think that he may have adversely influenced only rather tiresome people. Not a word was said about Cefalu . . . I was fully prepared to believe that he had his own magic; but it wouldn't be "mine." It would have embarrassed me and had me floundering to have to tell him I simply could not take in things of that kind . . . So we just sat and slowly drank the whiskey and I remember he looked rather "deeply" at me. (Is that occult?) And then, having said something about "The Serpent's Kiss," which I had heard about, he asked: "Shall I give you the Serpent's Kiss?" This did slightly embarrass me. It seemed rude to say no, to ask ridiculous questions as to its meaning and, somehow, I felt

no apprehension. So I said "yes." He applied his teeth very lightly to the
inner edge of my right wrist and, after a few seconds, there it was: a tiny
triangle of reddish dots—three of them—unfelt. How do you suppose
he did that? There is certainly some kind of special process here! I knew
him so little that I am quite unaware to this day if this was some kind
of honour. It must have meant something distinctive? I found that I liked
his intelligence very much indeed. There was something a touch sad about
him and—to put it quite briefly—I found I was "for" him in a general
way, and not "against." And that seemed enough. (Cunard, 1954)

Miss Cunard goes on to tell of the public meeting she had gone to as intended, and that Crowley had accompanied her. She describes the few other encounters she shared with him over the next several years—never mentioning any other occasions on which she was bitten, or her contracting blood poisoning. As a matter of fact, I would like to point out that she says "three *reddish* dots," not "red" or "bloodied," and she does not mention blood or even that Crowley broke the skin. I do not presume that he did not, but there is not enough detail here to presume that he *did.*

In a personal correspondence written to Nancy Cunard, apparently in response to this account, Gerald Yorke writes:

. . .What a great pity you did not meet Aleister more often, reminiscences
of him brought him back sharply to life for me. I saw so much of him as
he really was in your account. Particularly his habit of testing the psy-
chology of those he did not know well—poison in the "eagle tail," which
was his name for the cocktail you describe [and] the Serpent's Kiss for
another—it had no occult or special significance, except to give him the
reaction of the person so "honored," and to keep up the reputation of wick-
edness and unconventionality which he wove so carefully around him.
(Yorke, November 23, 1954)

This statement by Yorke carries the implication that there may have been other incidents involving the delivery of a serpent's kiss, but also points out that there was no special significance behind it. If there were other occasions, they were almost certainly rare, given that Miss Cunard is the only example that can be produced.

Crowley himself, a man whose inflated ego allowed him to write an autobiography that dwarfs the King James Bible, never mentions this or any other incident involving filing his teeth or delivering the serpent's kiss, nor is it mentioned in serious context by anyone else who actually knew him. This incident was just another opportunity for him to further his ominous reputation, as confirmed by Yorke, and in the hands of an unscrupulous biographer it has become one of many stories aimed at exciting the imagination and supporting Crowley's moniker of "evilest man alive" (even long after his death). Why then, if this rumor is so simply resolved, has it persisted fifty years after Crowley's death, being retold in new forms year after year?

To take a page from John Ford's classic western *The Man Who Shot Liberty Valance*: "When the legend becomes fact, we print the legend." Quite simply, the rumors are fun and exciting stories that thrill and shock readers. Biting the necks of young socialites and defecating on Persian rugs make for a much more entertaining read than volumes upon volumes of his mountaineering adventures.

Vampire versus Vampirism: The Semantics of Division

In *The Psychic Vampire Codex*, Michelle Belanger discusses many explanations of what a vampire is and why they *need* to feed. While her work focuses exclusively on psychic vampirism rather than sanguine vampirism, the metaphysics are essentially the same in that the crux of vampirism is a physical/metaphysical *need* to feed on energy (whether through psychic energy manipulation or from the vital forces contained within blood) in order to sustain one's own vitality. In contrast to this definition, the majority of ceremonial magicians define a "vamp" as someone who feeds on or steals energy from another living being—the difference being that there is no stipulation on *need*. Was Aleister Crowley a vampire? That depends entirely upon your definition of "vampire." Did Aleister Crowley practice vampirism? Yes, unquestionably.

I believe it is the differing definitions of vampirism that create the observable rift between the occult and vampire communities. While the majority of vampires believe feeding is an innate need, and is thus a value-neutral fact of life, most magicians believe it to be a choice that leads to the invasion of another's astral and physical vitality. They view it as something that must be defended against, thus assigning a negative value judgment. The opinion held by magicians is in no small part either directly or indirectly influenced by the examination of intentional vampirism and unintentional parasitism put forth by Dion Fortune in *Psychic Self-Defence*.

Fortune asserts that not only is vampirism an act of volition, but that "true vampirism cannot take place unless there is power to project the etheric double" (Fortune, 2001, p. 45). This view of the vampire as a psychically skilled, parasitic assailant strikes at the heart of the moral and ethical worldview of many magicians. While those of the vampire subculture maintain that the consensual exchange of vital forces (even if one-way) can be beneficial to all parties, to many magicians the very idea of "ethical vampirism" seems an oxymoron.

The reasons for this moralistic attitude may also arise in part from the influence of the occult revival of the late nineteenth century on modern ceremonial magick. The Victorian worldview, both in and out of the occult community, placed great stock in the importance of personal vitality. For example, Victorian attitudes held that the loss of semen, whether through nocturnal emissions or masturbation (the ever-popular "Sin of Onan"), and in some more extreme views even in the union of lawfully wedded couples, was not only grievously degenerate but a dire threat to the health, sanity, and very life of any young man who did not vigilantly strive to retain his precious fluids. Similarly, medical science of the day had a tendency to label any medical condition of an uncertain nature as simply a "disease of the blood." To the Victorian occultist, then, to willfully sacrifice one's own life essence would be an act of unfathomable self-destructiveness in the service of a most degenerate predator, making "ethical vampirism" or consensual feeding as much of an "abomination" to the self as a psychic or physical vampiric attack. Given that modern ceremonial magick was born out of this period, the correlation between period views on masturbation, intercourse, blood impurities, and vampirism are, perhaps, not insignificant.

Also worth considering:

- Samuel Taylor Coleridge's poem "Christabel" condemns female homosexuality with the introduction of the lesbian vampire to English romantic literature—just over two hundred years after the trial of Elizabeth Báthory, "the Blood Countess."

- Charles W. Webber wrote *Spiritual Vampirism: The History of Ethered Softdown and Her Friends of the 'New Light'* in 1853.
- In 1894, at a time when mesmerism had been dismissed as the work of charlatans, and yet hypnosis was giving the Victorian world an uncomfortably intimate look into the unconscious, Arthur Conan Doyle produced *The Parasite*, a work that linked vampires with hypnotism.
- Negative Victorian attitudes toward aggressive women and homoeroticism were forever intermingled with the loathsome vampire in Sheridan Le Fanu's 1872 *Carmilla* and Florence Marryat's 1897 *The Blood of the Vampire*.
- Meanwhile, in the world of nonfiction, Cesare Lombroso put forth theories on the genetic make-up and indicators of the natural-born criminal in his 1876 *L'Uomo Delinquente*, and Jack the Ripper terrorized London with his bloody killing spree of 1888.
- Bram Stoker, an initiate of the Golden Dawn, demonstrated some study of both of the latter events in his research for *Dracula*, also published in 1897.
- Aleister Crowley remarked that Stoker had gotten it right in his portrayal of the Count while *Dracula* scholar Elizabeth Miller comments that the Victorian anxieties concerning the displacement of religion by science, the immigration of foreigners, sexually aggressive women, and artistic decadence are clearly visible in this work.
- Madame Helena Petrovna Blavatsky's gross misinterpretation of the Hindu concept of the left-hand path as the evil shadow of the right-hand path created a black and white, good versus evil theme that still permeates magickal thought today.
- The vivid images of night-stalking demons such as the incubi and succubae that feed on the essence of young men and women in their sleep, which were commonly and graphically described by the predecessors of the nineteenth-century occult revival, lent imagery to the developing vampire mythos.

So why would a long list of fictional works and the religious superstitions of over one hundred years ago be relevant to the current attitude of ceremonial magicians toward vampires and vampirism? Simple: while the fictitious representation of vampires may have mutated with the changing cultural mores over the century and the emergence of the vampire subculture put a "human face" on vampirism in recent decades, this Victorian image of the vampire as ultimate evil has become embedded in the occult paradigms that were born out of that period.

Crowley on Vampirism—in His Own Words

The legend of the serpent's kiss was born out of a need for attention, not energy; however, Crowley recognized vampirism as a magickal act. There are several portions of Crowley's work that touch on the topic of vampirism. He writes the following in *De Arte Magica*:

> *Of a certain other method of Magick not included in the instruction of O.T.O.*
>
> *It may not be altogether inappropriate to allude to a method of vampirism commonly practiced.*
>
> *The Vampire selects the victim, stout and vigorous as may be, and, with the magical intention of transferring all that strength to himself, exhausts the quarry by a suitable use of the body, most usually the mouth, without himself entering in any other way into the matter. And this is thought by some to partake of the nature of Black Magic. The exhaustion should be complete; if the work be skillfully executed, a few minutes should suffice to produce a state resembling, and not far removed from, coma.*
>
> *Experts may push this practice to the point of the death of the victim, thus not merely obtaining the physical strength, but imprisoning and enslaving the soul. This soul then serves as a familiar spirit. The practice was held to be dangerous. (It was used by the late Oscar Wilde, and by Mr. and Mrs. "Horos"; also in a modified form by S. L. Mathers and his wife, and by E. W. Berridge. The ineptitude of the three latter saved them from the fate of the three former). (Crowley, 1989b)*

This passage is very reminiscent in tone of the instructions given in the same work for a particular sexual rite, under the heading "Of Eroto-comatose Lucidity," in which he states:

. . . Nor should the attendants reck of danger, but hunt down ruthlessly their appointed prey. Finally the Candidate will sink into a sleep of utter exhaustion resembling coma . . . The Initiate may then be allowed to sleep, or the practice may be renewed and persisted in until death ends all. The most favourable death is that occurring during orgasm, and is called Mors Justi. (Crowley, 1989a)

The relevance of this correlation becomes clear when compared to Crowley's advice on vampirism in *Magick Without Tears*, in which he informs his student that "there is a difference between living and dead protoplasm" (Crowley, 1994b, p. 400) and goes on to say ". . . best of all are fluids and secretions, notably blood and one other of supreme importance to the continuity of life" (Crowley, 1994b, pp. 400–401). Within the same letter, he tells his student that "there is a mighty volume of theory and practice concerning this and cognate subjects which will be open to you when—and if—you attain the VIII° of O.T.O. . . . further when you enter the Sanctuary of the Gnosis . . ." (Crowley, 1994b, p. 400). The significance of this is that these are the degrees known to be firmly connected with the secrets of Crowley's methods of sexual magick. Regarding the consumption of vital energies and the integration of higher and lower energies, he refers his student to "*Magick,* Chapter XII"—referring to *Magick in Theory and Practice*.

In the definitive "tome de Crowley" that is *Magick in Theory and Practice*, vampires and vampirism have three entries. The first two references are quoted here:

In the case of The Master Therion [referring here to himself], *he had originally the capacity for all classes of orgia. In the beginning, He* [sic] *cured the sick, bewitched the obstinate, allured the seductive, routed the aggressive, made himself invisible, and generally behaved like a Young-Man-About-Town on every possible plane. He would afflict one vampire with a Sending of Cats, and appoint another his private Enchantress, neither aware of any moral oxymoron, nor hampered by the implicit incongruity of his oaths.* (Crowley, 1994a, p. 229)

His need to check the vampiring of a lady in Paris by a sorceress once led Frater Perdurabo [again referring to himself] *to the discovery of a very powerful body of black magicians, which whom* [sic] *he was obliged to war for nearly 10 years before their ruin was complete and irremediable as it is now.* (Crowley, 1994a, p. 235)

The third mention in this work occurs under the heading "Other Books, Principally Fiction, of a Generally Suggestive and Helpful Kind," where he lists Bram Stoker's *Dracula* as "valuable for its account of legends concerning vampires" (Crowley, 1994a, p. 454). These passages have very little to do with ceremonial magick or vampirism, but go a long way in demonstrating Crowley's opinion of both himself and vampires.

Chapter XII of *Magick in Theory and Practice*, the chapter he refers to in *Magick Without Tears*, is titled "Of the Bloody Sacrifice: and Matters Cognate" and opens with, "The blood is the life. This simple statement is explained by the Hindus by saying that the blood is the principal vehicle of vital prana. There is some ground for the belief that there is a definite substance, not isolated as yet, by whose presence makes all the difference between live and dead matter." The chapter then goes on to discuss various aspects of blood offerings, human sacrifice, and self-sacrifice in the form of the Rosy Cross.

It is important to understand through the reading of this material that Crowley often used the word *blood* to mean semen and "sacrifice" as simply the offering up of such fluids, just as his use of *death* often translates to "orgasm." In light of this, it is plain to see that the majority of his comments on vampirism are really comments on sexual magick and the energy exchange that accompanies such workings. Given the implications of these passages, one must ask: Are the sex magician and the vampire so very different from one another? After all, they are each using the vital/subtle energies, either their own or that of another, for their own purposes.

The Rituals of the Ordo Templi Orientis

"The best blood is of the moon, monthly: then the fresh blood of a child, or dropping from the host of heaven: then of enemies; then of the priest or of the worshippers: last of some beast, no matter what."

—*The Book of the Law III*, 24.

Crowley used the consumption of blood and sexual fluids in many of his rituals, including certain initiation rites of the Ordo Templi Orientis. The two most publicly observable instances of this are the Gnostic Mass and the Mass of the Phoenix. The passage above is taken from the list of ingredients used to form the host for the Gnostic Mass. In order of significance, Crowley (or Aiwaz, the preter-human being who reportedly dedicated *Liber AL vel Legis* —*The Book of the Law*—to Crowley) mentions menstrual blood, then that of a child, the host of heaven, an enemy, the priest, and then any sort of animal. (Let me insert a reminder here that Crowley mixed the terms blood and semen freely.) This ingredient is to then be baked into the Cake of Light, consecrated through the Miracle of the Mass, and consumed by the congregants.

On the other hand, it bears mentioning that the seemingly obvious representation of blood consumption, drinking the wine, is not blood consumption at all within the context of the Gnostic Mass. In the context of the Roman Catholic Eucharist, the wine is transubstantiated—it becomes the physical blood of Christ. Within the latter context, the consumption of the Eucharist is literally the consumption of blood and flesh. In the former context, the bread and wine are consecrated and imbued with the significance of the "blood" and "body" of God; however, this is not a physical, earthly god but rather the Sun. Thus the "blood" and "body" are not physical, earthly blood but rather the "essence of the joy of the Earth" and not physical, earthly body but rather the "essence of the life of the Sun" (Crowley, 1988, p.382). The actual transmutation of the bread and wine into body and blood occurs within the body, after consumption, when the bread and wine quite literally break down into the energy that fuels the body and generates cellular matter: physical body and blood.

In the Mass of the Phoenix, the magician is instructed to carve a sigil upon his breast and stanch the blood with the host (created using the same recipe and thus already containing blood within it), and to then consume this bloodied Cake of Light. The eucharistic act in the Mass of the Phoenix differs from that of the Gnostic Mass in two significant ways: It is made more personal by requiring self-sacrifice rather than the sacrifice of the priest or priestess, as the magician is consuming his own blood; and it confronts a more ominous taboo in that he is consuming fresh (e.g., uncooked) human blood.

Crowley has already mentioned the eighth and ninth degree rituals in the earlier excerpt from *Magick Without Tears*. According to Francis King's *Secret Rituals of the O.T.O.*, at least two lower degrees of the Ordo Templi Orientis, when performed as Crowley wrote them, also contained the consumption of blood in their initiations.

The third degree initiation, as written by Crowley, had both the candidate and initiator consuming a mixture of blood and laudanum. In the ritual of the sixth degree, Crowley had the initiator ask the candidate to seal the oath with his "heart's own blood" (*The Secret Rituals of the O.T.O.*, 1973, p. 119). Once the candidate consented to this, his blood was drawn by carving a St. Andrew's Cross on his right forearm, and it was drained into the chalice. The oath was then sealed with a bloody thumbprint and "the blood [offered up to] our lady Babalon" (*The Secret Rituals of the O.T.O.*, 1973, p. 119), who then drank of the blood-filled chalice.

The Ordo Templi Orientis' current stance on blood magick and the consumption of bodily fluids has changed quite a bit, and the rituals have been greatly reworked since Crowley's day. The many excuses include fear of litigation and transmittable diseases, but I personally believe the change stems more from an unwillingness to confront, or ask members to confront, these taboos. If this is in fact the case, it reflects the reemergence of the moralistic Victorian attitudes toward blood and vital forces, even after Crowley's firm rejection of these attitudes. Reasoning aside, current policy discourages the use of blood in the Cakes of Light or public performances of the Mass of the Phoenix. The blood and laudanum (and even wormwood) have been banned from use in the third degree ritual. I am told that the particulars of the sixth degree ritual vary from location to location at this point.

Real Live Blood and Sex Magicians—Step Right Up, 25 Cents per Ticket

I am tempted to say that we are a dying breed, but I am afraid there were never really that many of us. We walk along the fine line between the occult and vampire subcultures. Blood and sex magick are a standard in our temple, and we make no apologies for it. Many ceremonial magicians would call us vampires because we do feed on energy and drink blood; we also embrace all the things that come with those acts. The phenomenon that we have termed "Metaphysical Kinship" is reflected perfectly in *The Psychic Vampire Codex*. This phenomenon centers on the link created when energy is exchanged, whether through psychic means or blood, and includes dreamwalking, "the calling," increased psychic connectivity, and emotional sensitivities. These are all things that we had experienced and worked with long before the publication of the *Codex* and never associated with psi or sang vampirism. Yet here they are, almost word for word, and put in the context of vampiric powers. So there, we are vampires—the book says so, right? Not so fast.

I think any vampire who meets us immediately knows that we are not an active part of their subculture either. Beyond the outward signs, or lack thereof, we do not share the foundational beliefs of the vampire subculture. We do not believe that our "feeding" or energy work is necessary to our continued strength or well-being, though it can become very addictive over time. We do not follow any established origin or cultural myth, as do some vampire houses. And though the acts and results are much the same, our aesthetic and psychological approach to this work is very different than that described by most vampires.

So where does that leave us? Unlabeled? An oddity among our peers? It leaves us in a very unique place, one that I hope will convey a message to both ceremonial magicians and the vampire community. There is no single definition or label capable of encompassing us all! I want ceremonial magicians to come away from this piece with the understanding that vampirism and vampires are not some terrible force that must be reckoned with or battled against. Nor are they weekend posers at a costume ball. There is no room in true magick for moralistic values that hold one paradigm above another or for taboos that are only whispered about in hushed tones. I want vampires to come away from this piece with the understanding that, regardless of their religious/occult beliefs or lack thereof, there is a long and well-established magickal tradition behind the type of energy and blood exchanges that they use to feed. I would personally like to see more of the vampire community embrace the magick behind the darkness, just as I would like to see more magicians embrace the darkness behind the magick.

I want to offer special thanks to the Harry Ransom Humanities Research Center at the University of Texas at Austin.

Reference List

Belanger, M. 2004. *The Psychic Vampire Codex: A Manual of Magick and Energy Work*. Boston: Weiser.

Booth, M. 2000. *A Magick Life: A Biography of Aleister Crowley*. London: Hodder & Stoughton.

Crowley, A. 2004. *The Book of the Law: Liber AL vel Legis*. York Beach, ME: Weiser. (Original work published 1909).

Crowley, A. 1988. "Liber XLIV: The Mass of the Phoenix." In I. Regardie, ed., *Gems from the Equinox: Instructions by Aleister Crowley for His Own Magical Order*, pp. 311–314. Las Vegas: Falcon Press. (Original work published 1912–13).

Crowley, A. 1988. "Liber XV: Ecclesiae Gnosticae Catholicae Canon Missae" (the Gnostic Mass). In I. Regardie, ed., *Gems from the Equinox: Instructions by Aleister Crowley for His Own Magical Order*, pp. 363–384. Las Vegas: Falcon Press. (Original work published 1918).

Crowley, A. 1989a. "De Art Magica: XV of Eroto-Comatose Lucidity." In S. Michaelsen, ed., *Portable Darkness: An Aleister Crowley Reader*, pp. 164–165. New York: Harmony Books. (Original work published 1974, written 1914).

Crowley, A. 1989b. "De Art Magica: XVIII of a Certain Other Method of Magick Not Included in the Instruction of the O.T.O." In S. Michaelsen ed., *Portable Darkness: An Aleister Crowley Reader*, pp. 167–168. New York: Harmony Books. (Original work published 1974, written 1914).

Crowley, A. 1994a. "Magick in Theory and Practice." In Hymenaeus Beta, ed., *Magick: Book 4*, pp. 121–290. York Beach, ME: Weiser. (Original work published 1929–30).

Crowley, A. 1994b. *Magick Without Tears* (I. Regardie, ed.). Tempe, AZ: New Falcon. (Original work published 1973).

Cunard, N. 1954. *Thoughts about Aleister Crowley* (by Nancy Cunard for Gerald Yorke). Unpublished essay (located at the Harry Ransom Humanities Research Center, The University of Texas at Austin). Credit: Harry Ransom Humanities Research Center, The University of Texas at Austin.

Fortune, D. 2001. *Psychic Self-Defense* (revised ed.). New York: Weiser. (Original work published in 1930 as *Psychic Self-Defence*).

King, F., ed. 1973. *The Secret Rituals of the O.T.O.* New York: Samuel Weiser.

Pincher, C. 1982. *The Private World of St. John Terrapin.* London: Sidgwick & Jackson.

Ramsland, K. 2002. *The Science of Vampires.* New York: Berkley Boulevard.

Symonds, J. 1973. *The Great Beast: The Life of Aleister Crowley.* London: Mayflower Books. (Original work published 1952).

Yorke, G. 1954. Personal Correspondence from Gerald Yorke to Nancy Cunard, 23 November 1954 (located at the Harry Ransom Humanities Research Center, The University of Texas at Austin). Credit: Harry Ransom Humanities Research Center, The University of Texas at Austin.

Alexzandria Baker, along with her husband James, is a consecrated Bishop of the Universal Gnostic Tradition. Alexzandria holds a dual B. A. in psychology and religion, and is pursuing post-graduate work in the field of anthropology. For more information on Alexzandria or Liberi Sanguinis Luciferi, visit www.solarphallic-cult.org.

The Aesthetics of Blood

A Brief Look at the History and Psychology of the Human Preoccupation with Blood

BY ALEXZANDRIA BAKER

*T*he creation drama contained within the menstrual temple rites and menstrual laws of the ancient Sumerians served as a constant reminder of the connection between man, woman, and the gods. Ianna, child of the moon, took these rites as her inheritance and fulfilled the role of Initiatrix to the budding girls of the menstrual huts. In a masculinized version of these rites, men imitated the menstrual flow by cutting their penises. Young men also had blood and sacrificial rites associated with becoming hunters (Grahn, 2005).

In ancient Egypt, one of the several meanings for the symbol of the *tyet* (or *tiet*) is "blood of Isis." This symbol resembles the ankh but with arms folded down, and like the ankh, its meanings center on the essences of life. The exact origins and meaning of this symbol are uncertain, but it was frequently seen in the form of a funerary amulet made of red stone or glass and it is speculated that it may represent the menstrual flow from Isis' womb. The 156th spell in the Egyptian *Book of the Dead* reads, "You possess your blood Isis, you possess your power, Isis, you possess your magic Isis. The amulet is a protection for this Great One, which will drive off anyone who would perform a criminal act against him." Amulets representing the girdle of Isis were also used to stem the blood flow after a miscarriage.

Despite these connections between a woman's blood and Isis, it was Sekhmet who was the goddess of menstruation. This is very possibly due to her blood lust in avenging wrongs and lending protection to the Pharaohs on the battlefield. Her wrathful connection with blood earned her honorifics such as The Scarlet Lady, the One Before Whom Evil Trembles, and the Lady of the Slaughter. Her priests dressed her statues in the color of blood and feared her displeasure. In the end, it was the color of blood that was her downfall, when Ra tricked her into becoming drunk by coloring beer with red ochre and thus transformed her into the gentler Hathoor. This signifies that not only did Sekhmet have a lust for blood, she also carried a thirst for it.

Blood continues to come into focus as mankind, and religion, move forward through time. From the near sacrifice of Abraham's firstborn child to the death of Christ on the Cross, from the use of blood as nourishment by Huns to the Holy Eucharist, from the fertility dances of menstruating women in medieval times to the precious royal bloodlines of autocracy, and from the gruesome sacrifices atop the Aztec pyramids to the piercing and scarification rituals of "modern primitives," blood has never been far from the human consciousness. Blood has meant life to some and death to others; in many cases, it has meant both simultaneously. It is impossible to even scratch the surface of mankind's connection and fascination with blood throughout history, but I want to briefly touch on three important aspects of that connection: the Quest, the Sacrifice, and the Continuity. To represent these aspects, I have selected only a handful of examples out of countless instances.

The Quest

The greatest quest, that of the Holy Grail, is firmly rooted in blood. The alternate term for the Grail, *Sangreal*, may be the oldest surviving pun—*sang rial* meaning "royal blood" and *san grial* meaning "Holy Grail" in Old French. There are practically infinite theories regarding exactly *what* the Holy Grail is, including these: a stone, usually an emerald but sometimes a bloodstone (from the translation of *sang*), which had been sanctuary for the neutral angels during the war in heaven but fell from heaven when God cast out Lucifer; the dish or cup used by Christ at the Last Supper, which was also used to catch his blood as he died on the Cross; the family bloodline of Christ's descendants; and the uterus, vagina, or collective female reproductive system, just to name a few. Legend has attributed many magical powers to the Grail, including immortality. The Grail has been seen as a symbol of male potency, female fertility, hope, life, death, and resurrection. It was searched for by King Arthur's knights and rumored to be the hidden treasure of the Knights Templar. Regardless of which theory concerning what the Holy Grail is on the physical plane you choose to believe, or what powers you might attribute to it, the stories maintain two vital elements: the Grail represents the ultimate desire of man's heart, and it is inseparable from the human fascination with blood.

The Sacrifice

Human history is riddled with stories of blood sacrifice. There was Isaac/Ishmael's narrow escape, the sacrificial bull of Roman times, and the blood libel leveled against the Jews and the multiple incarnations of the Dying God. But possibly the most complex and intense example of blood sacrifice is seen in the development of Mesoamerican cultures. Evidence shows that during the Classic (220–900 CE) and Post-Classic (900–1500 CE) periods of Mesoamerican culture, bloodletting was practiced both privately and publicly, in both the temples and in homes. Priests drew blood from tongues, earlobes, thighs and sexual organs using implements such as obsidian blades, fish spines, and, as in the case of Maya lords, knotted strands of thorns (Carrasco, 1990, p. 140). In both Mayan and Aztec times, even the central form of recreation led to sacrifice. Ball games that vaguely resembled modern basketball were played regularly, and often resulted in the sacrifice of the losing team or a representative thereof. During Aztec times, the I-shaped ball court came to represent the narrow passage that the sun took as it journeyed through the underworld, and the sacrifice of blood and life by the losing players offered up the energy needed to give birth to a new sun (Carrasco, 1990).

In the cosmovision of the Aztecs, the human body was considered a center of "vital forces and change" and "the earthly container of divine energy." The two primary forces recognized in the human body were *tonalli* and *teyolia*. Tonalli refers to vigor, warmth, solar heat, summertime, and soul. The

Aztecs believed that tonalli resided in the head. The sun was believed to be the central, most vital and visible source of tonalli, but in war, warriors would decapitate or grab the hair of an enemy because taking this from enemies increased one's own tonalli. In public sacrifices, enemies were decapitated to release the tonalli and thus increase the tonalli of the people as a whole through the ceremony (Carrasco, 1990, p. 171).

Teyolia resided in the human heart. This force animated the human body and shaped the person's sensibilities and thinking patterns. This was the "divine fire" in the heart and was in every person, but it was thought to be particularly strong in priests, artists, *hombre-dioses*, and those who impersonated gods in festivals. This energy, teyolia, is also the energy that fuels the sun. In the Aztec heart sacrifice, the priest slashed open a warrior's chest, took out his heart, and threw it into the fire. This released the warrior's teyolia and allowed it to rise up to heaven, as in the cremation of Topiltzin Quetzalcoatl. In the open chest cavity, the priest would light a new fire that would then be used as the source to rekindle all of the home fires in the surrounding region (Carrasco, 1990, p. 172).

As in many other cultures throughout time, these rituals were a means of world-centering and world-renewing for the Aztecs. They were a people who truly lived and died according to the forces within the blood.

Possibly more familiar to modern readers is the Roman Catholic Eucharist. Many would shudder at the comparison of this ritual with the often gruesome and violent sacrifices of Mesoamerica; however, regardless of its refinements, the Eucharist is still very much a blood ritual based in sacrifice.

Sharing of the Eucharist was, at the conclusion of the fourth century, an initiatory rite, and it still is the primary communal experience of the Catholic Church. Throughout the Christian community, it is still the ultimate mode of sharing in the life and experience of Jesus Christ (Cooke, 1983). It has alternately been viewed as a sacrifice, a means of giving thanks, a moment in the true and actual presence of the Lord, a sacred meal in the tradition of the apostles, and a remembrance of the Last Supper.

The communal meals shared by the Apostles were consistent with earlier Jewish tradition. At the Last Supper, the sacred meal shared between Jesus and the apostles just prior to his death, Jesus gave instructions on how to continue the communal meal once he was gone. The translations and interpretations of those words—"This is my body . . . this is my blood"—led to many later theological debates. Nonetheless, Jesus had instructed the apostles to eat and drink in remembrance of him. More than seventeen centuries of theological debate have still not settled the question for all Christians concerning the physical versus the symbolic presence of Christ in the host. Paschase Radbert, the ninth-century theologian, determined that the literal blood and body of Christ must be present on the altar during the Mass, and this began the trend away from congregants partaking in the communion and toward the visual and distant worship of the host (Martos, 2001).

Scholars have since examined and reexamined the reality and the metaphysical action of the Mass. Theories and terminology have gone through transmutation, transfiguration, transelementation, transformation, consubstantiation, and transubstantiation. Transubstantiation—the idea that the substances' presence truly changes into the blood and body of Christ, though their appearances remain as that of bread and wine—is the currently accepted theology within the Roman Catholic Church. This term was first used by Hildebert of Tours, and its use by the Fourth Lateran Council was later perceived as an ecclesiastical endorsement (Martos, 2001).

Actual body and blood of Christ on the altar? Here, there is first and foremost the blood (and body), which is consumed. Secondly, there is the presence of God, which in a sense is also consumed. The psychological and ritual significance behind these ritualized acts strongly reflect the Mesoamerican rituals, as well as the many, many other blood rituals that mirror this innate need for life and the consumption of life, seen in places all around the globe from the beginning of civilization all the way through last Sunday's sermon.

The Continuity

The most remarkable quality of the human fascination with blood is its continuity, even in its transformations. From ancient Sumer to the vampire and occult communities of the twenty-first century, blood has held a place of reverence and power. It has been used to heal the sick, protect the weak, honor the gods, and nourish both the body and the spirit. In Tibetan Buddhism, there is a particular ritual tool of note: the skull cap (*kapala* in Sanskrit). This vessel finds its parallel in the much older clay pot of Vedic sacrifices. The kapala is held by wrathful but protective deities, usually seen in artistic renderings as being held at chest (heart) level, and it can be filled with warm human blood; blood and brains; blood and intestines; human flesh and fat; the heart and lungs of an enemy; or a mixture containing the blood of Rudra (originally a god of storms and wind or a god of death from the Hindu Vedas but also an early form of Shiva as lord of destruction) and the heart of Mara (the goddess of death in Hindu mythology, better known as the lord of misfortune, sin, destruction, and death in the Buddhist tradition). Given this list of contents, the connection between this ritual implement and blood is obvious, but it is the source of the kapala itself that I want to examine here. Nitin Kumar details the preferences for obtaining this tool in his article "Ritual Implements in Tibetan Buddhism: A Symbolic Appraisal":

> . . . The selection of the right skull is of immense importance for the success of the ritual. The skull of a murder or execution victim is believed to possess the greatest tantric power; the skull of one who has died from a violent or accidental death, or from a virulent illness, possesses a medium magical power; the skull of a person who died peacefully in old age has virtually no occult power. The skull of a child who died during the onset of puberty also has great potency, as do the skulls of miscegenated or misbegotten child[ren] of unknown paternity, born from the forbidden union of castes, out of wedlock, from sexual misdemeanor, or particularly from incest. The "misbegotten skull" of a seven or eight-year-old child born from an incestuous union is considered to possess the greatest power in certain tantric rituals. Here the vital force or potential of the skull's "previous owner" is embodied within the bone as a spirit, rendering it as an effective power object for the performance of tantric rituals (Kumar, 2001).

This hierarchy of the dead in their ability to provide both protective and wrathful energies has leapfrogged through various cultures and times, showing up in medieval folklore, Appalachian folk remedies, old wives' tales, and 1930s Chicago, taking on various forms ranging from the burning Hand of Glory to handkerchiefs dipped in the blood of notorious gangster John Dillinger as he lay dead in the street. The image of the blood-filled skull chalice echoes in the poetry of Aleister Crowley when he describes Babalon's blood-filled "Cup of

Abominations" with lustful and degusting imagery. We see here the practice of harnessing vital life energy from the dead, through blood and bone, extending from the oldest Vedic and Tantric traditions to the stylized imagery of the occult revival, and even to the memorabilia of twentieth-century superstition. I know a Haitian Mambo, a Vodou priestess, who has asked, only half joking, that her house initiates leave her in the ground for a year before they dig her up. These few examples show how blood themes both travel from culture to culture and also spontaneously arise in multiple cultures simultaneously with seemingly no connection.

This abbreviated trip through the history of blood is not even comprehensive enough to be considered a "crash course," but it does, I hope, give an idea of the set and setting behind blood rites, religious and otherwise, in many of their varying permutations. Possibly more important than the historic details of blood usage is the development and reasoning behind the many meanings humans have applied to blood.

What Blood Means to Us

Blood, from the very beginning, has represented human life. This is seen in the correlation between the menstrual cycle and the creation of the universe in Sumerian rites. Blood is, after all, necessary for human life. Menstrual blood in particular is a key element in the creation of life. Newborns emerge through blood. Generation after generation, we make ourselves immortal by passing our blood on through our children and their children. Blood transfusions allowed medical science to lend new life to patients who would have died otherwise. The heart is a symbol of love and life, and was once thought to be the driving force of the body and the seat of human thought and emotion. Blood flows through our veins, fills our bodies, fuels our hearts, and sustains our existence, but should we lose a sufficient amount of it we will die—and thus blood is also death.

Slain enemies lie in bloody pools on the battlefield, and miscarriages (the reversal of conceived life) are announced by the accompanying gush of blood. "Disease of the blood" was once the medical term for mysterious illnesses that would almost surely lead to death. The medical practices of bloodletting and leeching killed as many, if not more, than it saved. This life/death duality of blood is fully realized in the images of Kali, mother and also goddess of death and destruction, who dances on the back of her lover while wearing a necklace of skulls and a belt of severed arms.

Beyond the obvious physically related connotations of blood is the seemingly endless list of attributes connected to blood through human spirituality and expression. In an attempt to transcend both life and death, we attribute powers of resurrection, eternal life, and immortality to blood as well. It is by the blood of Christ that Christians shall enter the kingdom of heaven and realize their reward of eternal life in the presence of God. Blood is what allowed Count Dracula, and many other fictional vampires, to grow young and live for centuries. The blood spilled on Aztec altars assured the rebirth of the sun and thus the continuation of the entire species. We use terms like *blue-blooded* to indicate royalty, while saying the blood is *mingled* or *thinned* means a degeneration of royal purity. *Thin-blooded* also refers to someone old and easily chilled. *Hot-blooded* indicates a volatile temper, while *cold-blooded* indicates that one is calculating and without feeling. *Warm-blooded* means "vigorous," or at least "full of life," as does *red-blooded*. That last term has also taken on connotations of patriotism in the United States (e.g., *red-blooded American*). *Bad blood* refers to a grudge or problem between persons. *Blood kin* and *bloodlines* refer to one's biological relatives, while the terms *blood brothers* and *blood sisters* refer to a ritualized bond created between two people.

There are also certain values applied to blood. Some cultures believe that deities reside in the blood, thus making it holy and binding mortals with immortals. Other cultures prohibit contact with blood, especially the blood of the dead, as it is impure and holds the power to contaminate. *Blood on your hands* infers guilt. The blood of Christ "purifies" the sinner. Royal blood is meant to be pure, not mingled with that of outsiders or commoners.

Blood is the most sincere form of sacrifice. Blood sacrifice, as that described among the Aztecs, Romans, Jews, and early Christians, is the most precious offering that one can make to the gods. Literal blood sacrifice is still practiced in many religions, including Vodou and Santería. Symbolic forms of blood sacrifice, often in the form of incense or wine, are still practiced in a number of rituals by various modern groups from Christians to occultists. The blood sacrifice symbolizes an offering up of ourselves, a giving of our own life's essence to the heavens—even in the case of animal sacrifice or symbolic blood sacrifices, it is an offering of one's own life.

People throughout time have consumed blood to sustain life, both physically and symbolically (or spiritually). Warriors joining the Mongol armies were expected to bring with them three horses—one to ride and two to drink blood from for nourishment in the harsh desert climates. Some Masai of Tanzania still practice blood-drinking for nourishment. Many vampires, both fictional and actual, look to blood for sustenance. Many eucharistic rites, including that of the Catholic Church, represent the consumption of blood and flesh as a form of spiritual nourishment. Warriors in various cultures have consumed the blood or flesh of slain enemies for a variety of reasons, ranging from absorption of their enemies' power to the honoring of a fallen but brave opponent. Gods tend to be particularly bloodthirsty, most likely due to the human projection of their own unrealized blood lust. Deities like Kali, Sekhmet, Aries, and the Christian God (at least in older times), to name only a few, demanded blood sacrifices to satisfy their hunger and need for worship.

Blood, Psychology, and the Vampire

The image of the vampire, both fictional and actual, embodies the entire range of human thought on blood. For the vampire, blood is life. For the victim, blood is the life being drained and is thus also death. In many cases of vampire lore, *Dracula* being one example, blood keeps the vampire young or even reverses aging, and is thus a source of his immortality. In some cultural lore, and in some modern clans, vampires are related to, or are themselves, gods and thus blood, their sustenance, is holy ambrosia. There also appears, in both literature and modern houses, the willing victim who represents the blood sacrifice. The idea of evil is attributed to his draining of the victim's life, while good is seen in the ecstasy and transformation delivered through this same process.

In the present vampire community, there is a debate between psi and sang vampires regarding the consumption of blood. Some psi-vampires (those who feed on psychic energy rather than blood) view sanguinary practices as dangerous and crude. While the present dangers of blood consumption are more than valid concerns, I disagree with the idea that blood consumption is a crude practice engaged in by those who lack the ability or finesse to manipulate the more subtle energies.

The consumption of blood does offer a more tangible source for feeding, which lends itself to those with less experience in psychic energy work. However, there are certain aspects of blood consumption that play into the psychology behind intense energy workings to heighten the experience. I am no biochemist; however, many of the psychobiological responses to sanguinary practices are clear even to the layperson.

In order to obtain the blood, there must be some sort of physical damage done to the body. This might come in the form of a bite, a laceration, or an intravenous extraction. The anticipation of such damage is sufficient, even in the experienced practitioner, to excite the adrenal glands, thus intensifying sensation with the increased presence of adrenaline. The pain incurred during the actual extraction of the blood then causes the body to release endorphins—pain-thwarting hormones akin to morphine. Dr. Katherine Ramsland, author of *The Science of Vampires*, even goes so far as to speculate that the vampire's bite (and she bases this almost entirely on the details of fictional accounts) might increase the body's production of DMT, a chemical that, when increased in the brain, can cause floating sensations, spiritual experiences, and sensory hallucinations. On a primal level, self-mutilation is counterintuitive to the human brain. Going against this instinct produces a psychological conflict that can trigger a wide range of emotions along with the increased chemicals in the brain. In addition, first aid courses will teach that any accident or damage to the body, regardless of how small, places the body in a low-level state of shock. These biological and psychological processes occur naturally in response to the sanguinary practices even in the willing and experienced.

Combining these responses with the multiple meanings and views of blood that may already be in the mind and emotional history of the sanguine vampire or the donor, one can see why the act of blood consumption is to be considered an experience unto itself, beyond (or at least in addition to) the rush experienced from the metaphysical reaction to the intake of the subtle energies. Granted, this experience is not to everyone's liking and, given that the natural biological and psychological responses stem from innate defenses, this is understandable.

My personal experience with blood rituals is more from the perspective of a magician and a student than from that of a vampire, but my study of the meanings and history of blood comes from an intense interest in the human fascination with blood and blood rites. This article is barely a sketch of the topic and I highly recommend independent reading on the subject.

References List

Carrasco, D. 1990. "Religions of Mesoamerica: Cosmovision and Ceremonial Centers." In H. B. Earhart, ed., *Religious Traditions of the World: A Journey through Africa, Mesoamerica, North America, Judaism, Christianity, Islam, Hinduism, Buddhism, China, and Japan*, pp. 107–254. New York: HarperCollins.

Cooke, B. 1983. *Sacraments and Sacramentality.* Mystic, CT: Twenty-Third Publications.

Grahn, J. 2005. "Chapter 13: Narratives: Descent Myth and the Great Flood" (excerpts from J. Grahn, *Blood, Bread, and Roses: How Menstruation Created the World*, originally published in 1993 by Beacon Press in Boston). Retrieved 11 September 2006 from http://bailiwick.lib.uiowa.edu/wstudies/grahn/chapt13.htm.

Kumar, N. 2001. "Ritual Implements in Tibetan Buddhism: A Symbolic Appraisal." Retrieved 11 September 2006 from http://www.exoticindiaart.com/article/ritual.

Martos, J. 2001. *Doors to the Sacred: A Historical Introduction to Sacraments in the Catholic Church* (revised and updated ed.). Liguori, MO: Liguori/Triumph.

Ramsland, K. 2002. *The Science of Vampires.* New York: Berkley Boulevard.

Mora is a tarot reader, public speaker, writer, model, and modern-day philosopher. She has been published in the Immanion Press anthology Magick On the Edge: An Anthology of Experimental Occultism, *and is working with other publishers and editors for upcoming works of both fiction and nonfiction. Future aspirations include completing a Therian Tarot deck with anthropomorphic artist K. Lawrence, and writing a book on the basics of her belief structure. For more information about Mora, visit her website at http://solitaire.empire-of-sin.com.*

A Vampire Amongst Pagans

BY MORA

When I first began my journey into Paganism, I was curious about other religions, spiritual paths, and belief systems. I went to the local bookstore and perused the religion section. The first book I stumbled upon was Scott Cunningham's *Wicca: A Guide for the Solitary Practitioner*. I purchased it, took it home, and began reading. Many of the concepts were common sense; many more were completely new and I had trouble wrapping my brain around them. However, the ideas resonated with me on an intrinsic level, as though I were finally remembering something I had long forgotten. I began the puzzle of my spirituality with solitary practice and study for a couple of years, making sure I had a decent handle on the theory and practice before moving on. I read through and studied not only Cunningham, but also other authors I stumbled upon via the occult section, and I became comfortable in my new beliefs. Books can only tell one so much; therefore, I also sought out others of a like mind and service.

I joined many mailing lists and websites, looking for others in my area with whom I could get together over coffee and chat with to share ideas. At first I could find no others in my area, and I stuck primarily to online venues until others came forward. During this search for area Pagans, I found a world of Pagan beliefs being practiced every day in the rest of the world that I had never before encountered and wouldn't have known about without the Internet. It was during this time that I discovered Druidry. I had always felt a pull to the archetype and, finding an online program, I began learning the path from those professing to be modern-day Druids. Although the path called to me when I began, I realized Druidry didn't quite fit what I needed any longer. Insatiable for knowledge and finding nothing to suit my needs, I began a study group and a Pagan Pride Day in my area. I realized others were afraid of coming forward and searching openly for other Pagans. If others wouldn't come forward, I would thrust myself out there and allow them to find me. I signed my name onto the banner of Pagan Pride in 2003 and came out of the broom closet in May of that year, openly displaying my pentacle.

Through exposing myself as a Pagan, I had several aspirations. First, I wanted to be able to find others who practiced. Not only did I want a group of people to share ideas and knowledge with, but I also wanted to draw many others out into the open. My desire was for Pagans to join together, share knowledge and information, and grow together as a local community. By posting messages on various websites and message boards, as well as posting flyers in local venues, a small group of people came together. We met not only as a study group, but also as the first members of the core group who would pull together Pagan Pride 2003 and 2004. Via these first members, I continued my research and shared what I had learned with those in my group, including the study of other religions. It was during this time I began researching Dark Paganism.

Having connections to the Gothic subculture, I learned of a site called Gothic Personals and its sister site Pagan Personals (and now Vampire Personals). One of the co-creators of the site, John Coughlin, had written a book about Dark Paganism called *Out of the Shadows: An Exploration of Dark Paganism*. In researching the concept, I found it was not an "evil" path, but rather a path focusing on introspection, self-realization, and self-actualization, as well as allowing for darker lifestyles. Reading the book was a wonderful change of pace from the standard how-to books generally populating the occult shelves. This was a book focusing on the philosophy behind Dark Paganism and comparing and contrasting the belief system with other related subjects, including

Satanism, BDSM, and the Gothic subculture. Further study led me to pick up *Nocturnal Witchcraft* by Konstantinos. Excellent practices and a lack of beginner jargon lined the pages and I was thrilled. I embarked on a journey of self-discovery using the ideas within this book, as well as other ideas I had picked up here and there along the way to form my own belief system. Although the puzzle of my spirituality was not complete, I had a majority of it pieced together. Still, I quested for the missing pieces.

It was through my journey into Dark Paganism that I found the concept of vampirism. I was invited into a Yahoo group for vampires and Dark Pagans to come together and find fellowship in one another. My first reaction, typical of many in the Pagan community was, sadly, that the group was populated by kids in capes pretending to be vampires with Halloween fangs and whiteface. Further research into the group, however, led me to the idea of psychic vampires. Having run into a few psychic vampires myself, they were usually believed to be people who spent their time causing senseless drama and problems so they could feed off of that energy generated by the people involved. They were portrayed as unhealthy individuals who were too lazy to produce enough energy on their own, and who were compared to parasites and leeches by their family and friends as well as within the Pagan community. In talking to the members of the vampire community, however, I found these ideas to be decently far from the reality. While there were some individuals who seemed to thrive on causing angst among those they were involved with, the rest of the group was friendly and was interested in learning more about the condition, just as I was.

Being thrown a new definition to a familiar term, I began to research. The owner of the group sent me to an online copy of Michelle Belanger's *Vampire Codex* published in the online archive at www.sacred-texts.com. As I read about the caste system, the pieces began falling out of thin air and snapping into place via phantom hands. Finally I had answers for what I had been experiencing. I knew why the doctors could find nothing wrong with me when I complained of deep body aches and severe flu symptoms that antibiotic and holistic means couldn't heal. Believing I had, perhaps, been feeding off of people unconsciously, I delved into research for feeding techniques and practices. Nothing online seemed to be very credible. Most of the websites were strangely lacking in anything other than dark motifs, lots of animated bats, and *Interview with the Vampire* quotes.

This was when I stumbled upon the Strigoi Vii, a vampire group based in New York who stated they had information in a forthcoming book titled *V*. I jumped at the chance to read something written by self-professed vampires instead of people "researching" the culture. Inside the book was a copy of the *Codex* complete with changes. Although the *Codex* was informative, the rest of the book left me wanting. While it included terminology, it told me nothing of what the group taught, and urged me toward membership. I contemplated seeking membership, but I didn't feel it would be in my best interest to join when I had no idea what I would be getting myself into.

I initiated conversation with a few of the members and found them to be very closed and rather secretive. Somewhat daunted, I began researching again, stumbling onto House Kheperu's website and the "Coming Soon" announcement for the *Psychic Vampire Codex*. I was hesitant at first to buy the book, wary of coming up empty-handed once again, but after perusing the website, I decided to give it another shot. I ordered a copy of the book, receiving my copy on Mother's Day in 2004. As soon as I had a copy in my hot little hands, I tore through it, finally finding the information I had been so desperately seeking. I immediately put the techniques I found into practice. Far from proficient, I went seeking others of a like mind and service to talk to on matters concerning vampires. Unfortunately, there weren't many reputable websites. Many of the sites I stumbled upon were by the same misguided Goths I had thought the mailing list was populated with. It was then I set to experimentation. Much like my journey into Paganism, I had done research, I had practiced, I had a feel for what I was doing—and I sought out others to share ideas with.

Many groups claiming to be populated by vampires wanted to charge for their information or seemed so completely ludicrous in their claims that I passed them by without a second glance. The groups I could find who seemed at least partially decent were secretive. Most insane of all, there were "vampire hunters" who sought out vampires and, in some cases, assaulted them.

In the same vein, I went to members of the local Pagan community and asked their opinions of psychic vampires. What I met with was completely unexpected. My friends had been accepting, but the general public at large seemed to fear psychic vampires or have many crackpot schemes of ridding a person of their vampirism through chakra cleansings, energy or psychological healing, or Reiki therapy. They defended themselves against them by creating energetic shields, or they feared vampires due to their "drama queen" natures. I was completely floored and slightly put off. The light in which vampires were portrayed was definitely not positive, and a complete mismatch for me. The community who had accepted me had shunned my newfound solution, and I no longer felt that I was part of the community. Not only was I facing dissension for my darker spirituality and my Gothic leanings, I was now at odds with them on a deeper level.

A split occurred in my study group in late 2003 due to my interest in knowing more about Satanism and other "dark" religions or spiritualities. After disbanding the group and turning Pagan Pride over to more capable hands, I stepped out of the community entirely. I only interacted with close friends and another newly awakened vampire via the Pagan Nation message boards, letting the stink from my old study group finally peter out and getting my feeding habits under control. I practiced gathering ambient energy while at a Goth night in a local bar. I found ready donors and utilized their energy. I didn't get sick any more, the headaches I suffered with for years were gone, and I could get out of bed in the morning without severe body pain. I was productive again. I continued to ask questions about vampires and vampirism in general, watching to be sure I wasn't doing any of the negative things many vampires were believed to do. Before I came out as a vampire, I wanted to be sure I knew exactly what my faults were.

I came out fully as a psychic vampire in 2004, and offered a class on psychic self-defense from the vampire's point of view at my former Pagan Pride Day. I pulled heavily on Michelle Belanger's work as well as personal experience, and I offered a class on psychic shielding. People were more interested in learning about vampires than in how to defend against them, and I spent most of the downtime between classes chatting with the various attendees about what being a vampire meant and how it affected me and my dealings in the community. By and large, I was well received. I was amazed. Although the title of *vampire* lends itself to some strange ideas, the community has come a long way in a short amount of time. People were curious instead of afraid.

In the time I had come out as a vampire, a friend of mine who was part of the online Pagan website Pagan Nation contacted me about a person who believed she was a vampire and needed help. No one had responded to her questions or her well-thought-out post. She had linked to posts others had made about psychic vampires and their negligence and disrespect for the well-being of others. These people continued bashing vampires—yet when this young woman posted her concerns about possibly being a vampire, no one offered suggestions. I was the first to offer forward suggestions for her. While I was not publicly flamed for being a vampire, I was made to understand any "instances of vampirism" while around any members of their community would not be tolerated and would be handled as they deemed necessary. When I tried explaining my situation, I was ignored. It was soon thereafter that my newfound vampire friend and I left the site.

Since then, however, I have not run into many problems. Outside of a few individuals, I have been accepted as a part of the community, and my knowledge and assistance in furthering acceptance have been welcomed. Pagans are becoming more aware of the presence of vampires in the community and are curious—especially when they meet a good, solid, responsible, respectable member of the vampire community. I have been a presenter at Pagan Pride days throughout Ohio. I attend various study groups and small Pagan community groups as a speaker. Actions speak louder than words; therefore, I am a good example of the community. I involve myself in the Pagan community by giving classes on psychic vampirism and the benefits it can have. I sit and chat with people. I make myself available and known as a vampire. I show people we are not scary, so they don't fear us and are educated instead.

One thing worrying me as I was trying to promote acceptance was the knowledge that not all vampires are responsible. I had a hard choice to make. Would I rather assuage the fears of the community at large and have them fall victim to the irresponsible, or would I rather have vampires feared and hated when we could provide the balance many communities seemed to think was lacking? I settled on a middle ground, offering forward my advice: do not take a self-proclaimed vampire at their title. Many times, misguided people will claim the title for shock value or out of a plea for acceptance. These people are seeking to find themselves and, as such, are often "going through a phase." Not every vampire is a good example of what a vampire should be. However, don't discount all vampires as energy leeches who do nothing but cause senseless drama. Vampires are essential to cleaning the outdated energy that can stagnate and create problems, and they allow it to flow again. Just as not all Pagans represent the whole community, so too it is the case with vampires.

With time, tolerance, and understanding, there is no reason the two communities can't function together as a unified whole. That day is quickly approaching, and I look forward to it wholeheartedly.

The Mystic Foundation
Understanding & Exploring the Magical Universe

CHRISTOPHER PENCZAK

The sheer number of mystical traditions out there can be overwhelming to seekers new to the metaphysical world. Summing up the universal truths underlying many mystic institutions, *The Mystic Foundation* is an initial step toward understanding the wisdom of each.

This nondogmatic primer outlines the mystical teachings of Paganism, Christianity, Islam, and other spiritualities spanning Eastern and Western traditions. Penczak transforms complex subjects and ideas—such as the powers of creation, life forces, elements, the world beyond, spirit entities, sacred space and time, magick, and metaphysical skills—into easy-to-understand concepts. Each chapter features exercises—including meditation, aura cleansing, chakra balancing, and psychic travel—to help seekers "go within" and ground themselves in a variety of mystic beliefs. By the end of the book, readers will have a solid foundation in mysticism for choosing a path of their own.

Christopher Penczak is a faculty member of the Northeast Institute of Whole Health (NEIWH) in Manchester, New Hampshire. He also teaches classes throughout New England on Witchcraft, meditation, Reiki, crystals, and shamanic journeys.

978-0-73870-979-6
336 pp. , 7½ x 9⅛ $15.95

The Urban Primitive
Paganism in the Concrete Jungle

RAVEN KALDERA &
TANNIN SCHWARTZSTEIN

Modern neo-paganism is primarily an urban movement, yet few books exist for city pagans, specifically city pagans on a budget. *The Urban Primitive* shows how every disaffected urban pagan can use magick to survive and make good in the city.

Find practical recommendations not found anywhere else, including how to protect your back in the combat zone, defend your house from intruders and lousy energies, find jobs, keep your car running, locate good parking spaces, and use the city's energy for sorcery. There are even chapters on body decoration, urban totem animals—such as sparrows and cockroaches—and old gods in new guises, including Skor (goddess of Dumpster treasures) and Slick (god of fast talking).

978-0-73870-259-9

288 pp., 6 x 9 $14.95

Goth Craft
The Magickal Side of Dark Culture

RAVEN DIGITALIS

When Paganism and Gothic culture collide, a powerful blend of indepen-dent thought and magickal transformation is often the result. Raven Digitalis explores this dynamic intersection and what draws us to the "dark side."

Digitalis introduces many kinds of Goths and Witches, and the philosophy of each. Practical as well as insightful, *Goth Craft* covers the basics of magick, with special attention to blood magick, death magick, and necromancy. You'll also learn how to channel dark emotions, express yourself through the dark arts (clothes, hair, makeup, body modification), choose appropriate Goth music for ritual, and myriad other ways to merge magickal practice with the Goth lifestyle.

From working shadow magick to spellcasting on the dance floor, *Goth Craft* revels in the exciting convergence of two vital subcultures.

978-0-7387-1104-1
316 pp. , 7½ x 9⅛ $16.95

Magickal Mystical Creatures
Invite Their Powers in to Your Life

D. J. CONWAY

(Formerly titled *Magickal, Mythical, Mystical Beasts*)

Unicorns . . . centaurs . . . gorgons, and gargoyles. Long ago, strange and fabulous beasts filled the tales of storytellers and the myths of many cultures. In those times, humans not only believed these creatures truly existed, but they also credited them with great knowledge and called upon them for aid.

These mythical beasts do exist, and they're alive and well on the astral plane. This one-of-a-kind guide describes how you can enlist the special energies and talents of over two hundred of these fabulous creatures to empower your magickal workings, rituals, and potential for success. Call upon a Magical Serpent for that financial windfall. Let the Phoenix help you resurrect your hope and energy. Invoke the Centaur for artistic inspiration. The mystical beings in this book are waiting to enhance your life with their legendary wisdom and power.

978-1-56718-149-4

272 pp. , 6x9 $14.95